N●B.S.
RUTHLESS
MANAGEMENT
OF PEOPLE & PROFITS

2nd Edition

NO HOLDS BARRED
KICK BUTT
TAKE NO PRISONERS
GUIDE TO REALLY
GETTING RICH

Dan S. Kennedy

Ep
Entrepreneur
PRESS®

Publisher: Entrepreneur Press
Cover Design: Andrew Welyczko
Production and Composition: Eliot House Productions

This publication is designed to provide accurate and authoritative information in regard to the subject matter covered. It is sold with the understanding that the publisher is not engaged in rendering legal, accounting or other professional services. If legal advice or other expert assistance is required, the services of a competent professional person should be sought.

Library of Congress Cataloging-in-Publication Data
Kennedy, Dan S., 1954–
        No B.S. ruthless management of people and profits: no holds barred,
    kick butt, take-no-prisoners guide to really getting rich/by
    Dan S. Kennedy.
            p. cm. — (No B.S.)
        Revised edition of the author's No B.S. ruthless management of
    people & profits, published in 2008.
        ISBN-13: 978-1-59918-540-8 (paperback)
        ISBN-10: 1-59918-540-7 (paperback)
        1. Management. 2. Supervision of employees. I. Title.
    HD31.K4544 2014
    658.4'21—dc23   2014028083

Printed in the United States of America

18 17 16 15   10 9 8 7 6 5 4 3 2 1

Contents

Something Different— Straight Talk

What does it really take, to get productivity from people and, by doing so, maximum profits from and success for a business?

In the time elapsed between the first edition of this book and now, much has become known about some revered entrepreneurs who built and led giant companies and who were or are extremely tough-minded and I would say, ruthless managers. Steve Jobs and Jeff Bezos are two great examples, known for being harsh, brutal, enraged by incompetence, mercurial, willing to embarrass executives in front of others, imposing autocratic rules and disciplines, and making it "my way or the highway." They built two of the most successful and valuable companies in the world with this leadership style. Theorists argue they succeeded despite this. I insist, because of it. You can place Donald Trump in the same place. I have personally witnessed his unrestrained ire toward employees who disappointed on two occasions. If you go back in time and really study Walt Disney, you discover a guy who, very often, created the *un*-happiest place on earth for his executives. Walt was dictatorial, confrontational, unreasonably demanding, hated being told "no," and was prone to rage. The Disney parks are run with an iron hand, with strict rules and discipline for employees, and swift elimination of those who can't cut the mustard.

If you read this book, which predated most of the books on Jobs, including Walter Isaacson's incredible biography, *Steve Jobs,* and predated the first in-depth book on Amazon and on Jeff Bezos, *The Everything Store: Jeff Bezos and the Age of Amazon* by Brad Stone, then read those books, you will see the commonality. There is no laissez-faire.

I must begin with a confession: I have only one employee and she is at an office thousands of miles away that I never visit, and we both like it that way. But this happy fact does **not** disqualify me from writing this book. You can relax; I'm not a fuzzy-headed academic, metaphysical softie chock full of personal growth axioms, ex-coach into team-building, or any other sort of theorist. I'm a *very* battle-scarred veteran. I've had as many as 48 employees, had a dozen for a number of years, then 5, then 3, then 1. I've had 'em in manufacturing, retail, direct sales, and publishing businesses. I've employed my parents, my brothers, my wife, my ex-wife, but mostly strangers. MBAs and minimum-wage earners. You will *know,* when you read this book, that I am "real," that I have been where you are, that I am talking from bloodied-nose experience, not ivory-tower theory.

My clients employ hundreds of thousands of people. I have clients with as many as 1,500 stores, large field sales forces, and, more commonly, 10 to 100 mixed employees—clerical, sales, customer service, fulfillment. At the time that I wrote this, I personally worked, in-depth, hands-on, with owners of 34 different businesses ranging in size from $1 million or so a year to $30 million. However, through my networks of consultants and coaches, I am in touch with over 1 million small to medium-sized business owners each year. And one thing they all have in common: gripes, complaints, disappointments, frustrations, pain, and agony with regard to their employees. Much of this has to do with unreasonable expectations and a misunderstanding of the actual nature of employer-employee relationships. Some of it lies squarely at the fault of the business owner for failing in one or more of the Three Requirements For Having Employees: Leadership, Management, Supervision. Some is unavoidable if you must have employees.

I do tell my clients: the fewer, the better—none if possible. I'm much happier without them, and you would be, too. And most businesses have many more than they need. But if you insist on having them, they come with responsibility; there are things you must do continuously to keep them from stealing you blind, to force them to perform to your specifications, to reward those who do, to rid yourself of those who won't. This book is about all those things. For many it will be a bucket of cold water in the face, an eye-opening shocker, a loud, clanging wake-up call. I have been called the Professor of Harsh Reality for a reason. For some, it will be an overdue permission slip to finally start managing your business as if it really is *your* business. For many, it will lead to greater profits, its primary purpose.

This is the 18th book in my *No B.S.* series. It may be the most No B.S. of them all. Hundreds of thousands of my books have been bought by business owners all over the world, and, fortunately, these readers eagerly await the next title and keep coming back for more. From what they write and tell me, the popularity is thanks to the blunt, unvarnished truth telling, the frank talk, the unequivocal positions. You may not agree with me, but you won't have any confusion about where I stand. These days, that's something. If this is the first *No B.S.* book you're reading, give it a chance. I think you'll appreciate just how different it is from the other business books you've read. Let me know what you think. You can communicate with me directly, by fax, (602) 269-3113.

You will also meet Keith Lee in this book. Keith is a "management systems guy." From personal experience building and operating two different very successful companies, he developed—initially out of need and self-defense—micro-detailed, fail-safe systems spanning selection and hiring of the right people for each purpose to managing people, information, and activities by the navigational star of maximum profit. These systems work so well, envious business owners who are customers of his companies or know him through association began asking him to share his secrets. The result is now a third company, working with small and midsize business owners nationwide, installing better management systems and coaching owners, CEOs, and managers. Keith is a nicer, kinder, gentler guy that I am. Yet, he is still about imposition of strict disciplines on every function of business and on the people who perform or administer those functions. I'm confident you'll find his chapters included here of great value.

Finally, I'd like to acknowledge that I am best known as an advertising, marketing, and direct-marketing expert, helping business owners and entrepreneurs skyrocket lead flow, sales, and growth. Some people are surprised to find me meddling in management. They shouldn't be. Pouring money in the form of leads, prospects, and customers or clients or patients into a bucket riddled with holes, leaking at its bottom, is miserably unproductive. Much of my good work is sabotaged by a business's people and its owner's lousy management of them. In direct marketing, everything starts unraveling at the first point human employees get involved. I once told a new client offering me $2 million to fix his advertising and marketing not to hire me and instead go get the way his stores' phones were answered fixed, the way his salespeople sold fixed, the way they followed up on unconverted leads fixed, and their own internal misinformation mess fixed. This advice was neither welcomed nor acted on. I took his money and did the best I could, but I witnessed a lot of sabotage and waste and tragedy. It was like bolting a rocket engine onto an old biplane made of rotting wood and held together with duct tape. You really can't separate marketing from management. And you have to understand that management is not an expense—it is a way of *making money.*

—Dan S. Kennedy

PS: There is an important FREE GIFT OFFER from me on page 379 of this book. This gift can really skyrocket your profits. It's also the way to continue our relationship beyond this book. Please take a minute to act on it.

Important Notices

1. *The opinions expressed in this book are those of the author, not necessarily those of the publisher.* Some of these opinions are exaggerated in order to make a point, be provocative, or be humorous. The book is intended for people with a sense of humor. One of the author's beliefs is if you don't offend somebody by noon each day, you aren't saying or doing much. He has made sure to exceed the quota here. If you are easily offended and do not have a sense of humor, you probably should NOT read this book.

2. *For those of you who are gender- or political-correctness sensitive, to head off letters:* The author has predominately used *he, him,* etc., throughout the book with only occasional exception, rather than awkwardly saying *he or she, him or her.* He does not mean this as a slight to women, only as a convenience. He is not getting paid by the word.

3. *This publication is designed to provide accurate and authoritative information in regard to the subject matter covered.* While every effort has been made to ensure factual accuracy, no warranties concerning such acts are made. This book

is published for general information and entertainment purposes only. It is sold with the understanding that the publisher is not engaged in rendering legal, accounting, or other professional services. If legal advice or other expert assistance is required, the services of a competent professional person should be sought.

4. *Employment law is complex and tricky.* This author is not a lawyer or expert in employment law. This book is not intended as legal advice of any kind, including advice regarding employment law. You're on your own. Neither the author nor publisher accepts any responsibility or liability whatsoever for any decisions you make or actions you take as an alleged result of something you read in this book, especially if it involves homicide.

Copyright © Dan Kennedy 2007

Vincent Palko
www.AdToons.com

CHAPTER 1

Gobbledygook
"R" Us

"Because of the fluctuational predispositions of your position's productive capacity as juxtaposed to government standards, it would be momentarily injudicious to advocate an increment."

—ALEXANDER HAIG WHEN SECRETARY OF STATE

"I don't get it."
"Exactly."

—CONVERSATION BETWEEN ALEXANDER HAIG,
THEN SECRETARY OF STATE, AND HIS AIDE

I hold in my hand a brochure sent to me in the mail from a highfalutin' university's school of management, attempting to sell me on attending its $4,950.00 two-day seminar titled "Managing the New Workforce: Leadership and Strategy."

This brochure, as well as the seminar it pitches, represents everything that's wrong with at least 90% of everything being fed to business owners and executives about managing people. It is, in a word, B.S.—but let me demonstrate.

First, it's chock full of vague, meaningless gobbledygook. Nice sounding, until you critically analyze it. Here are a few priceless examples:

Expand your own perspective and deepen your understanding of how to learn and act on the values and needs that drive a growing portion of your workforce.

Huh? What, exactly, is the take-away, practical value there? After all, you aren't really interested in running a group therapy program for your employees, are you?

It gets better . . .

With demographic shifts come new demands on leaders who must be prepared to find, develop, and retain the New Workforce.

This is a statement of fact, not a promise of a solution. The brochure is full of these and actually only lists five benefits, one of which is that "expand your perspective" thing. And, really, what is this "New Workforce" anyway? It's gobbledygook. It makes it sound like aliens from outer space have arrived and suddenly replaced all your employees. Hey, demographic shifts in available employees aren't anything new. They've been a constant since at least the Industrial Revolution. Lincoln freed the slaves. Off we went. Women came into the workforce. Asians, Hispanics, attention-deficit-disordered youth. Pfui. And you don't want to be prepared (with deeper understanding!) to find, develop, and retain any New Workforce anyway. That misses THE point. You want to be prepared to find, develop, and retain a productive workforce that produces maximum profit for your business. You see, the professors' very idea of the purpose of employing people, even of owning a company, is misguided. Certainly not in sync with yours.

And I'll bet you'll be wildly excited about this . . .

A multigenerational panel discussion will provide an opportunity for participants to interact with undergraduate

junior and senior students majoring in business. With an aim toward highlighting both differences and similarities among the generations, participants will come away with a deeper understanding of what makes these young employees tick.

There sure is a lot of talk here about "deeper understanding." Meaning you, the guy handing out the paychecks, have to more deeply understand the gentle, fragile, difficult-to-motivate, complex individuals entrusted to your care. Gee, sounds like you're running a day-care center.

Now here's what is NOT mentioned anywhere in this brochure: managing people for PROFIT. I read every word very carefully. Since I was occasionally convulsed with laughter, I reread it. The word "profit" does not appear. Not even once.

I wonder why?

Because—like virtually all these university-sponsored seminars, most other management seminars, most management books, most newsletters for managers, etc.—this puppy's being taught by people whose management experience is limited to organizing their sock drawers. No claim is made of even one day spent in the real world, dealing with real employees and real problems—let alone an imperative to create profit. This particular $4,950.00, two-day excursion into the theoretical world of psychobabble has four speakers:

An Academic Director (whatever that is) who is a visiting lecturer at the school of management. That's it. That's all that's said about her in the brochure. Presumably because there's nothing else to say.

A Chief Marketing Officer and an Adjunct Associate Professor of Marketing at, of course, the school of management. Hmm, Professor of Marketing—maybe he put this nifty brochure together.

A Diversity Coach who wrote a book, *Managing Differently.* Honest to Mabel, a "Diversity Coach!" "Go be diverse for the Gipper!" I wonder, are the Diversity Cheerleaders going to be there too? Maybe a marching band. Okay, that's harsh. Heck, I run business coaching programs myself. But this diversity scam has gone way, way too far. It's replaced the sexual harassment and gender sensitivity scam that previously sucked fortunes out of scared corporate coffers. And the fad before it. Enough already. We're diverse. Get over it. Get to work. The *job* isn't diverse. And the *coach* word has become the most overused term since *excellence.*

Nowhere does it say any of these "experts" ever took over a troubled company with horrid employee morale and massive quality control problems and turned it around. Or managed a workforce in a way that led to any measurable accomplishment, like increasing profits by 30% over a year. Or even managed a Dairy Queen. It doesn't say any of these things because it's selling *professors.* (If any of them have actually accomplished anything worth bragging about, managing a *real* workforce, failing to mention it is still telling. It reveals a certain mindset about the relative importance of practical experience and street smarts vs. academic theory and philosophy. There's a smugness to it. The folks with the leather elbow patches on tweed jackets and tenure looking down their noses at us sleeves-rolled-up, boots-in-the-muck folks.)

Of course, YOU are a real business owner in the real world, very unlikely to fall for this. I imagine a bunch of corporate executives who also can't spell *p-r-o-f-i-t* go on their companies' tabs and have a grand old time playing eight-people-at-a-table workshop games with their Diversity Coach, then head for happy hour. I doubt you'd catch an entrepreneur in here on a bet.

But the trouble is, this buffoonery and charlatanism seeps out of the colleges' little side businesses and infects the thinking of business owners in many other ways. This sort of academic gobbledygook and classroom theory finds its way into the articles you and I read in real business magazines, into the books on management we might turn to for help. These professor types actually get hired to come in and screw around in real companies we own or invest in or rely on as vendors. They get hired to speak at our associations' conventions. And if you hear this stuff enough, you might think it has a place in your business.

It's actually a cancer on corporate America. Untold millions of dollars and millions of hours are wasted on this sort of thing. Everybody's in meetings and group discussions and quality circles and deeper-understanding retreats when they should be *working*. Managers are embroiled in trying to implement this feel-good, talk-in-circles, meaningless stuff when they need to be *managing*.

I've watched otherwise intelligent CEOs and top executives sit in meetings, listening to this silliness, none willing to state the obvious—that the professor has no clothes. I guess for fear of appearing unsophisticated in front of the others. So budgets get approved by people who won't, themselves, have to suffer through the exercise, who can't clearly explain what they're buying, and who have no way of holding it accountable for increased profits.

It's sad enough this permeates big, dumb companies.

Whatever you do, keep it out of *yours*. You really need to put up barriers. Inoculate yourself. As a good start, any suggestions about managing your business or the people in it coming from somebody who can't show his success at managing businesses (profitably)—like a professor—ought to be ignored or viewed as comedy.

I'll go further. Be cautious about bringing "the gobbledygook culture" into your company with your hiring. In his book *Car Guys vs. Bean-Counters*, Bob Lutz uses the term "the MBA virus" to describe a takeover of a business by academic, management, and marketing theory, producing a permanent cloudiness of needless complexity. I have one client, two partners who began as kitchen table entrepreneurs, who now own a billion-dollar-a-year enterprise. I frequently spot their ads in the marketing journals, advertising open positions. Most include "MBA required." One of these men is a college dropout, the other never attended college. I have, a number of times over 30 years, been one of their highest paid advisors, and I never attended college either. None of us could get hired at their company. In recent years, in my occasional work with them and participation in meetings with various teams within their company, I find the MBA virus. When it infects a business, as it has this one, decision-making has slowed, bureaucracy has grown like vines on a brick wall, and it's hard to find anybody managing things with entrepreneurial background or directing marketing who has sold its kind of products to its kind of consumers, nose to nose. People entrusted with millions of dollars have opinions birthed in classrooms but zero experience in actually making real money.

Of course, you want to surround yourself with people smarter than you are if you can. But "better educated" does not necessarily mean "smarter."

Oh, and to keep picking on the management school's brochure for its seminar because it's such an easy target: There's one thing other than mention of profit that you won't find anywhere in it: a guarantee. My own company and dozens of my clients often conduct seminars for business owners, with fees ranging from less than $4,950.00 to four times that much. These seminars are always guaranteed, often by more than your money back: If, at the end of the first day, you aren't thrilled with the practical value you're getting, say so, leave, and get a full fee refund plus your airfare and hotel tab reimbursed. Why do *we* do such a thing? Because we can. Why don't the professors? I leave you to your own conclusions. **But here are the litmus tests you might consider whenever shelling out your hard-won dough for business advice:**

1. It's from somebody who's been where you are and done what you hope to do.
2. It's from somebody with real business battle scars.
3. It's from somebody who can prove profit comes from his advice—preferably in his own past or present businesses as well as others'.
4. It comes with a guarantee.

Two of the management books I now recommend as required reading (see page 363 for complete list) are by Bob Lutz, veteran of four different automakers but best known for his tenure at GM: *Car Guys vs. Bean Counters: The Battle for the Soul of American Business* and *Icons and Idiots*. He recounts tales of corporate dysfunction that will send chills up your spine and get you laughing out loud. The outright silliness that permeates corporate America, affecting management and marketing, is truly amazing. Much of it comes from academia, from MBAs, and from big-name consulting firms stocked with freshly graduated MBAs. It seems CEOs are as susceptible to fads as teenage girls, and as easily bamboozled as illiterate small-town farmers were by traveling medicine men at the turn of the last century.

This book is not for any of these people. Its first edition was absolutely shunned by the business media that serves the corporate world—from *Fast Company* to *Fortune*, despite my dutifully getting copies into the hands of a dozen such periodicals' editors, and despite buying full-page ads in several of these media. One took the time to send me a nasty note about how brutish and unenlightened it was. I researched him, and you can guess his story. Journalism degree. From the campus to editorial positions. Nary a day actually managing a business that had to turn a profit. That grubby matter left to others.

Well, a pox on 'em all. I don't work or write for that crowd anyway. My relationship is with the business owner who is armpit deep in it, day in, day out, fighting to wring profit out of his business. There is no place in your life for leadership *theory*, for psychobabble gobbledygook, for feel-goodism. This book is for you. A reality check. A *harsh* reality check. Clarity. Permission to manage rationally and, yes, ruthlessly when needed to achieve *your* objectives. Specific strategies that may rankle many, but can save you a lot of losses and headaches, and make you a lot of money. Which is the point of it all: to make you a lot of money.

Diversity Company Non-Fight Song

With new awareness we worship the gods of
Diversity, Sensitivity, and Flexibility
And cheerfully pretend Kwanza is
a real holiday.
Go D-I-V-E-R-S-I-T-E-E!

No Christmas trees, no Easter candy
But time off with pay to fight global warming
is fine 'n' dandy.
Go D-I-V-E-R-S-I-T-E-E!

At this company men can look pretty,
oh so pretty
'cuz we have classes in
sexual orientation sensitivity.
Go D-I-V-E-R-S-I-T-E-E!

For the new youth we must take special care
never to upset their delicate disposition
Criticism or be-back-from-lunch-on-time . . . beware
hostile workplace litigation.
Go D-I-V-E-R-S-I-T-E-E!

If he wears his backward hat indoors or
brings his goat to work
your new managerial imperative is to overlook.
Respect his unique cultural dignity.
Practice flexibility!
Go D-I-V-E-R-S-I-T-E-E!

Diversity Company Non-Fight Song

Demanding uniformity
stifles their creativity;
at the assembly line
it's the new hate crime.
Go D-I-V-E-R-S-I-T-E-E!

Clearly the new management think works so well
with all the cars we make recalled,
with customer service exported to India.
You may think you died and went to business hell
and wonder why truth and common sense so mauled,
but you just need to be more Mahatma Gandhia!
Go D-I-V-E-R-S-I-T-E-E!

Performance standards show no sensitivity.
Productivity is culturally subjective.
Tough-minded management, not a feasibility.
Only a Neanderthal would make profit the objective.
Go D-I-V-E-R-S-I-T-E-E!

CHAPTER 2

The True Nature of the
Employer-Employee
Relationship

*"One friend in a lifetime is much; two are many;
three are hardly possible."*

—HENRY ADAMS

F ew people ever want to acknowledge that the
relationship between employer and employee is inherently *adversarial.*

It is adversarial because your agenda is in conflict with
theirs, and you are constantly interfering with their ability to act
out their agenda. To impose your agenda, you must displace or
disrupt their agenda. Bluntly, you are a giant pain the ass.

Here's what might surprise you: I am *not* suggesting there's
something wrong with this, or that the employees are bad people
for having 13 or 30 or 300 things on their minds ranking in higher
priority, interest, and importance to them than the one thing
on top of your mind. I do not fault them at all for having their
agenda. To expect otherwise is simply stupid.

FIGURE 2.1: Conflicting Agendas

ON THEIR MINDS	ON YOURS
1. Taking care of kids	1. How much profit can we produce today?
2. Holding marriage together	
3. Planning for upcoming vacation, holiday, etc.	
4. Planning for upcoming weekend	
5. Planning night out with the girls/guys	
6. Getting bills paid	
7. Grocery shopping	
8. Finding out who Sue slept with over the weekend/office gossip	
9. Who will win *American Idol*?	
10. Social relationships at the office; who's a bitch, who's my friend	
11. Social activities at the office: lunch, football pool, birthdays	
12. Getting to work on time	
13. Getting off work right on time or early if possible	
14. Compliance with "The Program"	
15. How much profit can I produce for the company today?	

"Ownership Mentality" Is B.S.

They do not own your business. You do. Expecting employees to have "ownership mentality" is bull crap, despite the idea's popularity with some management gurus. It's irrational. It's like trying to make the zebras on display at Disney's Animal

Kingdom® park care deeply and profoundly about how many tickets were sold at the front gate today! The zebras care about getting enough good food to eat and not being eaten by a bigger animal. You can put 'em in team-building retreats all you want; they're still coming back with eating as #1, not being eaten as #2, finding warm sun to lay in #3, and it's a long, long way down their list before ticket sales comes up.

Your business is your life and your life is your business. They are intertwined and inseparable. Not so for your employees. Shocking as it may be to you, they have lives all their own. They think about all sorts of things a lot that you barely think about at all, like the price of gas or lettuce or movie tickets. They think *T.G.I.F.* You think: *I need another day this week to work.* They hope no customers wander in 15 minutes before closing time to delay their escape; you pray somebody comes in. You care passionately about profit. They probably don't think about it at all or, if they do, they resent how much of it you make at their expense, through their sweat and blood.

You own the zoo. They are zebras.

Their agendas are often at opposition with yours, as in the example: They want to hurry customers out 15 minutes before closing whether they buy anything or not, so they can get out the door a minute early to meet their friends over at Applebee's® before the chicken wings get cold. You want every customer treated like fragile china, made to feel welcome, courteously helped, never rushed, and sold something, even if your employee has to close 15 minutes late. You are not on the same page here and never will be. Not even with employees paid commissions or bonuses. I have been hurried out of an OfficeMax store 15 minutes before closing but I've also been rushed out of a car dealership at 3:00 P.M. on a Sunday afternoon. At home their spouse, who they sleep with, and depending on how long married occasionally have sex with, who therefore has more clout than you do, is leaning on them to be home or at the restaurant or at Johnny's T-ball game ON TIME. Angry if they aren't. And, of course, completely uninterested in your agenda.

On top of all that, there is the unavoidable resentment that comes with disparities in wealth and power. Consequently, if you could be privy to their discussions behind your back or among friends and family, you would hear that resentment bubble up and expressed constantly, many different ways, and agreed with and encouraged by those around them. I've even sat forgotten in clients' waiting rooms or small offices near enough to the front desk to eavesdrop and heard these conversations taking place on the employer's time. Your employees tend to believe they are doing all the work and you are getting all the money, and they count gross, not net. They see your new car, hear of you redecorating your house, see you away from the store at your beach house while they toil in the hot sun in the fields, and they resent you for it. The very fact that you can fire them but they can't fire you, that you dictate when they can take a vacation but you take yours whenever you feel like it, pisses them off. They think they are smarter than you are, know better than you do, and resent having to go along with your crazy schemes and new ideas.

This mindset is reinforced incessantly in and by the media. The mainstream media eagerly reports on something like the fast food workers' wage complaints, its commentators wringing hands and weeping crocodile tears over these people's need for a "living wage." Little is ever said about these people's need to educate themselves, develop more valuable skills, and raise themselves up to a living wage. No context is provided about the business owner's investment, risk, shrinking profit margins, rising taxes, and rising costs for each employee. It's a one-way presentation. Overall, the demonizing of Producers and of the rich that has been inflamed during the Obama years has furthered the difficulty in getting people to do their best work for the pay they agreed to take. The resentment toward work and toward the "slave masters" who try to compel work is greater than I've ever seen it. This is not helpful to you.

Finally, their minds have been captured by their very mobile toys. Shopping at Amazon, playing Angry Birds, or sneaking looks at porn sites on the desktop computer on company time *was* the problem when I wrote the first edition of this book. It still is, but multiplied exponentially and made infinitely easier, thanks to the proliferation of pads and smartphones and constant, uninterrupted connection to the online amusement park. Also, interruptions were calls and emails, now, added, texts—and many people get during work hours from 50 to 300 that have nothing to do with work, not to mention Facebook updates, Twitter, etc., etc. All this ranks high on their agenda for their day. Way higher than how can they be most productive and create the greatest profit for their employer?

No B.S. Ruthless Management Truth #1

Employees are employees.

They are *not* your friends. You can and, to a degree, should be friendly with them and encourage them to be friendly with you. You want whatever foxhole camaraderie can be created as you go. Just don't lose sight that if trapped together in the foxhole when all the food runs out, they won't hesitate to carve you up for dinner. Of course you should recognize their birthdays, childbirths, and anniversaries and genuinely care about their health and well-being. Just know that the birthday cake they bring in for you has arrived only partly due to friendship but partly due to obligation and compulsion.

They are *not* your family. You can be familial to a degree if you like. But don't con yourself. They will not be visiting you at the assisted living center after the paychecks stop. They have a family, and you aren't in it.

They are your employees.

The Requirement of "Accurate Thinking"

In his books, including *Think and Grow Rich*, Napoleon Hill presented principles practiced by the hundreds of great industrialists and entrepreneurs of his time. The one least interesting to his books' millions of readers is Accurate Thinking. Everybody likes the Desire one, but nobody seems to like the Accurate Thinking one. They like the pleasant ones. But Hill didn't mean his principles as a cafeteria, any more than Moses meant to report the Ten Suggestions as a mix 'n match, pick 'n choose menu. On Hill's list, it's my opinion the least liked Accurate Thinking is the most important. If you refuse to think about your real relationship with your employees accurately, rationally, and realistically, you are forever doomed to disappointment, frustration, rage, and financial losses throughout your busi-ness. If

> "ACCURATE THINKING is one of the most important foundation stones of all enduring success. This separates 'facts' from mere 'information.' It teaches you how to build definite working plans, in the pursuit of any calling, out of facts."
>
> —NAPOLEON HILL, IN *LAWS OF SUCCESS*

you acknowledge the true relationship and think about it accurately, you will manage your business and the people in it very differently than if you insist on thinking of these people as friends, family, team members, or even colleagues.

Recommended Resource #1

Napoleon Hill is best known for his books *Think and Grow Rich* and *Laws of Success,* and I recommend reading or re-reading what he has to say in them about accurate thinking. I also strongly recommend his last and least famous book, *Grow Rich with Peace of Mind.*

On TV, I think on The Discovery Channel, I saw this report about a guy who went into the woods to live with bears. He believed the bears had intelligence and souls and were caring individuals. He projected onto them human characteristics, just like we do to our pets, and just like we project onto our employees the characteristics we want them to have. He grew his hair, made himself smell like bears, and actually did move into a cave with a big family of bears. He made this into the relationship with the bears that he wanted to have with them. (This was my dad's downfall in his brief experience in sales management, in network marketing: He had a very different relationship with his distributors in his mind than existed in reality.) One day, with no apparent provocation, the bears ate this guy. His family and the people making this

Copyright © Dan Kennedy 2007

Vincent Palko
www.AdToons.com

documentary were properly horrified and much moaning and hand wringing went on. *Why oh why would the bears do such a thing?*

Because they are bears.

And wild bears' perception of dull-witted, foolish, and slow humans is: They're food.

The only sensible question is: Why did the bears wait so long to eat him?

CHAPTER 3

Shelby's Excuse
List

"I had thought very carefully about committing
hari-kari (ritual suicide) over this,
but I overslept this morning."

—FORMER JAPANESE LABOR MINISTER TOSHIO YAMAGUCHI

F or several years, I had an interest in a small
chain of cosmetic salons. We were not required to have
licensed cosmeticians because our employees only talked
the customers through the process of applying their own glop.
They were really salespeople in lab coats, primarily selling
a nonsurgical face-lift kit, then selling for about $300.00. The
biggest of the salons, and the one where the weekly batch of
new hires came to work their first couple of weeks, was in our
office building, just down the hall from my office. With my door
open, I could hear our rather coarse sales manager, a guy named
Shelby, yelling every morning: "Just give me the damn number!"

On the wall in Shelby's office, there was a large poster board
with a numbered list of excuses for being late for work. #14: My

dog swallowed my car keys. #37: It's my time of month. #41: I got on the wrong bus. He said it saved a lot of time just having them tell him the appropriate number.

This was comedy at the time. I thought Shelby was funny, the situation funny, actually the whole business funny.

But it's also symbolic of something that's not funny at all: accepting unacceptable behavior.

My speaking colleague of nine years, friend, and famous motivational figure, Zig Ziglar, told an old story about how a frog can get cooked in the squat. Since a frog has the ability to jump quite high, if you take a frog and toss him in a big pot of boiling water, he'll jump right out. But if you put the frog in a pan of room temperature water, he'll stay there. Frogs like water. Then if you ever so slowly turn up the heat on the stovetop he may sit there still, not really noticing the water getting warmer and warmer and warmer until—in spite of his God-given ability to save himself—he gets cooked in the squat.

This is how a lot of business owners get cooked in the squat by their employees. The employees' behavior worsens gradually over time. Little by little by little, one bad one poisons the others. Occasional tardiness becomes frequent tardiness, then constant tardiness. Sloppy appearance goes from rare to occasional to routine. Work left undone, rare, occasional, common. And the business gets cooked in the squat.

If you occasionally accept occasional unacceptable behavior, it's only a matter of time before you are routinely accepting routine unacceptable behavior.

Copyright © Dan Kennedy 2007

Vincent Palko
www.AdToons.com

CHAPTER 4

The Willy Loman Syndrome
Moves to Management

"I have 14 other grandchildren and if I pay one penny now,
then I'll have 14 kidnapped grandchildren."

—J. PAUL GETTY,
EXPLAINING HIS REFUSAL TO PAY A RANSOM

illy Loman is the lead character in Arthur Miller's play *Death of a Salesman*. The death of a salesman is a desperate desire to be liked, above all else—including making sales. This is so common a disease among failing sales professionals it's called the Willy Loman Syndrome. However, it is contagious beyond salespeople. Managers get infected, too. A manager is severely handicapped, dangerously vulnerable, and certain to be ineffective if he is an approval seeker, a person who needs to be *liked* by his subordinates.

Why the word *ruthless* in this book's title? Isn't that a bit harsh? Most business owners are anything but. They give chance after chance after chance, tolerate incompetence and insubordination, twist themselves into a pretzel trying not to fire even the worst employee ever to walk the earth. Most business owners try too hard to be "a good boss," meaning a boss liked by the employees, rather than an effective boss, or one who sets and enforces standards and procedures in order to create maximum possible profits. I find even ex-Marine tough guys who are pretty ruthless in other aspects of their business soft as mashed potatoes when it comes to managing the people they pay. Many enunciate fear statements, like "If I demand she does that, she'll quit" or wimp statements like "My people just won't do that." Even though in my consulting and coaching relationships I'm supposed to be dealing with marketing, I find myself fixing these travesties, helping business owners grow a pair. So I think *ruthless* is the direction most need to move in.

One of my favorite stories from the trenches involves the owner of a company with 22 offices scattered over three states, and a corporate office really running three businesses in one. After about three years of working with me, his longtime executive assistant came out and told him: "You were a much nicer guy before you started listening to that Kennedy guy," and "I don't like working here anymore." Notably, his company's profits had increased nearly 35% over those three years. He correctly suggested to her it would be most appropriate for her to find a different place of employment where she could be happier. As an accountant, he was able to grasp the fact that there's no bonus added by the bank to his deposits nor extra contribution made to his retirement fund because Bertha is *happy* . Of course I'm not advocating intentionally making everybody unhappy. But somehow, employees and opinion makers have gotten it into their heads that it's your job to make your employees happy. They forget you are paying them to work and generate profits. There are businesses that make people happy, ranging from Disneyland® to Nevada brothels. They all charge fees *for* doing so.

So, yes, I very deliberately used the word *ruthless* to grab attention. One person's *ruthless* is another person's *sane* approach to business. After you read this book, you can draw your own conclusions.

I expect some very harsh, critical reviews. I expect about 33% of the business owners to recoil from what I've put between these pages as they might if finding a bevy of large snakes busily consuming rats under the bed sheets. If that's you, I offer no apologies. Only sympathy. I will probably hear from some of you. It won't be fan mail. You might want to know before writing that I practice as policy "immunity to criticism."

I expect about 33% to rejoice that—*finally*—somebody is speaking the truth and providing both permission to behave in a sane manner as a business owner toward employees and honestly practical advice for doing so. I expect to hear from a lot of you. Of your relief. Of being emboldened. Of your success.

I expect the middle 33% to just be perplexed. But then, the middle 33% is pretty much perplexed 100% of the time about 100% of everything. You know who they are, in your company and out on the street. Easy to spot. They have that perplexed look on their faces.

If you're in the 33% who are rejoicing, congratulations and welcome.

What you need to know most is that Willy Loman would be even more of a failure as a manager than he was as a salesman. There is absolutely no evidence whatsoever that a manager liked by the employees creates more productivity or more profitability for the company. In fact, in sports it's rather common to see underperforming players rallying around the unsuccessful coach they like, trying to keep him from being fired. Not only is the boss who's liked by everybody not any more successful than the boss who's not liked at all, he may even be less successful. It's okay and probably advisable to take "being liked" off the table altogether. There are a number of other more important priorities.

The new-style "fun palace" workplaces can't go without comment. This is a popular fad, born of Google® and its workplace environment, and academic theorists' love for it, and media infatuation—including creation of a plethora of awards for "best place to work" in a given city or industry. There are even "most fun place to work" awards. So, companies are busily putting in playrooms, nap rooms, having recess and nap times, and employees are zipping around on electric roller skates and *playing*. I am a founding stockholder in a fast-growth software company that has a "Cereal Bar" for its employees, with a range of flavors of cereal and milk, free, and this firm has won some "best place to work" awards. It makes me nervous over my investment. I actually cashed out a lot of my equity during a round of expansion financing with Goldman Sachs because of this.

I *guess* you can't argue with Google's success, but everywhere else I've seen the "care and feeding of" approach taken, it has ruined productivity and profits. As I was writing this, Facebook was publicly discussing plans to build its own town for its employees to live in, where they can be cared for 24/7, have their laundry done, their refrigerators stocked, and have little buses ferrying them to and from work. This is something of a throwback to the company towns of the early steel, coal, and other Industrial Revolution companies. It suggests these people dare not be left to care for themselves, and that the best productivity might be obtained by waking them up, getting them up, getting them dressed, feeding them, and bringing them to a job as if the mother who must get her small, utterly unreliable child to school. Amazon took and takes a very different approach.

The workplace as kindergarten and the coddling of employees as little children may be uniquely necessary with tech-tots in Silicon Valley. I suspect it also reflects some egotism of certain companies' founders and leaders, a new form of bragging right—look how progressive we are!

With 40-plus years' long backward view, I count it as just another management fad, in a long line of such fads, most that have come and gone. I am with Jeff Bezos. When you come to work, you should be in a workplace, and you should work hard, fast, and intensely. You should be laser-beam focused. You should be under pressure of urgency. In the book *The Everything Store: Jeff Bezos and the Age of Amazon,* its author, Brad Stone, who has reported on Amazon for 15 years, says that a great many past and present Amazon employees bemoan the fact that Bezos is *extremely* difficult to work for. Stone reports that despite Bezos' cheerful public persona, he is capable of the same kind of acerbic outbursts as Steve Jobs—who could terrify any employee who stepped into an elevator with him. Bezos is a micromanager who reacts harshly to efforts that don't meet his rigorous standards. About working for him, one former executive referred to the company motto, "Get Big Fast," and said, "There were deadlines and death marches." I can tell you that my most successful clients surround themselves with very self-reliant people, not babies who need to be brought their blankies and warm milk, cooed at, sung calming songs. I am also right there with Marissa Mayer who took the very unpopular position that Yahoo! employees should actually come to work at Yahoo!, rather than at Starbucks, the park, or at home. Her move on this is somewhat akin to Bezos' unpopular banning of prepared PowerPoint presentations at all meetings, instead dictating that employees be able to enunciate and argue for their ideas, be interrupted and challenged, and think on their feet.

A big entity like Google, with extraordinary profit margins, with no manufactured goods costs, and unlimited access to other people's money, can conceal a lot of dysfunction. It can afford four people to do the work of one. Growth can mask a lot of sins. It's when growth levels off, and profitability becomes the governing mandate, that a lot of chicanery and foolishness gets exposed. This, a version of Buffett's line: You can't really tell who's naked until the tide goes *out*.

Your company is probably not anything like Google. It's unlikely that you have access to an unlimited ocean of investors' money. You probably have to make things, inventory things, deliver things. You probably don't have anything close to monopolistic power. You probably need to make real profits, consistently, day in and day out, and for you to wind up taking home enough to grow and stay rich—your reason for being in business—those profits need to be substantial. They must cover reinvestment needs and growth financing, a dizzying array of taxes, the occasional trauma or crisis. You probably do not have the luxury of throwing money about carelessly. Therefore, being "inspired" by Google or some similar "magic enterprise" in managing your workforce, your workplace, or your money is a bad idea.

There will be a day, mark my words, when some turnaround guy with a steel spine and a bloody hatchet has to be brought into Google, as well as to companies copying its culture, to ruthlessly slash away at all the accumulated, out-of-control fat and waste and sloth. Harsh accountability for costs will occur. Demands will be made for proof that happy-making expenditures are producing profits.

So let's be clear. You can't have *as goals* being beloved by your troops, being the provider of the coolest place to work, being recognized as a cool place to work by media, or being envied by your peers for your progressiveness. The last item's even juvenile, like Chevy Chase's character trying to best his neighbor with the biggest and most elaborate Christmas light display. If these things occur naturally as byproducts of you creating and managing (and policing) the most productive workplace and the most profit-producing workforce, fine, take the plaque and hang it proudly. But you can't afford to pursue that award plaque.

CHAPTER 5

The Program

"I believe in benevolent dictatorships,
provided I am the dictator."

—Sir Richard Branson

A lot of business owners get the performance from their employees they deserve because they have no real Program. As in "Hey, what's the Program around here?" You've asked it when you first reported to a new job at a new place. So does everybody else.

The Program is the way things are supposed to be done.

If you don't have a Program, you can't very well expect anybody to follow your Program, can you?

I'm not talking about the deadly dull, from a boilerplate template, with legal gobbledygook employee manual. I'm talking about clearly stated, illustrated, and taught expectations for how Bill and Betty are supposed to talk, walk, act, do. If you don't have a Program, your employees make up their own. They tell the new guy what their Program is. If you leave people to their own devices, you leave your outcomes to chance.

CHAPTER 6

Random and
Erratic Acts

"We can tell our men: Here is a certain amount of money you can realistically set out to make every week because we have a system for doing so—a system that never fails. Without such a system, goals are empty goals."

—W. CLEMENT STONE

I often accuse business owners of living by random and erratic acts.

This occurs with their advertising, marketing, and sales. They are often reacting belatedly to trailing facts, like a slump in last week's or last month's sales. They'll somehow stimulate a surge of new business, neglect present customers while serving the new, and then see a huge drop in sales after the brief rush is over. A lot of small businesses create that trouble with a Groupon promotion. You really aren't managing marketing this way. You are starting fires and putting out fires, but not managing.

To be manageable, a business's marketing, to obtain new customers and to monetize customers on an ongoing basis, has to have a solid foundation of systems. For example, there has to be a system for lead management that all new and prospective customers or clients are processed through in the same way, with Step 2 occurring on the fourth day after Step 1, Step 3 occurring eight days after Step 2, etc., and a series of "nexts," so any yes triggers a next yes or no, and any no triggers a next yes or no. Similar manageable systems you can diagram are needed for new customer retention and orientation, upsells for each product or purchase, rescue and reactivation of inactive customers, and, situationally, 5 to 50 more. You also need a system that predictably and steadily feeds new leads or prospects into your website, workshop, showroom, or store. Key word: *steadily*. I have probably offered a $100.00 bill to at least a thousand business owners, theirs if they can show or diagram and describe these systems in their businesses—and I have only twice handed it over.

A great marketing management system lets you know, within a small and acceptable range of variance, how many new prospects will start with you next week, how many new customers will buy from you next week, how many current customers will purchase next week, even how many referrals you will get next week. One restaurant owner says: "I hope we have a full house Friday night three weeks from now." Another can say: "We'll have between 'x' and 'y' number of customers here on Friday three weeks from now." And he can say this before a single reservation has been booked.

As this is not a marketing book, I'm not going to delve into the details of all this here. I simply use it as an illustration of the power of systems.

Living by random and erratic acts extends far beyond marketing.

Few people have a system for accumulating savings. Most business owners make contributions to their pension plans once or twice a year, and often have to borrow money in order to make the maximum contribution the week their accountant calls and tells them to. People will set aside money after a big, unexpected sale or some other windfall. A system is to direct a pre-set-in-stone percentage of every dollar that comes to you over to an untouchable "Wealth Account," and from that invest. That's one-half of a wealth-building system fully described in my book, *No B.S. Wealth Attraction for Entrepreneurs.* At the end of a multiyear term, who do you think will have accumulated more money—the person randomly putting money into his Wealth Account when there is money "left over" to put there or when occasional windfalls occur or the person systematically putting 7% of every inbound dollar into his Wealth Account?

Few people have systems for managing their businesses or their people, and even fewer have such systems tuned to maximum productivity and profit. Some have basic operations checklists and *specific* operations systems, but very few are fully systemized. A carpet cleaning company may have a specific procedure for the way its technicians are supposed to enter a home, quote a job, clean the carpets, but do they have a system for insuring the techs actually do it as prescribed? No. Do they have a system for consistent feedback to technicians about that performance? No. And you might be surprised at how many such companies have five technicians out there with five trucks, each doing things differently. A few years ago, when starting consulting with a large health products company, with over 1,000 offices, I got transcripts of recordings of actual face-to-face sales presentations delivered to consumers by ten of their purportedly best representatives, in ten different offices. If you reviewed them side by side as I did and weren't told they were all representatives of the same company, selling the same product, you'd never guess it!

The less freelancing by your people, the more order, the more consistency experienced by your customers, and the better your feedback loops are with your people, the better your business can handle growth and the greater your profits will be.

In the next three chapters, my friend and a client I advise, Keith Lee, has experience-based insights and important advice on systems. You'll find discussions of systems in general, a staff management system, and a customer service management system. Keith has built and now operates four different, thriving businesses of significant size. They are not businesses that lend themselves to hands-off management, yet he has engineered them to be self-operating, with very little day-to-day dependence on him. Most business owners can only dream of this. Instead, they are the prime creators of random and erratic acts inside their businesses.

There is a restaurant I patronize often enough to sense and correctly deduce whether or not its owner is on the premises or not within 30 seconds of entering. The difference is palpable. It then reveals itself more fully in a variety of ways, particularly in the quality of the service. A lot of businesses are this owner dependent. It is why the owners of service businesses are reluctant to add more trucks and technicians, dentists are reluctant to add associate doctors and open additional offices, and why, overall, businesses' growth or expansion is so often fraught with peril and pain. The business and its staff are full of randomness, of freelancing, of "Well, I have *my* way of doing things," and of coaching by crisis. Keith has developed effective means of replacing this chaos with *organized effort*. I think that's a key term. Lots of people and lots of teams of people do put forth a lot of effort but never really get any better at what they're doing or get to their desired goals. Effort's not it. *Organized* effort is. I think you'll find these three chapters illuminating.

Most people even lack systems for managing themselves. Business owners take and process information randomly. They go to their place of business and react to whatever each day brings. They do not budget time as they would money. Frankly, if you can't or won't manage yourself, what makes you think you should or can manage others? If you can't or won't measure, daily, your progress toward specific goals, how will you persuade anybody else to do so? If you won't hold yourself ruthlessly accountable, how dare you hold anyone else accountable? "Sloppiness" is not a privilege or perk of being the boss or the owner. You are entitled to a lot of privileges, but being a hot mess of disorganization isn't one of them. Running in and out of your business like a whirling dervish creating chaos or reacting randomly to whatever and whoever pops up are not the marks of a creative leader—they are dangerous behaviors.

There is a popular approach involving various kinds of personality assessments and tests, so that the business owner— who thinks of himself as a creative visionary who can't be bothered with organized effort—can match himself with staff of different temperaments, who will chase after him, clean up his messes, and fill in the details of his vague ideas for him. This is a dumb way to use personality typing. There's really no excuse for sloppy dysfunction. I'm an "idea person" myself, but I don't use it as an excuse. I have systems to manage myself, and even systems for production of ideas. It is a lie that creativity requires spontaneity and defies methodology.

My book, *No B.S. Time Management for Entrepreneurs* might better be titled *Self-Management*. It describes, in detail, my system for managing myself. It applies to my lives as an entrepreneur, as a consultant to others, as a direct-response marketing copywriter, and as a writer. It can apply to anyone in any field, because you have more power when you have more control.

Being self-employed, running an office of three, a salesforce of 30, or a company employing 300 can be a manic, high-stress, random and erratic acts dominated torture, incorrectly accepted as a necessary evil. That same situation can, instead, be a means

CHAPTER 7

How to Control Your
Business and Your Life

By Keith Lee

"No person will make a great business
who wants to do it all himself or get all the credit."

— ANDREW CARNEGIE

A s Dan Kennedy points out, employees can be a nightmare. I agree, but in almost all businesses employees are needed to really grow, and when managed properly, they can create the ultimate leverage, job security, and wealth for you.

You're likely reading this book for one of three reasons. In regards to managing your business you think:

1. You have become a slave to your business. It seems like you're always responding to things and taking care of problems. You have no time for yourself, and you're certainly not having any "fun."

2. Your business runs well, but if things ran smoother and you didn't have to do so many "regular everyday menial

things," you could work on the important thing, on actually improving and growing your business.

3. Your business is great, but you're always looking for ways to improve your efficiency and effectiveness.

You know that if you could control your business better you could accomplish a lot more. That's what this, and the next two chapters, are all about, taking control of your business and your life. **You will take total control of your business when you create systems to control your business.**

> **"All wealth is based on *systems*."**
> **—Dan Kennedy**

> **"Let systems run the business and people run the *systems*. People come and go but *systems* remain constant."**
> **—Michael Gerber**

> **"For a business owner, *systems* set you free."**
> **—Keith Lee**

I doubt this is the first time you've heard that systems are the key to controlling your business. The bestselling business book *The E-Myth Revisited*, by Michael Gerber, is all about systems, and Gerber has it exactly right. You need to "let systems run the business and people run the systems" because "people come and go but systems remain constant."

Gerber's book is excellent, and I suggest you read it. With that said, there are some big problems with *E-Myth*. I've met hundreds of business people who have read *The E-Myth Revisited*, but I don't know any who implemented what they learned there to create the systems they needed to truly control their business. They don't create those systems because they think systems take a tremendous amount of time to create, and they are complicated.

At emyth.com/business-coaching.com, they describe a Business Management System as follows . . .

It's a complex system of people and systems that are all evolving at the same time. To build a great business—to get out of survival mode—you need an outside perspective to help you see it clearly, someone who'll call it like it is and who won't waste your time and money with band-aids and tricks.

That Is Complete and Total B.S.!

Sure, an effective business management system evolves, and you want to use advisors like your CPA, attorney, banker, etc., at times. But it is **not** complex, and you sure as heck don't need an outside perspective (nursemaid), other than your own employees (team), to implement an effective business management system in your business.

Ask yourself, why does a business coach want you to believe that an effective business management system is complex, and you need an outside perspective?

It's simple: If it's complex and you need an "outside perspective," you need to hire him, paying him hundreds, maybe thousands of dollars a month, maybe forever.

Here's the Truth—Systems Are Simple

Dan Kennedy uses this example to show just how simple systems can be. When he used valet parking at a particularly well-run business, he got a business size card from the valet. It is printed with the six things you should expect when you use the valet. It's a very effective system that lets the customer know what to expect and tells the valet exactly what they should be doing. That's a system. Sure, some systems may need a longer explanation, but everything you do in your business can be written into easy-to-understand instructions.

It's that simple. You create a System when you document—put in writing—something that needs to be done in your business.

You create an Effective Business Management System when you have *everything* you do documented and you have an Effective Performance Management System in place.

STOP . . .

I know, I've probably scared you off by saying Performance Management System, but let me assure you I don't mean Performance Reviews because . . .

Performance Reviews Suck

In the next chapter I'll show you how to replace demotivating, demoralizing, and worst of all, counterproductive, Performance Reviews with motivating Personal Development Interviews that actually lead to the results you want.

But that's for the next chapter. Let's get back to systems.

Here's why you need systems. When you hire someone, over time, the knowledge the person has at that job rises. Without systems (everything in writing) what happens when that person leaves? The knowledge is gone, and someone is back to training the new person **one-on-one** in everything that needs to be done (see Figure 7.1).

But what if you have systems? That is, written documentation for everything that person does. What happens to knowledge when someone leaves and you have systems? (See Figure 7.2.)

It's that simple. When they leave, and every single thing they do is documented, how hard is it to replace that person and get the new person up to speed? Just think of the amount of time you'll save.

FIGURE 7.1: Without Systems

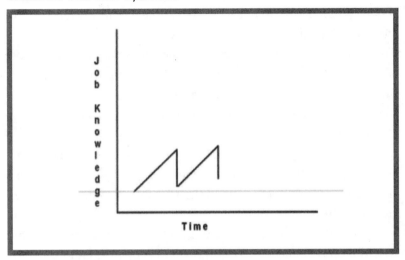

FIGURE 7.2: With Systems

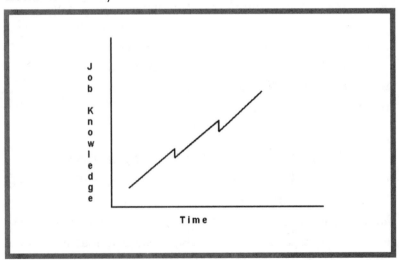

Dan Kennedy Says, "All Wealth Is Based on Systems"

When it's time to sell your business, what is it worth if you're critical to it? Not much!

What if you're not only not critical, but the business gets better whether you're there or not? What is your business worth now when it's time to sell? You know the answer.

When you have Systems in place for everything you do, Personal Development Interviews implemented (next chapter), and systems to consistently deliver world-class customer service (chapter after next), your business will improve whether you're there or not.

The goal I have with all my clients is to make them irrelevant to the day-to-day, then week-to-week, and then month-to-month operations of their business so they can create real wealth.

I recently went on a three-week Mediterranean cruise. I told our operations manager what cruise line I was on and the ship. That's it.

I knew I wasn't going to get a phone call. That's why I didn't need to worry about giving her any more information or getting an international phone number for three weeks. For the last 15 years, while on vacation, I've never gotten a phone call from work. That's the freedom you have when you have systems in place.

Frustrated, I Went Looking for the Answer

I started managing American Retail Supply (one of the businesses I now own) in 1981. By 1992, I was burnt out. It seemed I spent all my time solving problems, fixing things, working on menial everyday tasks, and not on the important activities that would allow us to continue to grow.

From 1981 to 1992 the business had grown dramatically, but so had my headaches. There had to be something better. I was a business school graduate for crying out loud. Why didn't what I had learned in college and from previous managers work?

I found this guy named W. Edwards Deming. He was a statistician in World War II. After the war he tried showing American manufacturers how to build quality products, but they weren't interested. There was so much demand for their products that it didn't matter if they made top-quality products or not. Deming took his ideas to Japan—**Toyota listened**.

Deming became a hero in Japan, and even today, the highest award for quality in Japan is the Deming Prize.

I read everything I could about Deming and his management methods. Most of it made sense, but it didn't really fit into a people business. So I read other management gurus—Joseph Juran and Phil Crosby, and it started to come together. But it still didn't quite fit.

Deming, Juran, and Crosby taught *manufacturers* how to produce quality. **When you're a manufacturer you can dial in quality**. You can build a better machine with closer tolerances and hire the best engineers to dial in quality, but in people businesses you can't dial in quality.

In people businesses quality is meeting, and preferably exceeding, your customer's expectations *every time*. You do that when you have systems in place to make sure you do each task correctly every time.

Actions Speak Louder Than Words

When I introduced our new management system at a companywide meeting in 1993, I told our team, "I know what you're thinking. You're thinking *this too will pass*. Keith has been at another seminar and got all jazzed up about this. I'll humor him, pretend it's the greatest thing since apple pie, but I know this too will pass. I want to tell you, this will not pass. This is how we will manage the business in the future, and I think you'll be excited about it."

But I still had to back it up with actions, and I did.

A number of years later the Make-You-Happy Management System led us to being named "The Best Small Business to Work for in Washington State" by *Washington CEO* magazine.

We didn't earn that honor because we had the highest pay, the greatest benefits, a child-care center, or any other bells and whistles. We earned it because *Washington CEO* magazine determined that the management of our company and our entire team were committed to the same Belief, Vision, Mission, and Goals.

Someone had nominated us as the Best Business to Work for in the state. I never found out who nominated us, but I decided to apply because the magazine promised to tell us how we did and why. I just wanted to know how we stacked up. I thought everyone here liked our systems idea, thought they built a better business, knew that we as a management team saw them as experts at their jobs, and that we truly valued and wanted their input to make the business better.

Washington CEO magazine asked me to give them the names of three people they could interview in the company. Again, I hadn't entered the contest to win. I entered to find out how we were doing, so I sent them our entire employee (team member) list. The next thing I knew the magazine staff was calling me to do an interview because we were named the "Best Small Business to Work for in Washington State."

They told me we did a lot of things right, and the number-one reason we were named the best small business to work for was because our management philosophy and company goals and objectives could be verbalized and were committed to by our frontline people better than any other entry.

We Were All on the Same Page—We Had BUY IN.
Here's How We Got There.

Right after I told my team that "this will not pass," I showed them my management system. Here's how I explained it to them. This is a participative exercise, so work through it with me.

Answer the following question right here. Don't read any more until you answer this question. What are the eight steps of solving a problem?

1. _____

2. _____

3. _____

4. _____

5. _____

6. _____

7. _____

8. _____

Assume you have the same question, but now you're part of a group with four other people and you have two guidelines:

1. Everybody must participate.
2. You need to achieve consensus with the answer. Consensus means that you can all agree that you have a very good answer. You may not all agree with everything in the answer, but you accept it as a very good answer.

Also assume that one of the members of the group is trained to facilitate these meetings and get consensus; and the group is filled with people who work at solving problems for a living. The people you're working with know, from working experience, not theory, how to solve problems.

Now the question is, which of these scenarios gets a better answer to the question, "What are the eight steps to solving a problem?" By yourself, or in the group?

When I do this exercise with groups, 95% of people say they get a better answer in the group.

Which takes longer? The group, of course. You need consensus in the group. You can make your own list lots quicker.

Can we afford to do this with everything in our business? Absolutely not. But you'll want to use this type of system on the important things, the complicated things, the things that affect more than one department in your business.

Why did I ask, "What are the eight steps to solving a problem?" Because it's like many business decisions you need to make. There's no right answer. There's no wrong answer. There are some really bad answers. There are some really good answers. And there's everything in between.

Here's an example. Many years ago we purchased new computer software, and we were supposed to be able to enter orders online while talking with the client. Months later our staff was still writing orders by hand and entering them when they got off the phone. If the customer didn't change his mind during the order, didn't order both a custom product and a stock product on the same order, or one of dozens of other scenarios, the software was fine. But for far too many orders, it was much easier to write the order down and then enter it.

We decided to redesign the software from the ground up and get the input we needed to make it truly client- and user-focused.

The salespeople were involved during the entire process, and we got accounting involved with issues like the customer being on credit hold when he placed the order. When it came to processing nonstock orders, we got purchasing involved. When it was time to address shipping issues, we got the warehouse staff involved.

There are three management types:

1. **X Theory** says, "I'm the owner, I'm the boss, I've built this company with my blood, sweat, and tears, do what I say and don't ask any questions."
2. **Y Theory** is what I learned in college. It says, "I'm the owner, I'm the boss, I built this company with my blood, sweat, and tears, this is what I want you to do; tell me what you think, and I'll tell you whether it's OK."

At this point in the training, whether in person or on DVD, we ask the employee, "Which would you rather work in? X or Y theory?" Almost everyone answers Y. They want to have input.

We then ask, "Which gets *better answers* to important issues, X or Y?" Everyone answers Y.

So virtually everyone would rather work in Y and almost everyone thinks you get better answers in Y theory.

But there's a third management type:

3. **Z Theory** says, "I'm the owner, I'm the boss, I'm the manager, I built this company with my blood, sweat, and tears. I know a lot, and when we have something that's important, I understand that my team knows a lot also. In fact, in regards to their job they likely know far more than me. On those important decisions that involve others, I'm going to get stakeholders involved and find the best answer."

Again, at this point in the training we ask, "Which would you rather work in? Y or Z theory?" Everyone answers Z. We then tell them if they would rather work in "X" or "Y" they might be in the wrong place because we hired both you and your brain, and we want you to use your brain.

We then ask, "Which gets better answers, Y or Z?" Again, almost every one answers Z.

Here's where real freedom comes for you. In the DVD and live training, I then ask, "If we have a problem or an opportunity and we're an X theory management organization, whose problem is it?" The answer, "The boss'."

"If we're a Y theory management business, whose problem is it?" "The boss'."

"If we have a problem or opportunity and we're a Z theory company, whose problem is it?" The answer, "Ours!"

With this we get, and we expect, everyone on the same side of the table working together to solve the problem. Once you create "buy in" for this with your actions, you'll have real freedom, a business that gets better every day with or without you there, and the ability to go on vacation for three weeks and come back to a business running better than when you left.

You can't use Z Theory Management for everything. Your staff would spend all its time in meetings. But the reality is after it's been implemented for a while, not only will your business run much smoother and more efficiently, **you'll spend far less time in meetings fixing things.**

When we get a group of stakeholders (those who are affected by the problem or opportunity) together to solve a problem or capitalize on an opportunity, we call this a **Make-You-Happy Action Team**. The result of their work is the written documentation (System) of how to do a particular job. We call this written documentation a **Make-You-Happy Job Requirement** (MJR). Just like the Make-You-Happy Management System, that features Systems and Employee Empowerment, Personal Development Interviews that replace counterproductive performance reviews, and The Happy Customer Handbook; these Make-You-Happy Action Teams and Job Requirements make you—the owner— happy, make your clients/customers/patients/members happy, make your team (employees) happy, make your managers happy, and even make your vendors and suppliers happy.

Here Is When You Should Use Z Theory Management and Make-You-Happy Action Teams

- Whenever you're working on one of those big issues that will get a better answer when you get the group of stakeholders involved.
- When you have an issue that is causing conflict or problems in your business.
- When the results of what you decide will significantly affect another group. If what the salespeople are deciding is going to affect the warehouse, we have at least one stakeholder from each group on the Make-You-Happy Action Team.
- When someone asks for one. They say, "I've tried to get this changed, and I can't get it done. Can we get a group together and find out the best way to do it?"

As I said earlier, creating systems is not complex. Figure 7.3 on page 52 is an example that applies to everyone in our company.

We created that on February 22, 2000, and we've never had to address the issue again. If someone brings a fundraiser to work and approaches others, they are simply reminded of the MJR.

The first problem I discussed with the concepts in the *E-Myth* is the idea that systems and an effective business management system are complex and you need an "outside perspective." They're not!

But there's another problem with Gerber's concepts in the *E-Myth*. Gerber calls his system "the franchise model." In his model **you** create all the systems and give them to your employees.

That means that all of your business' improvement is dependent on you!
I hate to break this to you, but you just ain't that smart.
You and your team are that smart, but you, alone, ain't!

FIGURE 7.3

Make-You-Happy Job Requirement

MJR-ALL-26: Fundraisers

Position: All

Created: February 22, 20XX

You are welcome to bring your fundraisers to work and advertise and display them using the following guidelines:

Advertising

- You may use your email to announce the product. Example: My son Joey's fundraiser for his baseball team is in the lunchroom. Good Candy!

- You may use voice mail.

- You may put a note in everyone's bin.

- You may display the product in the lunchroom with a small sign.

No No's

- Nothing other than ARS products are to be displayed in the showroom. An ARS product is a product ARS sells to make a profit. The VP of marketing is responsible for showroom display.

- Do not approach anyone directly with requests for donations.

The franchise model works fine if you're McDonald's and you have a bunch of people dedicated to creating all of those systems, and testing this vs. that, but you don't have that luxury.

In the Make-You-Happy Management System **your team, and you**, are the experts. There is no question that the guys in my warehouse know more about what works in the warehouse than I do. The employees in purchasing know their problems and issues better than I do. And there is no question that my combined team is a whole lot smarter than I am.

When your entire team knows that you value their input and expect their help to make things better every day and you get their input on the big issues bulleted above, you'll truly control your business and your life.

Today, we have about 1,000 MJRs in our various businesses, and I'm sure you're wondering how we got that all done. We got it done the same way you eat an elephant, one bite at a time. Managers wrote some, frontline people wrote some, some were created by Make-You-Happy Action Teams, and early on I even wrote some. Regardless of who creates them, before it becomes "an official MJR" we ask everyone who's affected by it to read it and tell us how it can be improved.

We initially implemented the Make-You-Happy Management System in American Retail Supply (ARS), a distribution business. When it worked at American Retail, we implemented it at Superior Display (www.superiordisplay.com) and Eureka! We found that even though the two businesses operate independently of each other, most of the MJRs transferred from one business to the other with no, or minor, changes. Now we use the System in all my businesses, and the majority of systems (MJRs) in all the businesses are the same or very similar.

After using this management system for 20 years and telling other business owners how I control my business and my life, I was literally begged to turn it into a system that any business owner could implement. You can learn more about the management system, and shortcuts to creating the Systems you need to run your business, in my book *"How to Control Your Business and Your Life"* at www.HowToControlYourBusiness. com. Enter Dan Kennedy in the promo code, and I'll send you the book for free.

KEITH LEE owns five businesses. The systems that Keith and his team have created allow him to spend more than 95% of his time working on his businesses: on the important, rather than in them, on everyday menial tasks. Keith shares exactly how to create all the systems you need for your business in his book *How to Control Your Business and Your Life*. You can get a free copy of Keith's book when you enter the promo code Dan Kennedy at www.HowToControlYourBusiness.com. You can also learn more about Keith at www.KeithLee.com.

CHAPTER 8

Performance Reviews
Suck

By Keith Lee

"Make the other person feel important,
and do it sincerely."

— ANDREW CARNEGIE

*S*hortly after starting Keith Lee Business Systems we had a friend over for dinner. My wife, Patty, had told her that I had been in Florida and then Michigan giving presentations on my management system, so she said, "Tell me about this management stuff you're doing."

She was retired from a large aerospace company in the Puget Sound area. I knew she had never been in management, so rather than talk about systems, management theory, and all of the problems managers face, I took another approach.

I said, "When you were at B*****, you did performance reviews, right?"

She rolled her eyes and said, "Yes."

I asked, "What did you think of them?"

She replied, "They sucked!"

I speak to a lot of groups, and I often ask how many of the people in the room have been on the giving or receiving end of a performance review. Most of the people in the room raise their hand. Then I ask, "How many of you like performance reviews, think they are motivating, and lead to the results that the organization wants?" Once in a while a hand or two will go up, but most often no one raises their hand.

In this chapter I'll tell you why performance reviews not only suck but also don't help the organization, and I'll introduce you to Personal Development Interviews (PDI).

Going back to my conversation with Mary, I told her a little about PDI and said, "Just listening to what they're called, a Performance Review or a Personal Development Interview, which would you rather have?"

Her reply, "A Personal Development Interview."

If you've ever been on the giving or receiving end of a performance review you know they suck. Everyone hates them, they're demotivational, discouraging, and, most importantly, don't lead to the behavior you want.

Performance Reviews Are Like Driving Your Car by Looking in the Rearview Mirror

Whether you've ever been the parent of a teenager or not, ask yourself: Do you think you could get the behavior you want from a teenager if you had a performance review with him once a year? Every six months? Quarterly? Of course, your employees aren't teenagers, but we're all human. Self-knowledge tells you that only stopping to contemplate your own thinking, actions, and progress once a year is too little, too late. Still, many companies stick with these belated performance reviews. It's even possible you operate without any formal performance reviews because you know they're useless but you don't know what else to do. My own informal survey indicates more than half of small businesses are operating without an organized means of measuring performance and giving fair and useful feedback about it to their staffs.

In 1993 when I created my management system discussed in the previous chapter and the customer service system in the next chapter, I took control of my business, and my life, but I knew there was something missing in my system.

The system set expectations for exactly what needed to be done, but in regards to Performance Management we were still doing Performance Reviews. While trying to put on my "best face" for our team in regard to performance reviews, the truth is I hated them. I knew they were demotivating, and finally determined that they were actually counterproductive and stopped doing them.

I met Vince Zirpoli in 2005 and knew immediately that I found **the missing link.** My management system was complete with a Performance Management System that actually worked. I was now ready to answer the pleas from my business owner friends and create my management system for others.

How to Replace Demotivating, Discouraging, and Counterproductive Performance Reviews with Motivating, Inspiring, and MOST IMPORTANTLY Productive Personal Development Interviews

Vince's Performance Management System replaces Performance Reviews with Personal Development Interviews.

Just listen to what they're called. Which would you rather give—a Performance Review or a Personal Development Interview? Would you rather review someone's performance, or develop someone?

What if you're on the receiving end? Would you like your performance reviewed or would you rather have someone work proactively to develop you?

Which do you think gets better results, developing people and coaching them or reviewing their performance after the fact?

Traditional management focuses on catching people doing things wrong. If every time I do something wrong, the boss catches me, but he doesn't catch me when I do things right, my creativity is stymied and I stop using my creativity, stop stepping out front, and stop helping the organization grow.

Conversely, when we start catching people doing things right, we encourage empowerment. People start to do things in the organization. Productivity improves on an ongoing basis. Improvement doesn't just come from management but from the whole organization interacting with each other and picking each other up. This is a motivating environment.

Another benefit of this type of management is you create a learning organization. Researchers tell us that as we move forward, people are going to stay with organizations where they have an opportunity to grow and learn. There are going to be many more skilled positions than there are people to fill them. And if there are a lot of skilled positions and not enough people to fill them, money isn't going to make the difference. Money is going to be a given. You have to pay in the competitive market to get good people. But they want to work in a place where they can grow, where they can enjoy themselves, where they can use their creativity to help the organization grow, and that happens in a learning organization. That's exactly why my company, American Retail Supply, was named the Best Company to Work for in Washington by *Washington CEO* magazine.

Before we discuss Personal Development Interviews in depth, it's important to understand a couple other concepts. The first is, in all organizations, systems at a minimum influence and at a maximum control the behavior of individuals. It's critical to understand this because if you don't, you'll take a band-aid approach to correcting situations rather than finding what system is controlling the behavior and changing it.

The second concept is *the 5 percenter*. If you look at any organization, what you find is that about 5% of the people are self-starters. They are self-motivated. They join the organization and management says go in that direction, and they go in that direction. They plan, they organize, they motivate themselves, they control their activities, and they go in that direction. They do a super job.

The *5 percenter* is often selected to move into management. **You are probably a 5 percenter.**

When *5 percenters* move into management, they're told they have to coach, motivate, train, and develop people; and their automatic response is: "No one had to watch me. No one had to tell me how to do it. I just did it."

They don't understand that they are managing the *95 percenters*. The *95 percenters* are good people, but they need coaching, leadership, development, and follow-through. The key is the manager has to understand this, and understand he is more than a manager, or a director. The manager needs to be a trainer, a coach, a facilitator, a developer, a motivator, a counselor, and an administrator.

With that said, it's critical to understand that all development is self-development. You cannot develop another person. You cannot motivate another person. You can create an environment in which they motivate themselves and you facilitate their development. As you facilitate their development, you've got to know that you cannot be the know-it-all guru. Managers who believe they have to be the know-it-all guru do not develop people.

You want them to use their creativity. You want to empower them. You want them to come up with ideas. You teach them the process that leads to the objectives you want. Once they've proved to you that they can get the results, it's time to turn the process over to them.

In short, you want your team displaying initiative, improvement, and self-development, so that they can be relied on more and can rely on each other more and depend on you less. That can only happen with an effective performance management system. Ours has seven components:

1. Personal Development Interview
2. Objectives
3. Objective Focused Activities
4. Feedback
5. Measurement
6. Reinforcement
7. Coaching

The Personal Development Interview

The Personal Development Interview (PDI) is the powering source of an effective performance management system. PDIs need to be regularly scheduled, and held weekly, every other week or—at the very least—monthly. In areas where you want to see a lot of change, a lot of improvement, have a lot of opportunity, or have challenges you'll have them more often. In other areas that are very much under control, you'll have them less often.

Typically the lower the job function, the shorter the meeting. This is one of the places where you'll catch people doing things right. Your job is to encourage them, keep them excited about their job, and discuss corrective action. When you're discussing corrective action, it's critical that you frame it properly. When you frame it properly and sandwich the corrective action between positive reinforcement and catching them doing things right, you'll see improvement.

But How Much Time Does All This Take?

When I talk with business owners about Personal Development Interviews, the first question is, "Who has the time for that?" The real answer that they're not ready to hear is, people who use the systems and employee empowerment I talked about in the previous chapter, and people who use the Customer Service System I'll discuss in the next chapter. But again, they're not ready for that.

Here are the facts: I own four businesses and conduct PDIs with the six people who report directly to me. I meet with each person, every other week, for about 20 minutes. So, on average, I spend one hour a week in PDIs. That means, because of the systems we have in place, I spend one hour a week managing four businesses. I spend the rest of my time working on the important things that grow my businesses, and the things I enjoy and want to work on.

Research has shown that the average executive interacts with subordinates at least 37 times a week—two, three, five minutes at a time. What if you and your subordinate got into the habit of discussing only critical issues right away and left the others for your regularly scheduled PDI? You will find that PDIs actually free up time for you, your managers, and your entire team.

As I mentioned before, for the most part you don't want to be the know-it-all guru during PDIs. No doubt, there are times when you have to be the know-it-all. For instance, when you're putting on a brand-new person and they don't know the processes, someone has to show them the process. But shortly thereafter, it turns into a meeting in which you're eliciting ideas from them. You're priming the pump to help them, but each week, when they realize that you're giving their ideas consideration, they'll get better at it.

When that interview is running properly, the interviewer (you or your managers) will be talking about 20% and the subordinate will be talking 80%.

Let's assume you, or a manager, are having a PDI and the subordinate comes up with an idea you don't like. We discussed "framing" of corrective action above. You also need to "frame" your response here. If your response is, "That won't work," they're going to close their mind. What if you responded with, "Well, you know, that could possibly work, but what will you do if . . ." and then introduce the reason you know it won't work.

Maybe they have thought about your objection and found a way around it. Now two people have grown. If they haven't found a way around it, then they'll come back with, "Yeah, I hadn't thought of that, okay." Now it's time for the manager to ask, "How do you think you'll solve that problem?" The responsibility for finding solutions lies with the interviewee, not the interviewer. This is the way people grow in the organization.

Another key to effective PDIs is that the person being interviewed should leave pumped up, ready to go after every interview. Your job, as the interviewer, is to make sure they are pumped up, ready to go, and achieve their objectives. The only time they should leave a Personal Development Interview disappointed is if you're ready to fire them.

I Need To Tell You I Didn't Believe That at First

I couldn't understand how you could get the behavior you want without constructive criticism, but when I practiced what I learned from Vince I was blown away. That's why I teamed with Vince to add Personal Development Interview training to my management system.

I don't have room here to discuss the other six components of an effective performance management system because I want to introduce you to the incredible concept of Situational Leadership. You can get a free copy of my book *Performance Reviews Suck* at www.PerformanceReviewsSuck.com. The book discusses the final six components of an effective performance management system in detail and shows you exactly how to set up and conduct your Personal Development Interviews that replace counterproductive performance reviews.

Situational Leadership

I'm mostly a black-and-white kind of guy. There's good, there's bad. There's right, there's wrong. There's proper behavior, there's stupid behavior. You succeed or you fail, and you don't blame anyone else.

So when I heard the term Situational Leadership, I thought, holy cow, another feel good, politically correct excuse for not performing. I was wrong—way wrong.

Relationship Behavior is the extent to which the leader engages in two-way communication; in other words, your interaction with people. High relationship means you're highly engaged. You're giving them additional training and support on an ongoing basis. You're interacting with them quite frequently.

Low-relationship behavior means that you're not as engaged in two-way communication.

Task Behavior is the extent to which the leader is engaged in spelling out the duties and responsibilities. High-task behavior means the manager is more detailed and directive telling the subordinate step-by-step what to do.

Low-task behavior is when the manager assigns the task, delegates the task, and is not involved with actually getting the job done.

Look at the Four Quadrants in Figure 8.1 on page 64. A new employee (team member) typically starts in Q1 (on the lower right side), and the manager does a lot of **Telling** (high task, low relationship). There is a lot of instruction, showing him how to

FIGURE 8.1: Four Quadrants

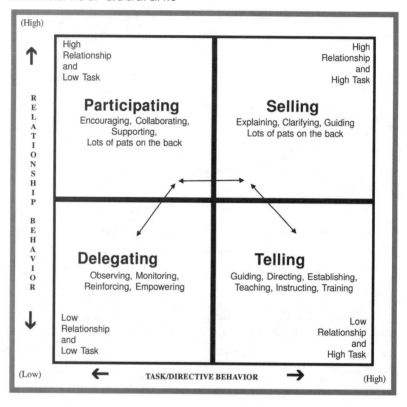

do the job. You're not patting him on the back yet because he hasn't shown anything yet. You're teaching him and training him, so there is not a lot of relationship behavior.

After a few months the new employee is making some progress, and it's time to move from telling to **Selling** (high task, high relationship). The manager is still directing and showing, but the communication is more two-way. The manager gives a lot of reinforcement while explaining, clarifying, and persuading. The manager is mining for ideas from the team member and teaching him to think on his own. The leader still defines the roles and tasks, but seeks ideas and suggestions. The leader pats him on the back. The more you can guide him to thinking things out **the more beneficial it is to you in the future.**

As the individual grows, it's time for the manager to move from selling to **Participating** (high relationship, low task). The person understands the job, knows how to do it, but doesn't have a lot of confidence yet. He needs reinforcement on an ongoing basis until he develops confidence. The manager gives the individual a lot of support, pats him on the back, and stays very close. Because the individual knows the job, there is much less directive behavior from the manager.

As the team member becomes more and more competent, he becomes a true expert at the job, and the relationship moves to **Delegating** (low relationship, low task). The team member is doing 80% or more of the talking during the PDI with the manager. The manager is observing, monitoring, and reinforcing.

Your goal as the manager is to get your staff to Quadrant 4, but as the graph shows, it's not a one-way street. Depending on the job or task, you may move back a quadrant or even two. In one of my businesses one of my vice presidents is fabulous at her job, and my management style is almost always Delegating. But when it comes to working with numbers, my management style with her moves to Participating and sometimes to Selling or even Telling.

It's also important to understand that you're working with people, not machines. We all have personal lives away from business, and for all of us, even us *5 percenters,* our personal lives influence us at work. Sometimes it's critically important to move back a quadrant when a team member has personal problems. Leaving your empathy and understanding behind, you have a lot invested in someone who's in Q4. Moving up on the relationship scale to Participating or even to Selling is sometimes critical to get that person back up to speed. And, of course, if things get worse, you may need to return to Telling.

As I mentioned, the powering source of an effective Performance Management System is its first component, the Personal Development Interview, that replaces demotivating and counterproductive Performance Reviews. You can learn the next six components, and learn exactly how to implement Personal Development Interviews, in my book, *Performance Reviews Suck: How to Replace Demotivating, Discouraging, and Counterproductive Performance Reviews with Motivating, Uplifting and Most Importantly; Productive Personal Development Interviews.* You can get the book for free when you enter the promo code Dan Kennedy at www.PerformanceReviewsSuck.com.

KEITH LEE owns five businesses. The systems that Keith and his team have created allow him to spend more than 95% of his time working on his businesses: on the important, rather than in them, on everyday menial tasks. Keith shares exactly how to create all the systems you need for your business in his book, *How to Control Your Business and Your Life.* You can get a free copy of Keith's book when you enter the promo code Dan Kennedy at www.HowToControlYourBusiness.com. You can also learn more about Keith at www.KeithLee.com.

CHAPTER 9

Implementing Customer Service That Gets Repeat and New Business

By Keith Lee

"We see our customers as invited guests to a party, and we are the hosts. It's our job every day to make every important aspect of the customer experience a little bit better."

—JEFF BEZOS, CEO, AMAZON.COM

You might be wondering, why a chapter on customer service in a management book? If you have anything less than exceptional customer service in your business, you're wasting the time of, creating extra work for, and frustrating your frontline people, other staff, managers, and yourself—and that's poor management.

As the author of *The Happy Customer Handbook*, I'm often asked, "What is the number-one thing business owners can do to improve their customer service?" Another question I get is, "Why is customer service so poor?" The answer to both questions is the same.

When I speak to live audiences I often ask this question, "What *should* you be doing when it comes to customer service training in your business?"

1. We tell our staff to deliver good customer service. They should know what that is.
2. We tell our staff to deliver good customer service and give some examples sometimes but nothing formal.
3. We have meetings about customer service once in a while and tell everyone they should give good customer service.
4. All new staff gets customer service training when they are hired.
5. Everyone has gone through our customer service training, and they are consistently and persistently reminded about our customer service expectations.

With every audience almost all hands go up for answer 5.

We've surveyed thousands of business owners before they purchase my book *The Happy Customer Handbook.* We ask them, "What best **describes** customer service training in your organization?"

1. We tell our staff to deliver good customer service. They should know what that is.
2. We tell our staff to deliver good customer service and give some examples sometimes but nothing formal.
3. We have meetings about customer service once in a while and tell everyone they should give good customer service.
4. All new staff gets customer service training when they are hired.
5. Everyone has gone through our customer service training, and they are consistently and persistently reminded about our customer service expectations.

Only 2% answer 5. How is that? Why is it that everyone knows their team should have customer training upfront and consistent reminders, but almost no one does it?

Here's what happens in most businesses. With the best of intentions, the business owner has a "rah rah" meeting about customer service, and the service improves for a few weeks, and then without reminders you're back where you started. And it's simple. The reminders don't come because you're a busy business owner and you have lots of other things to do. In addition, it's likely you're a *5 percenter* (see previous chapter) and can't understand why people don't always do what they're supposed to do.

But this may even be more amazing. More than 75% of all businesses have no upfront, consistent customer service training for new employees.

The answer to both questions, "What can business owners do to improve their customer service?" and "Why is customer service so poor?" is the same:

1. Train your entire team to deliver exceptional customer service.
2. Consistently reinforce your customer service expectations with your team.

To start, your entire team needs to get trained with your exceptional customer service expectations. This is the "rah rah" training I talked about above. But it can't stop there. You need to consistently and persistently reinforce those expectations. Zig Ziglar quoted, "Repetition is the mother of all learning." But learning something doesn't necessarily lead to behavior change, so when it comes to customer service in your business I tweak Zig's quotation to, "When it come to customer service, repetition is the mother of all learning and permanent behavior change."

When you have your entire team trained and you're consistently reminding them of your customer service expectations, you need to make sure every new employee (team member) gets the same initial customer service training that your entire team received.

You Never Have a Second Chance to Make a First Impression

The best thing you can do to show your commitment to Make-You-Happy Customer Service to every new employee is train them about your customer service expectations immediately. After your new team member fills out the required government employment forms, what do they do? In most businesses, it's not customer service training, but it should be. Whether you create your own training, use the training we have available at www.KeithLee.com, or invest in another training system, be sure that the very first training every new employee receives is in customer service.

If You Have Anything Less Than Exceptional Customer Service, IT'S YOUR FAULT!

Previously, when my wife and I got poor customer service in a retail store, she would say something about the individual. She finally got tired of me telling her that the real blame lies with management and now tells me, "The manager of that store needs to read your book."

Anything less than exceptional customer service is your fault. YOU haven't trained properly, or reinforced properly, or have the proper systems in place, or don't have good feedback systems to monitor customer service, or you haven't fired someone!

Regardless of how well you implement the Systems and Employee Empowerment discussed in the chapter before last or how well you implement Performance Management with Personal Development Interviews discussed in the last chapter, if you're not committed to exceptional customer service, your business will never achieve its potential for profitability or sustainability.

When It Comes to Customer Service, a Goal of "Good" is NOT Good Enough

Dan discusses it throughout this book—when the cat's away, the mice will play. The very best customer service any customer will ever get in your business is when you're there, right next to your employee. The fact is, if at that point you accept good, the service when you're not around will, without question, be less than good, and that's not healthy for your business.

When you're committed to exceptional customer service, you'll fall short sometimes, but when you do, you'll often still be providing good customer service. In addition, when your customers are used to getting exceptional customer service, they'll be much more likely to forgive you in the rare instance when your customer service falls below good.

You cannot rely on the absence of customer complaints as your standard. You have to determine the appropriate definitions of "exceptional" and of "good enough," and train and coach accordingly, and have systems in place to insure those standards.

The reality is that the huge majority of customers who are disappointed with any business won't complain to anyone, they just leave. How does that sound to you? **"They just leave."** It should send chills through your blood.

It's reported that for every 25 dissatisfied customers only one complains. Twenty-four don't complain, and on average the noncomplainers tell 10 to 20 other people. In the *Harvard Business Review,* Frederick F. Reichheld and W. Earl Sasser Jr. report that a 5% increase in customer loyalty can produce profit increases from 25% to 85%. With numbers like this, you have to love customers who complain because they give you a chance to make them happy and fix your systems. But you need to be much more proactive than waiting for complaints.

My mom worked for Sears when I was growing up. For years, maybe decades, its motto was, "Satisfaction Guaranteed." Where did that get Sears? Customer satisfaction isn't enough.

Satisfied customers are . . . satisfied. If someone else has a little better price or opens a store that's a bit more convenient, they're gone. Just think of it, if your goal is a satisfied customer, even if you and your staff do everything perfectly, the best you'll get is a satisfied customer—that's your goal.

Customer satisfaction is not good enough. Your customer service expectations need to be exceptional, and you need to create not just satisfied customers, but happy, loyal customers.

When I say loyal customers, I don't mean customers who stay with you for some nebulous touchy-feely, feel-good reasons. They are loyal for specific reasons: your product knowledge and advice, "your product mix," they know you'll always take care of them, "they know you won't oversell them," they know they'll always see a smiling face, receive a pleasant greeting, get a sincere thank you, and be *SERVED* with an attitude of sincere appreciation. They will never be promised something that you don't really think you can deliver. The list goes on and on.

What happens when a happy, loyal customer finds a lower price? They're likely to stay with you or at least let you know. What happens when a competitor who's a bit more convenient moves in and your customer is happy and loyal? They're likely to keep coming to your store.

What happens when you mess up with a happy, loyal customer? Your happy, loyal customer knows that's not normal, and they're likely to tell you and let you make it right.

What happens when the subject of the products or services you offer comes up with a happy, loyal customer? They're likely to rave about you, and you're likely to get another new customer.

The biggest business of the five I own, American Retail Supply (www.AmericanRetailSupply.com), provides independent retailers and regional retail chains with the things they need to run their store(s): store displays, fixtures, the bags the store puts your purchase into, the computer systems they use, etc. Even though the number of independent retailers has free-fallen in the past 20 years, American Retail Supply is thriving because plenty of independent retailers know how to create loyal customers in the face of the onslaught of mega-chains, Amazon, wholesale clubs, and the like.

How many independent hardware stores do you see today vs. 20 years ago? How about drugstores?

While thousands of independent hardware stores have gone out of business with the assault of Home Depot, Lowes, and others, McLendon Hardware in Renton, Washington, has added stores and is doing very well. I and many of my neighbors drive right by one of the mega-hardware chain stores and go another three miles to McLendon because it has a great product selection, knowledgeable people in every department, and friendly service.

I drive right past one of the huge national drugstore chain stores to shop at Bartell Drug for the same reason, and it is doing just fine with competition from a mega-drug chain.

Don't Keep Your Standards a Secret

Truly outstanding businesses committed to exceptional customer service don't just make up slogans about it, they let their customers know what they're up to and put themselves and their employees on the hot seat by doing so. Secret #5 in my book, *The Happy Customer Handbook,* is: Your customers need to know your customer service expectations.

As I mentioned, we don't rely on complaints to tell us what to do or how to improve, but when I get them, I take them seriously. My American Retail Supply business sells to about 10,000 businesses each year, and all of those clients have my direct phone number to call if we're not taking care of them. Each year I get somewhere between three to six phone calls from customers who think they have not received exceptional service from us. Almost all of these calls start with, "I read in your newsletter that customer service is important to you, and I just wanted you to know . . ." or "A few months ago when I was on hold I heard that you wanted me to call if I had a problem that wasn't being taken care of . . ." or "I really didn't want to bother you, but in your Retail Tip of the Week, you said you want to be notified if I'm not happy . . ."

Find as many ways as you can to tell your customers that you want to know if they are not happy. Tell them when they are on hold on the telephone. Tell them with signs when they are at your place of business. Tell them in your advertising. Tell them when you communicate via email. Tell them on your website. Survey them by email or direct mail, and simply ask them, "What do you like? What don't you like? I'd like to know."

I repeat this often in client newsletters, email tips, package stuffers, etc. "If we ever let you down, please call us immediately at 800-426-5708 so we can make it right. If you're still not happy, please call me on my direct line xxx-xxx-xxxx." (Sorry, that number is for customers.)

But if you're going to ask for input from customers, you need to act when you get it. Whether it's a good comment or a complaint, every customer who contacts us gets a response.

But there's another great reason to share your customer service expectations with your customers and ask them to let you know if they're not thrilled . . .

The best reason for sharing your customer service expectations with your customers and for encouraging

customers to let you know of any disappointment is that your staff knows customers may come directly to you when they feel they have not gotten the promised level of service. You will also be much more concerned with having everyone meeting your customers' expectations if there is a direct path to you, and you have to get personally involved with every failure.

How Customer Service Links to Business GROWTH

If you're like most people, when you think about growing your business, you think about getting *new* customers. Mega-businesses spend millions of dollars each year trying to get new customers, and it continually amazes me that once they get me to try them, the customer service is often so bad that I won't ever go back.

When it comes to growing your business, Think Upside Down. To grow your business, rather than thinking about getting new customers first, think first about keeping your existing customers and getting them to buy more from you.

Let's look at the numbers. Assume that "Their Business" wants to grow by 10% this year. Let's further assume that its customer service is typical of most businesses, and two out of ten customers decide they are going to take their business elsewhere because of lousy or indifferent customer service. Let's assume another 5% go somewhere else for a multitude of reasons. So they lose 25% of their business each year. Now, rather than just growing by 10%, "Their Business" needs to grow by 35% to hit their target growth rate of 10%.

Now let's look at "Your Business." You also want to grow by 10%. But because you and everyone on your staff understands that customers give each of you your paycheck, and your vacations, and your raises, and everything else you get, you simply do not lose customers due to poor customer service. You do lose about 5% of your customers each year for a variety of reasons—they move, they die, misunderstandings, whatever. So for "Your Business," after you take into account losing 5% of your customers, you need to grow by 15% to reach your 10% growth rate.

The moral of the story is: It's a lot easier to grow your business if you take care of your existing customers.

When you think about growing your business, Think Upside Down. Think in this order:

1. What can I do to keep my existing customers?
2. What can I do to increase business with my existing customers?
   and finally . . .
3. How can I get new customers?

This was a lesson I learned early on. In 1978 my wife worked for a beauty supply wholesaler. It sold the products and supplies that beauty salons used, and the sales reps got commission on every sale. I was working my tail off for wages, and I saw that all these guys (yes, they were all guys) had to do is keep their current customers happy, and get another customer, and their income would keep growing and growing. I liked that idea so I went looking for a similar commission job and landed at Thompson Marking Service, the company that I renamed American Retail Supply when I became the owner.

Dick Thompson told me he thought my first month commission would be about one-third of what I was making at my current job. But I liked the idea of keeping existing customers happy so they continued to buy, getting another customer, and earning the commission that would never go down as long as I kept them all happy. In the first month I actually made about two-thirds what I was making at the previous job and within a few months made more than I did at the previous job and never looked back.

The obsession with getting new customers coupled with negligence and low investment in keeping and growing the amount of business you do with existing customers is one of the dumbest, most common mistakes there is. In my example here, the difference between needing 35% top-line growth vs. only 15% top-line growth to arrive at the same net growth goal is enormous. If you take just about any business and develop realistic, detailed plans for what has to happen to get a 35% increase vs. what needs to be done to get a 15% increase, you quickly see how much more daunting, difficult, and expensive, maybe also more risky, the first plan is compared to the second. In short, customer retention is the surer and more efficient means of growth than is relying much more on getting new customers. This is bad news for ad agencies, marketing companies, trade or consumer shows, social media agencies, and everyone else who lives by keeping you obsessed with and pouring money into chasing more and more and more new customers. It's good news for you if you embrace it, because you can do this internally with people you are already paying, and exercise much more control over it than you can over outside, external advertising and marketing.

KEITH LEE owns five businesses, including American Retail Supply. When Keith shared his secrets to his exceptional customer service with his customers via his Retail Tip of the Week, they clamored for more and asked him if he could put them all together. The result is his book *The Happy Customer Handbook: 59 Secrets to Creating Happy Customers Who Come Back Time and Time Again and Enthusiastically Tell Others About You.* You can get a free copy of the book, including FREE postage, at www. TheHappyCustomerHandbook.com. You can also learn more about Keith at www. KeithLee.com.

CHAPTER 10

The Two Most Crucial
Management Decisions of All

"I do not like broccoli and I haven't liked it since I was a little kid.
I am President of the United States and I am not going
to eat it anymore."

—PRESIDENT GEORGE H. W. BUSH

A crucial management decision is: What kind of employee do you want? When I ask that question of individual clients or groups of people, I usually get a litany of vague and nice-sounding responses. *I want productive employees. Employees that care. Loyal. Ambitious. Intelligent. With good communication skills. With good attitudes.*

This is akin to, when asked to define goals, answering with "I want to be happy." Not a target. Just an idea.

The only rational answer to this critically important question is: "I want a PROFITABLE employee."

Contrary to a lot of silly ideas, the only sane reason to have an employee is profit. Somehow you get more profit by having the employee than by not having the employee. The only reason to have an employee is that you make a multiple of what he costs by having him. Unfortunately, a lot of people pile up employees around them for remarkably irrational reasons!

In addition to all the management stuff to be discussed in this book, this goal requires four other things: 1) buying into the premise; 2) calculating true and total cost; 3) creating a means of measurement for return on investment (ROI); and 4) vicious intolerance for unsatisfactory ROI.

The Premise

Liberals, most Democrats, some Republicans, and most employees think you, the business owner, exist to provide people with jobs. This is bullshit. If you can make more money by employing fewer people, that is exactly what you ought to do. In fact, it is your responsibility to do so because your first and foremost responsibility as CEO is to maximize company income and shareholder value. If you own the thing, then you are CEO *and* shareholder. You have a responsibility to yourself to maximize profit. Only you are invested, only you are at risk, only you truly care. If you go belly up, they'll go get jobs someplace else. It is not your responsibility to provide Mary with a job, nor your responsibility to pay her enough to support herself, her uneducated and refusing-to-get-educated husband, three kids, dog, two cars, five cell phones, and cable TV with premium channels. It is Mary's responsibility to make herself so valuable your business can't live without her. It is Mary's responsibility to continue making herself more and more valuable so you keep paying her more and more. If she doesn't, if she's an interchangeable commodity, so be it.

It's really important for you to get clear about who owns which responsibilities. Mary might never get clear about this. Mary's family may never get clear about this. Liberals and media pundits will never face this. But at least you can get clear about it. A lot of business owners get bullied into having and keeping unprofitable employees because those employees need their jobs. It seems incredible but it's true. This sense of obligation or this guilt over doing so well yourself must be resisted with all your might.

The *only* reason to have or keep Mary around is profit.

The Other Reasons to *NOT* Have Employees

Other unforgivable reasons business owners have employees, more employees than they need, and unprofitable employees are ego, poor self-esteem, and a need for reassurance, social activity, and friends. Some equate success with having a bigger staff than the next guy. When the brother-in-law who's the doctor visits, the business owner doesn't feel good about showing him a 600-square-foot hole in the wall with one employee at a desk counting

More than half of McDonald's franchise owners and 40% of its corporate executives started out as crew in entry-level jobs, working in the restaurants. Chipotle, operator of 1,400 fast-food restaurants, has an aggressive promote-from-within program, allowing employees to rise to manager and qualify for educational assistance, paid vacations, stock options, even company cars. They have 300 managers who've risen from their ranks; their average salary is $90,000.00 a year. Do not let anybody convince you that people are imprisoned in entry-level, minimum-wage jobs or that we must make all such jobs pay a "living wage." Opportunity beckons!

(SOURCE: *NATION'S RESTAURANT NEWS*/NRN.COM. 5-13)

money—no matter how much money he's counting. The business owner wants to show his brother-in-law, the doctor, a big beehive of activity with worker bees buzzing about, flying hither and thon. Other business owners lack confidence in their decision making and need a bunch of people around who are paid to agree with them. Other owners can't stand working alone and need to populate a place with people. Instead, I recommend getting a dog. The only reason to have or keep an employee is profit. (There are lots of good reasons to have a dog. If you are unfamiliar with them, read *Marley & Me*, quite possibly the best book ever written by anybody about anything, period.)

It is your role to keep wage costs to the lowest possible number. That said, I do believe in Chapter 27's title, "Exceptions to All the Rules." I also believe in suppressing wages for ordinary people who deliver only ordinary performance or people in mundane jobs with inherently low value by any and all legal means necessary so that you, the owner, take home as much money as possible from your business. As I was writing this, by the way, much noise was being made about the U.S. wages for bottom-rung jobs in service sectors like hotels and restaurants actually declining in recent years. So there was a lot of noise about again raising the minimum wage. About it having to be a "living wage" that allows an employee to own a home, raise a family, and retire. This idea ignores two facts. First, getting certain jobs done is only worth a certain amount of money. Doesn't matter who does the job, how long he's been doing the job, or what his needs are. Getting those red things packed in that brown box is only worth $4.18, no more. Second, minimum wage jobs are not supposed to be *careers*. They should be called entry-level jobs or first-rung-on-the-ladder jobs. A place to start, not to stay. Many people do understand or learn that. To be very clear about where the responsibility for a good living wage lies, it is the responsibility of the person doing a job that pays an unsatisfactory wage to somehow move himself up the ladders of skill, value, and income. It is not the responsibility of any employer to pay more than a job is worth because of other people's needs.

When employers are forced to do so, they do other things instead. They automate. In *The Future of Employment: How Susceptible Are Jobs to Computerization?* Carl Frey and Michael Osborne of Oxford University forecast that 47% of all U.S. jobs are at risk of being automated. How fast probably depends on how much government, unions, and other sources raise the cost of labor. Amazon paid $750-million to buy a robotics company, making mobile robots to replace human workers in its warehouses. The fast-food industry is racing to replace counter clerks with self-order computer screens, just as supermarkets did and are doing with checkouts, airlines did and are doing with check-in, banks did and are doing with ATMs and online banking. Faced with Obamacare, countless companies, universities—even staunchly liberal ones—hospitals, and even unions began replacing full-time jobs with part-time jobs. The idea that employers/owners are just going to roll over, lie down, and have their profit structure forcibly changed without a reaction is ridiculous. The big companies can't and won't. They'll shutter their least profitable outlets, they'll

Bad, bad, bad news for humans who need to work for food: A recent survey indicates that 61% of consumers would be willing to shop in a fully automated store absent any humans, and 42% claim they would prefer it. 58% of shoppers are happy to have stores or online retailers keep track of their purchase history (now advertised as a benefit in Lowe's TV spots), so that a machine can serve as their memory, tell them what they bought, and tell them what to buy.

(SOURCE: CISCO CUSTOMER EXPERIENCE RESEARCH/RETAIL SHOPPING RESULTS. CISCO.COM.)

EMPLOYEES OF THE MONTH

JANUARY — ETHEL
FEBRUARY — MATT
MARCH — FRANK
APRIL — CAROL
MAY — MARJor

JULY — TOM
AUGUST — AUTOTRON
SEPTEMBER — AUTOTRON
OCTOBER — AUTOTRON
NOVEMI — AUTOTI

Kanin

shift investments overseas, they'll automate, they'll outsource, and they will even shrink in size if need be to protect net profits. After being held up by President Obama as a shining example of progressiveness in health care and used as the site for a speech and photo op, when actually faced with the costs, the Cleveland Clinic announced $300-million in budget cuts and erasure of as many as 9,000 jobs. Nobody can compel business to hire or to pay a set wage above value of job or to absorb newly invented costs. Business reacts, by raising prices, eliminating jobs, freezing pay, and reducing employee benefits.

You must react in a similar way. You can't be bullied. The last person at your place to ever take a pay cut has to be you. Make that your number-one policy. Don't let yourself be made to feel guilty either. Each individual chooses his income by his behavior.

No B.S. Ruthless Management Truth #2

Take home as much money as you can from *your* business. No nickel left behind.

There's a ton of B.S. spread around about money, including the idea that rich business owners are NOT working people. A few facts. The number of U.S. penta-millionaires (worth upwards from $5 million) has more than quadrupled in the past ten years, to more than 930,000. The people in that group are mostly entrepreneurs. None got there by working in secure jobs at the post office, the department of motor vehicles, or some big corporation. Only 10% of their wealth comes from inheritance, and only 10% from passive investments; 80% comes from *earned* income. Meaning, they worked for it. Quite patiently, too, as most made their fortune in a big lump, after many years of effort, sacrifice, and risk. Most employees work 40-hour weeks; most business owners work 60- to 70-hour weeks. Should *anybody* want much greater income and financial security, there is a known, clear, present, and rather formulaic path to getting it.

Little truth is plainly and publicly spoken about this. Politicians demagogue it. I'll reach back to the magnificently coiffed, JFK wannabe, brief darling of the Left, super-rich trial lawyer John Edwards. In a speech in Cleveland on July 4, 2007, the Presidential candidate Edwards flatly stated: "No one in America should work at a full-time job and still be in poverty." This is bullshit piled high and stinking strong. It ignores the fact that lots of folks put themselves in poverty and keep themselves in poverty by birthing multiple children they can't afford to care for; by engaging in money-wasting habits they can't afford, including smoking, drinking, and gambling; and most of all by refusing to move themselves up from a lowest-paying job to a better job and again to a better job. It focuses only on societal, government, and marketplace responsibility but not at all on personal responsibility. It ignores the fact that merely raising wages is inflationary and encourages downsizing, job exporting, and automation, thereby making things worse, not better, for the lowest-skilled workers earning the lowest wages. It is shamefully disingenuous or horribly ignorant or some of each. Having said that, I happen to agree that in a country as rich as ours is— especially rich in opportunity—it is a crying shame that anyone willing to work remains in poverty. But the answers will never be found in government forcibly raising wages. It's much more complex than that. And it has to start with truth telling in place of pandering. I believe I have a lot more honest compassion for the working poor than Edwards and his ilk, because I would tell them the truth instead of perpetually waving the utterly false hope in front of them that somebody else—Edwards, Obama, Hillary, government Robin Hood—is going to ride in on a white horse and lift them up out of poverty.

We desperately need to tell everybody the blunt truth about this. We need to say: You *shouldn't* make a good living wage to support your family cleaning the toilets and sweeping the floors at the local motel. That job was never designed or intended to be your career. You should use it only as a step to the next step to the next step. And you should step as fast as you can—like somebody stepping from stone to stone, crossing a swamp. You should haul ass over to the library at night or go on the internet or find a friend to advise you or save up money and take classes to acquire additional, more valuable skills.

You should beg your employer for a chance to step up and use those better skills for better income or move on to a different employer who offers a better ladder of opportunity. Maybe you should start a part-time, homebased business on the side and work toward the day you can be in business for yourself. But you shouldn't stay put in a low-value, low-wage job and somehow expect employers or the government to make your wages increase again and again.

We need to educate people that getting a certain job done has only so much value and that value does not increase by the number of years a person does it or by the person's need for income. We need to admit that our safety nets are severely flawed and porous and aren't likely to improve much, so you don't want to be dependent on them . . . but that our country offers enormous, varied, accessible opportunities. So you'd better pick one and get in gear. We need to say this as a unified voice: parents, educators, employers, civic leaders, white and black and brown and purple leaders, and politicians.

Since that's not going to happen, *you* probably need to stop watching and listening to all the politicians' and mainstream media's bleating about this. You dare not let it weaken your resolve. You need to focus on the fact that the only reason to have an employee is profit and the only kind of employee to have is a profitable one. Further, you want to use the overwhelming majority of your money available for wages to attract exceptional talent for your most important jobs and to reward truly exceptional performance. To do that, you have to be a Scrooge about paying the people who do commoditized, mundane jobs and the people providing only ordinary, barely profitable performance. You have to pay as little as you legally and possibly can for the lowest-level work, in order to, by market comparisons, grossly overpay, overincentivize, and overreward the highly profitable employees doing highly profitable work.

We Can Get Even Clearer by
Dehumanizing the Equations

Fundamentally, an employee is a rented asset. It has a monthly payment to be made on it. Just like a piece of equipment. So if you are renting a hay baling machine for $300.00 a month but it breaks down all the time, makes the bales the wrong sizes, is slow, and when it's all said and done only bales about $400.00 worth of hay, what should you do with it? Turn it back in. If it costs you $300.00, it better bale $3,000.00 worth of hay. Because we are in the hay-baling business for one reason and one reason only: to make as much money as possible. And you need to remember the hay business can be good some sunny years but bad some wet years or if there are too many sunny years, and it may even be ruined altogether before long if Al Gore's right about global warming. So in the good years you have to make enough profit for those years plus more, to cover the years you make poor profits or no profits or have to reach into your pockets and put money back into the business. Your hay baler better give you a big, big return on your investment in it. If it doesn't, you may need a different hay baler. Or you may need to get out of the hay-baling business altogether, turn back in all 100 of your hay balers, and find something entirely different to do. That's why it's good to only rent the hay balers, not buy them.

So every piece of equipment—that is, every employee—must pay off at a big multiple of his cost.

Which gets us to employees' cost. Few business owners properly calculate employee cost because they leave out several very important numbers. Every CPA, MBA, and others of their ilk I've ever seen gets this wrong. Every management book I've ever read gets it wrong.

Here's how they do it: wages + taxes + benefits + overhead. So, if an employee is paid, let's say, $12.00 an hour, taxes and Social Security and workers' comp and so on add, say, 30%, that puts us at $15.60 an hour. Then add the health care plan, the 401(k) matching contributions, the Christmas bonus, etc.—let's say that calculates out to another $1.00 an hour. Then some neglect overhead, but it belongs in there. Employees use up soap, toilet paper, steal office supplies, require heat and air conditioning, and take up space. If it costs this hypothetical business owner $2,000.00 a month for his space, utilities, and supplies, and he has four employees, that's $500.00 each divided by 160 work hours, $3.12 an hour. Now we're up to $19.72 an hour. But we are just getting started.

The REAL Costs

The first big number omitted is the do-over number. The cost of mistakes. Consider the episodically, repeatedly endangered American automakers. The most recent taxpayer-funded rescues weren't the first, and they won't be the last. This time around GM was the prime disaster into which we had to pour money, and the touting of it as a success just because the government has gotten much of its money back is a big con job. It ignores the fact that settled bankruptcy law was circumvented by President Obama, GM bondholders and shareholders had their money stolen and their rights ignored, assets obligated to them cavalierly transferred to a newly created entity in which new stock was gifted to the unions, numerous profitable dealerships summarily closed and their owners' rights ignored, and none of the core flaws in the business cured.

Among the ongoing problems guaranteeing future crises in this industry is a unionized, highly paid, grossly overpaid workforce incapable of or unwilling to actually do their jobs right. Consequently these companies are awash in recalls. Hundreds of thousands of cars have to be done over. None of that cost gets taken back out of the incompetent employees' paychecks. The company just eats it. Translation: Your employees make mistakes with zero consequences or cost; you bear 100% of the burden for their screwups. And screw up they will. When I took over a terribly troubled manufacturing company, that assembly line mimicked God's for snowflakes: Every item coming off it was different. Employees can, obviously, make and ship defective goods, ship goods to the wrong place, pack goods poorly so they break, damage raw materials, waste materials, annoy and drive away customers, not answer the phone until the eighth ring instead of the third as instructed thus letting prospects you paid money for give up and hang up, and on and on and on ad infinitum. More importantly, employees not only can but *will* do these things. There is a hard cost in all this that must be factored into the employee cost in advance, because you can't go charge them for their mistakes as they happen.

Obviously, this cost varies by business, by employee, and by employer. No formula for calculating it exists that I know of. But for the sake of this hypothetical example, let's conservatively say that our pretty good hypothetical employee costs us about $400.00 a week from waste, mistakes, and outright theft. Divide by 40 hours; add $10.00 an hour to the employee's cost. Now we're up to $29.72 an hour.

Next big number all the bean counters ignore and are ignorant of: the cost of YOUR time. With employees comes time *consumption*. In big companies, much of this is easy to see and can be cost controlled, because they employ professional baby-sitters at modest wages (called Human Resources or HRD professionals) and have layers of middle management baby-sitting each other. In a small business, however, the layers are compressed or not there at all, and you are definitely not going to pay $50,000.00 a year or so to an HRD person. So your employees are going to consume your time. As I lay out in this book, they require you to take on three jobs: Leadership, Management, and Supervision. You have to hire, fire, train, coach, police. Break up knife fights (I did that with two computer programmers), listen to marital breakup stories, and this list is long. Again I know of no formula. But let's just say it's an average of two hours a week per employee.

Now, what's your time worth doing the highest-value things you do? Mine is currently worth $1,600.00 an hour and up. So if an employee sucks up two hours of my time, that's $3,200.00 divided into her 40 hours, which adds $80.00 an hour to the cost of having her. Your time is, frankly, probably less valuable than mine. To be simplistic, let's assume you're happy making $100,000.00 a year divided by roughly 2,000 work hours, which makes your time worth $50.00 an hour. If she sucks up two hours of your time this week, that's $100.00 divided into her 40 hours, adding $2.50, which brings her total cost to $32.22 an hour. If, however, you want to make $1,000,000.00 a year . . . .

The final big number is the cost of her absence and replacement. I'm always amused when I'm in Washington, DC, in winter, when they announce that only the *essential* employees should brave the roads and report to work. Shouldn't only essential employees be coming in *every* day? Why is anybody employing a nonessential employee? This tells you a lot about the stupidity that blankets Washington, DC, but it's also telling about the reality of business. Any small-business owner can tell you, if the business can operate for three weeks while Mary or Billy Bob take family leave days, they aren't needed at all. But if they are needed, you have to replace them when they are absent. You do this by having other employees short and cheat their responsibilities to cover or taking your higher value time to cover or bringing in temps that cost double or triple Mary's wages. Will she be absent this year? Of course, at least 20 days, combining vacation, personal, and sick time. Then every few years, she'll quit or be fired, and you'll incur advertising, hiring, and training costs to replace her. Factor all that in. Let's guess: 20 days of your time used times your $50.00-an-hour value; $400.00 a day; $8,000.00 a year. Working backward, that comes to approximately $4.00 an hour added to her $32.22, bringing her cost to $36.22.

Well, you had no idea you were actually paying Mary $36.22 an hour, did you?

And that's my point.

I'll bet you'd require more of Mary and manage Mary differently if you did know. Now you do.

ROI

Now to ROI, return on investment. At $36.22 an hour, Mary costs you about $5,795.00 a month or $69,000.00 a year. What sort of return on that investment will be satisfactory to you? If you compare it to bank interest on CDs, then the hurdle is low. Mary need only cover her cost plus a measly $2,700.00 of profit. Of course, if you sold the business and put all the money in bank CDs, you'd never have to even see Mary or any of your other employees again. Chances are, you would like something superior to bank interest just for putting up with your people and occasionally stopping by your own office. But what ROI do you want? Two-to-one, three-to-one, four-to-one? At four-to-one, Mary has to produce $276,000.00 of profit. Is she?

This, finally, gets us to the second most critical managerial decision: How will you quantify and measure the profit produced by Mary? Most business owners will tell me they need Mary and are able to tell me what Mary does, but hardly any can ever tell me how much Mary makes for them.

CHAPTER 11

In the Wrong Place

"I married beneath me. All women do."

—Viscountess Nancy Astor, American-born British Politician

N apoleon Hill, author of the success classic *Think and Grow Rich*, derived from his 20 years of research into the lives of an era's most successful inventors and industrialists that: "Everyone enjoys doing the kind of work for which he is best suited."

If you have someone in your business engaged in work for which he is ill-suited, nothing you can do will ever make him productive or happy for long. You and he are best served by figuring out where he can thrive. If that is in different work within your business, fine. If not, getting him out of there—or avoiding hiring him in the first place—is the best thing for you and for him.

One of the smartest sales experts I've known, the late Bill Brooks, explained that there are four things an employer needs to determine about a candidate for a sales job or about a salesperson currently working for him:

1. Can he sell?
2. Will he sell?
3. Can he sell HERE?
4. Will he sell HERE?

The last two are defining. A football player can fail with one team but be a champion with another. The same with a salesman, or factory supervisor, or anyone in any other job. Someone might be miserable as my executive assistant and therefore do a miserable job, but thoroughly enjoy being your executive assistant and therefore do a great job. Different dental practices, stores, restaurants, car dealerships, etc., have different internal cultures, different kinds of clientele, different marketing and sales strategies, so, naturally, different people fit or don't fit. As I write this, I have three different clients who run competing training and consulting companies serving the dental profession: Jay Geier and The Scheduling Institute, Greg Stanley and Whitehall Management, and Dr. Tom Orent. They are amicable competitors. I know them well. I can assure you working as a key employee in the exact same position would be a very different experience with Jay vs. Greg vs. Tom. They are very different individuals, their company cultures are different, and their customers are different (although all dentists). Somebody could be ill-suited for a key position with one, but perfectly suited for the same role at another's company.

Let's step out of their businesses and into their clients' businesses—dental practices. If you're not a dentist, you are hopefully a dental patient. Every dental office has somebody who must "finish" the financial arrangements with existent or brand-new patients, after they've had diagnosis, exam, and recommendations from the dentist. In some offices, the dentist concludes his case presentation by fully presenting the fee or, more typically, fee options and discussing issues with payment, financing, and so on, then sends the patient to his money person to sign forms, get a credit card processed, or complete a financing application. In other offices, the dentist—maybe timid about asking for money—delivers the recommendations but delegates the entire fee and payment discussion to a staff person. In some offices, very high-end, premium price dentistry is performed, and case sizes typically range from $20,000.00 to $50,000.00. In other offices, bread 'n butter dentistry, with case sizes from $2,000.00 to $5,000.00. Some dentists believe in very aggressively closing these sales and use "hard sell" tactics, and expect staff support for those tactics. Other dentists believe in "nonselling," and handle the matter with kid gloves. I could go on, but just from this, you can see that a thoroughly knowledgeable and competent financial arrangements person could be ill-fitted to the job in either kind of practice.

Ruthlessness comes in, because you need to be aware of this, figuring it out as fast as possible, and ridding yourself of people ill-fitted to the way you define certain work or to you without hesitation or remorse. The same is true with vendors, and with anybody and everybody you depend on to facilitate your success. Even one around who is ill-suited to working with you is one too many. Try driving down the highway at 70 mph in a car with three right-sized tires and one tiny tire taken off a Moped. At best, it's a very bumpy ride. Getting the right people around you, and getting rid of the wrong people, is vital.

Peak Performance Comes from Pressure

One of the chief reasons a person is ill-suited for a driven, determined entrepreneur's environment is that person's inability to handle pressure. One of my clients, owner of the Texas Baseball

Ranch, Ron Wolforth, says that top athletes and top people in every field learn to be comfortable in uncomfortable situations. The first time I heard him say it, I knew he had summarized a lot of facts about what makes exceptional personal success possible, and what sabotages it. Some people thrive under pressure, and those are most likely the people you want around you.

Years back, I got to know the in-house trainer and coach for the waitstaff of an upscale, pricey restaurant. I sat in once on her 90-minute meeting that occurred before every shift, every day, at which the previous day's results were reviewed in detail, waitperson by waitperson, table by table, somewhat like the Monday-morning-after film session endured by football teams. To hold a prime-time position at this restaurant, the waitperson had to average no less than $9,000.00 a month in tips to hit $100,000.00 a year, or they were ejected and replaced. The trainer/coach/supervisor told me: "If they aren't good enough to make $100,000.00 a year in our environment, they're costing us at least that much because it means they are failing at giving our customers the kind of exceptional experience we've crafted and failing at selling appetizers, wines, and desserts—and they need to go work somewhere else *where they are a better fit*. We can't afford having them here." These people were under a lot of pressure. This was no place for somebody who couldn't work under pressure.

These people were critiqued, in every meeting, in front of their peers. This was no place for somebody with fragile self-esteem, with emotional vulnerability. These people were expected to prepare, memorize detailed descriptions of the day's features, know their regular customers, and *to sell*. This was no place for people who weren't smart or didn't want to work or had a bad attitude toward selling. It *was* a great place for somebody who sincerely wanted to make $100,000.00 a year waiting tables. It was a great place for people who thrive under the pressure to perform.

Backstage at an event where we were both speaking, former Dallas Cowboys all-star quarterback Troy Aikman, there during Cowboy glory days, when Jimmy Johnson coached, told me that playing for the Cowboys meant unrelenting pressure because they were absolutely expected to win every game. He said that is not really true of every team, of every locker room. Many teams, their players and even their coaches, are of the "you win some, you lose some" mentality. They look at the season's schedule and decide which games they can win and which they can't, and are resigned to at least a few bad games. The attitude: "Anybody can have an off day—and everybody will." Not so when Troy played for the Cowboys. Some players thrived under such expectations. Others melted. Others sulked. And they had to go.

The restaurant trainer's words: "We can't afford having them here" are absolutely accurate. You can't afford an ill-suited, underperforming person for even a day.

If you have a person planted in the wrong place, it's up to you to uproot them. People will often stay put in work they know they are ill-suited for, in jobs they dislike, in environments they find unpleasant, and basically do just barely enough, just well enough, not to get fired. Attempts at *motivating* such people are futile. It's like trying to encourage a cactus to thrive planted in a rain forest. Motivation isn't the issue. Motivation isn't possible. They Are In The Wrong Place! But they may not leave it of their own initiative.

Let's "Team Build." This Will Be Fun!

The first requisite for a successful team is to stock it with people who really, sincerely want to be on that particular team and fit with its coach or leaders and other team members. The second requisite is to eject those who are or who become weight others must carry. The third requisite is that everybody knows you will jettison weight. For high performers to have confidence in you, they must know you as ruthless toward poor performers.

You are no doubt aware of team-building exercises. There are all sorts of moonlighting college professors, retired executives, psychologists, and coaches who come into companies to run team-building workshops. There are games and group discussions. People put into teams, one blind-folded, the other guiding him by voice to finding the apple in the corner. There are even companies that take you and your team on campouts in the woods, mountain climbing (or rock wall climbing), kayak racing, into a circus tent to tightrope walk together, out to build a house for Habitat for Humanity. This is all *artificial*. It is orchestrated, choreographed, supervised, and held together for a very short time. The entire Amish community comes together and builds a barn in a weekend. That does not mean those same people could work together effectively on the same team building barns for a living every day. If you've got the wrong people or even one wrong person on your team, all the team-building workshops and adventures in the world won't fix your problem. They *may* have a grand old time in the woods taking turns putting marshmallows on sticks and applauding each other during rope climbing, but on Monday, back in the office, with the workshop leaders gone and real work in front of them, their true selves re-assert. A skilled human potential workshop leader can have everybody reading poetry aloud, tearing up, hugging each other, and acting like a close-knit family in perfect harmony for a short time in an artificial setting. That workshop leader then pockets his fee, gets out of town, and moves on to repeat the performance with different people. You need your people to perform well individually and as a team day in and day out.

Team building is clever charlatanism. It's a way of separating corporations from their money. And it is very old wine, constantly relabeled. There once was a field called "industrial psychology."

It was this. Briefly, imported from Japan, there was "quality circles." We now have "sensitivity training." Whatever you call it, if it is deployed with a group of people ill-fitted together or ill-suited to the actual work to be done, it is exercise in futility. My three requisites work better.

1. Stock the team with people who sincerely want to be on that particular team and fit with its coach or leaders and other team members.
2. Eject those who are or who become weight others must carry.
3. Be sure everybody knows you will jettison weight.

For high performers to have confidence in you, they must know you as ruthless toward poor performers.

CHAPTER 12

They ALL Go Lame

" 'Horse Sense' is the faculty that prevents horses from betting on people."

—UNKNOWN

I own racehorses. At any one time, 15 to 20 of them. I have day-to-day, hands-on personal contact with them. It is impossible not to form relationships with them, to bond more with some than others, to care about them, and to miss them when they leave the stable. Each horse has his own unique personality. Some are antisocial, but most are not only social but real characters. They are equine athletes, each trying his best to perform successfully. Most give it their all—for you. I also drive professionally in over 100 harness races a year, and always keep several of these racehorses to drive myself. With these, the bond can be even greater, as I and the horse are competing out there as a team. When I have retired horses, I have gone somewhere private and wept. There are several I miss often, even though they've been gone for years.

With all that said, they can never become pets. This is a business. They are professional equine athletes, and I own the team. I must trade players, I must force players to retire—if I am to keep my team competitive and my business solvent. Beyond that, the ultimate truth of owning, training, and racing horses is: They ALL go lame.

As the saying goes, it's not a question of if. It's a question of when.

With the horses, they mostly go lame physically. But some go lame psychologically. They lose their personal passion for competing; they lose their will to win. Or they become overly picky about the conditions required for their peak performance; they refuse to race well in rain or cold or peak summer heat or from outside starting gate positions. One way or another, at some point, they all go lame. If their lameness cannot be quickly and affordably resolved, then they must go. Some go on to other, second careers, as pleasure riding horses, Amish buggy horses, even police horses—as in a long ago Disney® movie. Others retire to the pasture. Wealthy people with big estates like having retired racehorses as living, breathing, walking lawn ornaments. An unfortunate few with severe and untreatable injuries or unresolvable vicious behavior must be put to sleep. Getting overly attached to any of them is a very bad idea because the day will inevitably come when you must make the decision to send them packing. Key words: *inevitably, must.*

So it is with your employees, associates, partners, and vendors. At some point, every single one of them will go lame. The number of times an entrepreneur goes the distance of his business life with the same person at his side or working for him productively or serving him as a supplier from beginning to end are so rare and extraordinary they are the stuff of business legends. Walt and Roy Disney and Rich DeVos and Jay VanAndel, co-founders of Amway®, come to mind in the partner category. Hardly any others do. The relative rarity of these long and happy business relationships should convince you not to wager a sou on having one of your own. Know that every single person in your business life will go lame inevitably and you will need to send them packing.

No B.S. Ruthless Management Truth #3

When a food is no longer edible, it must be thrown out. When an employee is no longer profitable, he must go.

There are even famously productive CEOs, executives, and legendary entrepreneurs who went lame and had to be sent packing by their partners, shareholders, and boards of directors. Famous business leaders celebrated in *Fortune, Forbes, Inc., The Wall Street Journal*, etc., go lame and must be sent packing.

I was a huge fan of Michael Eisner during 80% of his tenure at the Disney helm. He reinvigorated a moribund company. I did very well as a stockholder thanks to his confident and aggressive leadership. I tell Eisner stories to my clients and coaching group members. Roy Disney made a terrific choice in bringing him in. Roy also made a terrific choice in forcing him out. For whatever combination of reasons, Eisner went lame. He could no longer lead the company effectively, he was alienating critically important allies left and right, he was no longer a profitable employee, and he had to go. When a horse can no longer win, he has to go. When an employee is no longer profitable, he must go.

Lee Iacocca gave Ford the Mustang, one of its most successful products ever, and a product as iconic as the Model T. And he was fired. He subsequently saved Chrysler with decisive action, cunning, salesmanship, and dynamic leadership. That, however, does not mean that the folks at Ford were necessarily wrong in firing him. Sometimes a person who goes lame and is ineffectual in one environment can be reborn, re-energized, and highly effective in a new environment.

Why and How I Fired Myself

There's a famous Clint Eastwood movie line: A man's got to know his limitations. I think I'm fairly honest about my own limitations. Primarily with my strengths in advertising, marketing, and sales, I built a small but very successful and exceptionally profitable information-marketing business, incorporating my flagship paid-subscription newsletter, *The No B.S. Marketing Letter*, other publications, and seminars. It hit a wall, though, largely due to my managerial deficiencies and, even more so, due to my personal distaste for managing people, especially layers of people and vendors, and my unwillingness to do certain things necessary to take the business to its next logical, evolutionary level. I faced choices of impossible-to-sustain stagnation, riding the business slowly into the ground while siphoning out all the money I could before its last gasp, or firing myself and figuring out how to replace myself in a way much more profitable for the business and, hopefully, financially and personally satisfactory for myself.

I had basically gone lame. I was bored, irritable, and tired with the many business functions and responsibilities that did not play to my strengths, but completely unwilling to hire and manage key people to take over those responsibilities. Personally, I'd rather have a root canal without anesthesia than have employees—and if you think that's odd coming from the author of a book on No-B.S. management, please go back and read the book's introduction; I explain myself there. Anyway, I knew I'd gone lame and that I needed to be sent packing. Since there was nobody to fire me, I fired myself.

I found someone within my clientele who was ably qualified and willing, even eager, to move from running a small, niched business of our kind to a big, expandable mainstream business. He not only possessed marketing knowledge and skills comparable with mine but also had extensive experience hiring, managing, and firing staff; building infrastructure; and overseeing complex operations. He was willing to cross many Rubicons I was not, including ones having to do with staff size, capital investment, internet marketing, and managing thousands of online affiliates. I sold him the business via a formula involving a purchase price, a consulting fee, an ongoing royalty, and opportunities to create new joint ventures, and we reduced and narrowed my responsibilities almost entirely to those things I'm not only exceptionally skilled at but also enjoy and have a passion for doing. As soon as we got the lame guy (me) out of the way, the business began multiplying. I'm delighted to say that, after a first-year pay cut, each successive year provided me with an escalating income greater than it was when I owned the whole thing myself. Thank you, Bill Glazer.

Such arrangements are not easy to make, such people are not easy to find, and there are caveats about them too numerous and complicated to include here. The main point, however, is that I faced reality about having a lame employee on my hands, in this case the CEO, in this case me. And I not only faced the reality, I did something about it.

Fast-forward about ten years, and Bill found himself where I had been. He was going lame. He too did something constructive about it, with my assistance and support. After a year of discussion leading to a definitive decision, a subsequent year-long effort was made to find an appropriate, all-cash buyer for the company, which culminated successfully, to his gain and mine. Today, what was Glazer-Kennedy Insider's Circle is GKIC. It is owned by a private equity fund and a handful of other investors, and it is managed by a combination of people they put in charge and people I brought in. Bill is gone. I remain, as a well-compensated contract player, with specified roles but zero involvement in management and zero equity. GKIC continues as far and away the leading organization supporting entrepreneurs, small-business owners, private practice professionals, and sales professionals utilizing direct marketing. It will hopefully continue and grow and expand long after I am gone, too.

This solution is also not an easy one. Actually selling and walking away from a company, getting the desired financial results from the sale, and handling the emotional issues, often unexpected, of your diminished importance and influence is a minefield. A client of mine, Ted Oakley, specializes in advising sellers of midsize companies on the aftermath of the sale, from preservation of the liberated wealth to "what's next?" issues, and if you are nearing such an action, I suggest getting and reading his books and other materials, accessible at www.oxbowadv.com. When outsiders and absentee owners with money take over a business built from scratch by entrepreneurs, all sorts of troubles can occur within and for that business. Some businesses flourish under new leadership and with new capital and resources. Others fail, some quietly, some spectacularly. You'll be hard-pressed to find big companies who haven't acquired small ones that they have subsequently killed and made disappear. What occurs after the sale is not your responsibility. Your chief responsibility is to you. Selling a company you built, which employs people you know well and have relationship with, has customers you know well and have relationship with, and has a way of doing business you birthed has to be a ruthless exercise. All thoughts about all those things must take a seat in the back of the bus and be silent. Your present and future self-interest rule.

Regardless of these challenges, Bill faced his reality and did something about it. He was limping about, knew his value to his own company was ebbing, had other things he wanted to do, and did not feel merely replacing himself and overseeing as absentee owner was a practical answer. There were also timing considerations. This sale occurred shortly before the big recession, and both he and I were certain it was coming. The company was sold at a price based on its best years. There is, as Johnny Carson said, a time when it is time to go.

I titled this book "Ruthless Management of People and Profits." I did not specify *other* people.

I suppose that ruthless self-assessment is the most difficult of all entrepreneurial tasks. It is helpful to have a few key people around you who will tell you the truth about yourself, will posit difficult questions, will help you sort out options, a function I filled in the above scenario. Ultimately, though, you, as the Billy Joel song says, sleep alone in your own bed. It is quite common to see corporate CEOs, high-level executives, as well as entrepreneurs go from being terrific assets to their businesses to relatively uninterested caretakers or, worse, daring adventurers out of boredom, and finally, liabilities. It is common to see leaders who were visionary and creative become stuck in place, as their industry passes them by. In the field of books, think of Borders vs. Amazon. For everyone, there are seasons. For everyone, there is a time to go.

That's the lesson, or cautionary tale. They all go lame. Even you. When one does go lame, he must be sent packing. Even you.

"No farmer long keeps a cow that can't give milk.
There's a term for such a cow.
Burgers."

—TOLD TO ME BY A NEIGHBOR WHO OWNED SEVERAL FARMS

WHEN I WAS BUT A WEE TYKE

CHAPTER 13

The Worst Number in Business Is.....

"Only the paranoid survive."

—ANDY GROVE, FORMER CEO, INTEL

The worst number in business is one. One of just about anything is a bad thing.

In my little home office, where I work under deadline pressure as an advertising copywriter, I do not have one Mac. I have three. Why? So when Mac #1 freezes up, crashes, or requires an exorcism, I can move what I'm working on and urgently need to print out before the day's FedEx deadline to Mac #2. And in case Mac #2 has indigestion or PMS or leprosy that day, I have Mac #3. I keep them in different rooms to prevent contagion. My Mac is my employee. If Mac were a living, breathing human employee who, say, printed what I wrote in booklets on a printing press, I'd want at least two of those Macs and two printing presses. NEVER one.

Yes, this doubles your personnel cost. But that's an easier economic puzzle to solve than is suddenly, abruptly being without the one person absolutely required to deliver a job on time to your most important client or to get tax reports filed before you are fined up the wazoo or to staff your trade show booth this weekend, where you intend writing 30% of your business for the year. I've had clients report their number-one and only salesman calling in to quit the day he was supposed to be jetting off to McCormack Place in Chicago for just such a trade show. And, defying my own rule, by having my wife of some 20 years running my entire office, I was suddenly (and because of my own incredible myopia) served with divorce papers, a restraining order barring me from entering my own home, *and a* resignation notice. Fortunately, I had a capable replacement readily available, and my wife was cooperative about the transition. But even so it wasn't pretty, and it could have been a disaster. (For soap opera fans, we were divorced. We've remarried. All is well.) These are not freakish incidents like being bit in the butt by a snake escaped from your local zoo who has found his way up the pipe to your toilet—still, looking before sitting is prudent. You will be bitten by this "one thing" if you insist on leaving yourself vulnerable to it.

You still refuse to double up? The next best things, poor substitutes but better than no preventive medicine at all, are cross training and, when possible, job sharing or job rotation. Cross training means everybody is trained in everybody else's job. Job sharing means two part-time people doing one full-time job. This is a quietly growing, trendy practice in corporate America that actually seems to work. Job rotation means two employees swap jobs during each month, Bill gets Job A the first two weeks and Job B the last two weeks, and Betty gets A and B vice versa. If all that seems awkward to you, wait until you see just how awkward the "I had just one and one is gone" scenario can be.

As I was writing this, Obamacare was just coming to troubled fruition. Business owners were having to cope. It quickly accelerated and expanded trends of replacing full-time jobs with part-time ones, getting a job done by two or three part-time workers in place of one full-time one, as well as replacing humans with automation wherever possible. Obamacare is inarguably both a practical and psychological impediment to job creation and to business expansion requiring job creation. I am in total sympathy with the business owner made more resistant than ever to adding another employee by this leviathan. But, if you are going to have one who performs "x" duties, and they are essential duties, you need two. With two, you are the boss, and you can, if and when need occurs, be ruthless. With one, you are not a boss at all. You are a hostage.

Recently, a friend of mine with a small business found her assistant and office manager stealing untold amounts of time. Because my friend had taken my advice and had two assistants and co-office managers working for her at the same time, she was able to take the one out back and shoot her. Had she not taken my advice, she'd have been held hostage at gunpoint by her own dysfunctional and thieving employee. **You decide at whose head the gun is pointed.**

Just as a bonus point, one's the worst number for anything else, too. Too much of your revenue dependent on one key account, one product, one service, one advertising media, one calendar event, one means of distribution, one anything, anything, anything.

On the marketing and business development side, I teach: *Diversity equals stability.* Entrepreneurs often confuse an invention, a product, even a website with a business. Whenever your money is coming to you, funneled through one thing, you are in mortal peril 24/7/365, no matter how rich you may be or feel. A great business has diversity of success drivers in every aspect of the business. It has diverse sources and means of new customer acquisition, diverse means of monetizing those customers, a diverse portfolio of products and services, diversity in its distribution channels. The best businesses have equity in their control of their customers, not just in their products. Business owners and staffs tend to get lazy or cheap about this, and let the diversification narrow, relying over time on fewer and fewer sources, methods, means, media, and distribution channels over time, letting success lull them into false sense of security. The exact same thing occurs with the people in a business. Over time, more and more power and control of vital functions concentrates into fewer and fewer people's hands. In this way, power actually equalizes between the invested and at-risk owner(s) and the hired hands. This is one of the seven deadly sins—sloth—insidiously permeating a business.

The Happy Delusion That Bad Things Happen Only to the Other Man's Business

I used to speak 25 to 27 times a year for the largest, most prominent public seminar company in America, pulling crowds of 20,000 to 30,000 to each event. The entire business was wiped out almost overnight, thanks to 9/11. Two events were scheduled the week after, one in New York, both including a famous former U.S. President and other celebrities on the program. The chicken-shit former President and several other celebrities cancelled. Attendance was all but nonexistent; thus the vital on-site revenues from book, home study course, and merchandise sales cut from dollars to pennies. Refund demands through the roof. Business bankrupt. Why? Total dependence on one way of making money.

Of course, something like 9/11 would never happen to *your* business.

In a business I was running long ago, in a turnaround situation, desperate for every earned dollar, I had a client whose business we depended on tell me he was switching to a competitor over a price difference of several pennies a unit. Even though we had carried him when he had cash flow troubles, promoted him to our other customers, and he and I were personal friends. He said, "You understand, biz is biz."

Of course, *your* most important client would never do such a thing.

A client I'd warned and warned and warned and warned about this "one thing" business was wiped out by a change in the laws governing the use of broadcast fax as an advertising medium. He went from a fat 'n happy millionaire with hundreds of thousands of dollars flowing in every month to a businessman with no business in less than 30 days. The passage of the Do Not Call List laws decimated the mortgage refi industry, including many of its most successful companies overly reliant on cold-call telemarketing. The TV infomercials you see constantly today, that fueled one of my clients' growth of a billion-dollar-a-year business, were once illegal—you could not buy 30 consecutive minutes of commercial time.

Of course, *your* media that you rely on could never be taken away from you.

A friend of mine selling over $500,000.00 worth of his product on a home shopping channel, busily buying second homes and yachts with the money, with manufacturing established in China, and a boatload of goods en route, was abruptly told by the home shopping channel they'd no longer be selling his product. They'd knocked it off, to be sold under a brand name they controlled, by one of their most popular "house" personalities. In 24 hours he went from king of the world to owning a steamship full of doohickeys with no place to sell them.

There's a very big company I dare not identify by name, with a very interesting strategy for acquiring smaller companies at deep discounts. It's used the very same strategy at least 11 times that I know of. It finds a small manufacturer of a unique product or products well protected by patents that its huge direct-to-consumer salesforce can move huge quantities of, beginning with a huge surge when the product is first introduced. It gets the little companies' owners greed glands so stimulated by the prospect of going from making and selling a small, steady output of units and earning a good living to selling a huge, endless tidal wave of units and getting richer than Trump's ex-wives that these owners agree to onerous contracts imposing all sorts of dire penalties for tardy deliveries or product defects, exclusivity to the big company but with no certain, continuing commitments from them, and other draconian provisions. The big company then buries the small company in orders. The small company's owners scurry frantically to ramp up; they buy and lease equipment, lease more space, hire more people, and go deeply in debt to do it. They quickly cease worrying about their small accounts and leave most of them high and dry without product. Then the big company announces it's going to abruptly terminate the relationship and manufacture a substitute product internally . . . or they might, might consider buying the small company. The little company's owners can face horrible destruction, epic financial losses, quite possibly working for free for years just to crawl out from under all the debt, or they can sell the company for debt transfer plus a pittance of its previous, true value and get out alive.

Of course, *your* distribution would never be taken away from you. Of course, *you'd* never get taken advantage of in such a devious way. *You'd* never be blinded by greed.

Burglaries and fires happen only to the neighbors down the street. Only other people's teenagers get arrested for drunk driving or possession of drugs. Go ahead, live in denial. Believe your business somehow impervious to the myriad of "one thing" disasters that befall all others. Go ahead.

"Just because you're paranoid doesn't mean they're not out to get you."

—DR. CHARLIE JARVIS

CHAPTER 14

Hire Slow,
Fire Fast

"Whoever admits that he is too busy to improve his methods has acknowledged himself to be at the end of his rope. And that is the saddest predicament."

—J. OGDEN ARMOUR

I first heard "Hire Slow, Fire Fast" from Chuck Sekeres, the founder of a very successful company, Physicians Weight Loss Centers. He was attending my seminar, but when it came out of his mouth, I scribbled it down. It's at least as profound as anything Aristotle ever said. Its genius and its truth is in its being the polar opposite to what 99% of us do. (Oh, yeah, I've been guilty of this one a few times myself. And it cost me dearly.)

So, as an aside, here's the single most useful and empowering piece of success advice I have ever heard in my entire life. I've based most of what I've done in my own business life and in developing strategies for my clients on this single piece of advice. I heard this one while still a teenager, listening to a cassette tape by

Earl Nightingale. Earl said that if you wanted to do something—anything—successfully and you had no instructions, no role model, no road map, no mentors, all you needed to do was look around at how the majority was doing that thing, then do the opposite—because the majority is always wrong. Whenever I teach this, there's always one twit who challenges me with our own great American democracy as his sword. After all, he'll say, our system of government is based on majority rule. Well, no, it's not. First of all, the founding fathers originally had only people paying taxes—at the time, landowners—voting, as it should be today. Second, the electoral college got stuck in to provide a last line of defense against public stupidity—in case you didn't know it, the electors aren't legally bound to vote as their state's majority has. Third, fortunately, the majority does not vote. If the majority actually, directly elected people, Kim Kardashian would be President and the guy from Duck Dynasty would be Vice-President. So, no, thank our stars, our government is not majority rule. And the principle stands that the majority is always wrong, and you gain most by conforming to the majority as little as possible. (For more from me on this, visit www.GKIC.com/store and check out the Renegade Millionaire resources.)

No B.S. Ruthless Management Truth #4

The majority is always wrong.

Now back to this hiring and firing thing.

Most business owners fire slow. They manage like they go to the movies. Sitting through a three-hour-long movie that is rancid from 1st to 180th minute. Why? They think it has to get better. They keep hoping it will get better. Because I'm a Burt Reynolds fan, I once did this with the single worst movie ever made, *At Long Last Love* or something like that, in which Burt and Cybill Shepherd sing and dance. Bad employees do not cure themselves like ham hung in a barn. Hope isn't a sound business strategy. But that's what too many managers do. Wait and hope for a miraculous, spontaneous cure. Consequently, according to my admittedly unscientific survey of about a hundred of my clients, the average firing occurs somewhere between 6 and 18 months *after* the business owner *knew* the employee was consistently performing poorly, consistently noncompliant, poisoning the workplace, and negatively affecting others in it, or otherwise stinking up the joint. Ironically, most employees who finally get fired are mystified the axe didn't fall sooner. One told a friend of mine, "When you didn't fire me five months ago when you should have, I figured I could get away with just about anything." Some fired employees are even relieved and glad it's over; they've been visualizing the sword of Damocles overhead for months.

Being 6 to 18 months late doing anything in business is a very bad idea.

There is, sadly, one other reason the necessary firings occur so late. Sure, we're waiting and hoping for the bad movie to get good, against our best instincts and all our previous experience. But beyond that, a lot of owners delay firing people who desperately need firing because the business owner is lazy. He has permitted the bad employee to amass and control information only he knows, carried in his head or filed with his own unique code. One lawyer told me, "She's my worst employee, but I rely on her every time I go to court." Huh? And the business owner dreads the difficulty of finding and training a replacement. In this, he's like the single guy at home alone on an autumn Sunday afternoon in dirty underwear, watching football, who discovers he has no cash and his refrigerator has only a beer, a two-day-old half of a pizza, and some bologna going green around the edges. After weighing the options, he'd rather trim the green and eat the bologna and old pizza for dinner than find clothes, get dressed, go to the ATM, then go to the grocery store. Hard to have any sympathy for him when he's up half the night at the vomitorium.

Being 6 to 18 months late is inexcusable.

Next mistake: hiring fast. This is closely linked to the first mistake more often than not. Finally firing the toxic employee, you create a vacancy. It needs to be filled. You've done nothing proactive to be able to fill it until your urgent and desperate need has arisen. Thus the fact that your "best" applicant attracted from your first help-wanted posting at Monster.com has two nose rings, sports a tattoo that says "Kill The Boss," has no references, and occasionally interrupts her sentences by snarling like a dog is ignored. Hey, those phones need answering *today*.

This is the way almost everybody operates. Do the opposite.

CHAPTER 15

Leadership Is Vastly
Overrated

"A leader is one who makes an immediate decision
and is sometimes right."

—ELBERT HUBBARD

L eadership is a powerful buzzword, doubly so since the 9/11 attacks. In politics, we use it as a noun and as an attribute—as in "Rudy Giuliani exhibits real leadership." Supposedly the American public is longing for leadership. If challenged to define it, I doubt many could tell us exactly what it is that they want delivered under its banner. After all, at least half the country got to be thoroughly pissed off at President Bush, and many stayed that way, yet by most attempts at defining leadership, he exhibited plenty of it. He pushed forward a visionary idea of remaking the Middle East as the best means of safeguarding America and the world from ever-rising terrorism, stuck to his convictions despite criticism and opposition, and defied preferences of his own party as well as the opposing party to do what he believed right, and, on occasion, took what could only be described as bold action. His successor, President Obama, has a different style and different agenda, but otherwise can be credited with the same points: visionary ideas for home and abroad, sticking to convictions despite resistance from within his own political party as well as the opposing party, and, on occasion, taking bold action. He, too, has about half the country thoroughly pissed off at him. Bush got high marks for his leadership immediately after 9/11, but no other near unanimous support. Obama got applause after the orchestrated killing of Bin Laden, but no other near unanimous support. So why isn't everybody who loves *the idea of* leadership in love with Bush and Obama?

Because the *idea* of leadership is attractive, but the choices made by somebody acting out leadership are likely to be controversial, even extreme, and there's no way to objectively evaluate them. One man's leadership admired by some is just as easily criticized by others as pig-headed. One man's visionary leadership some find awe-inspiring, others find fantastical. In historical retrospect, President Kennedy is revered as a visionary and courageous leader for setting the goal of landing men on the moon and doing it. You heard and hear little if any criticism for misdirecting billions of dollars that might have been better deployed on the war on poverty or securing Social Security or researching cures for Alzheimer's or cancer, although I could certainly make that case. Why the absence of such criticism? JFK was a popular, charismatic individual who chose a mission built around a very simple idea that was subsequently achieved without significant problems, and no astronauts returned to earth as corpses in body bags. It made for terrific TV, too. The public likes good TV. Hates bad TV. President Bush's equally ambitious but land-based pet project and President Obama's wildly ambitious socialized medicine project have not been so well received. I only want to point out that, if you can be objective about it for a moment, there are far more similarities than differences in the three Presidents' grandiose schemes, and they could be shown as parallel examples of this longed-for leadership.

In corporate America, leadership—better yet, visionary leadership—is the all-time favorite idea people never tire of talking about. If you laid all the books written about it end to end, I imagine you could walk to the moon. CEOs are frequently glorified as great leaders, then later chastised as arrogant fools by the same media, and finally fired by their boards of directors. Still, everybody loves the endless pursuit of leadership. And that's the rub. The pursuit is endless because there's no definable, definite target. Leadership is so ethereal nobody can agree on what it is, nobody's sure if they've got it or not, and nobody can quantify its value. I've certainly worked with highly profitable businesses run by people I'd rank as pathetically inferior leaders. I've also known people who seem to exhibit all the characteristics ascribed to great leaders, who run businesses right into bankruptcy court. Repeatedly.

After much thought, I have come to the conclusion that leadership is vastly overrated. In business, to maximize profits, things that can be agreed on, accurately measured, and proven to deliver predictable results consistently—regardless of who has got their hand on the wheel—are far more valuable. One of these far more valuable assets is: systems and procedures, coupled with enforcement (see Chapters 18 and 19).

McDonalds® is able to deliver millions of products to millions of customers day in, day out, in outlets scattered all over the country, owned by independent operators, without poisoning a lot of people, with consistent (albeit mediocre but satisfactory) quality, at value prices, and dominate the field— all with pimply-faced, hormones raging, attention-deficient teenagers, NOT due to visionary leadership, charismatic leaders, and motivational speakers, or happy-talk team-building camp-outs. This improbable achievement occurs because of systems.

As an investor, I'd rather invest in a corporation with great systems than with great leaders. The leaders might all die in a plane crash and leave me with my stock certificates in one hand, hankie in the other. The systems live on. Disney®, a company I own stock in and admire, has had the benefit of CEOs generally viewed, at least for a time, as great visionary leaders, although I doubt you'd call Bob Iger "charismatic." However, I've really studied Disney® intently and in-depth. By far the company's greatest asset is its incredibly sophisticated, microdetailed, micromanaged systems for maximizing profits in every nook and cranny of its parks, with every intellectual property, from every job and every person.

You can probably win a lot of games with any offensive scheme if you have Peyton Manning or Tom Brady as your quarterback. But the reason the West Coast Offense originally designed by Bill Walsh is so much copied is it permits winning games not just with a Joe Montana but also with a Steve Young, and even a Steve Bono. Arguably it makes average quarterbacks better. Walsh made the game and the position less about individual personality or exceptional talent and more about the system. Of course it helps to have a Montana or a Young. But . . .

. . . the fact of business life is: you can't go far if you require *exceptional* people.

There aren't enough of them to go around. There's intense competition for them. They're expensive. They're damnably hard to keep. If you only need one or two, maybe. But if you need 10 or 20 or more, then you have to get the idea of finding and hiring only superstars and building a team of superstars out of your head.

In your key, top-level and critical positions, you want to do everything possible to find, recruit, and keep superstar performers. You want to build an inner circle team of such exceptional individuals. But if you have significant-sized troops, you'd better have systems that compel performance and that create sales and profits without requiring exceptional people.

One of the greatest "inventions" in the entire history of multilevel or network marketing, an industry entirely driven by and dependent on selling activity by frightened and timid, ineffectual people, is instructive. The companies need them to broach conversations, first with family and friends and co-workers (their "warm" market), but also with strangers. Most don't. Most won't. That's why Mark Hughes, the original founder of Herbalife, created the little button for distributors to wear, that read "Lose Weight? Ask Me How." If distributors wore the button, *somebody* would occasionally ask them how, and they would then be forced to talk to them about Herbalife. Today, I coach my clients with staffs interacting with customers in retail environments—fitness centers, dental offices, stores—to use this button tactic. With 50-cent buttons, Hughes drove up Herbalife's sales. Leadership wouldn't have the same impact. You could teach, train, demonstrate, incentivize, motivate, and lead people to open up conversations with strangers until you were working on your third lifetime and only affect a teeny-tiny percentage of exceptional people already possessing both confidence and sales skill. Or you could stick buttons on people and force selling on them by prospects. The buttons win.

Exceptional people respond exceptionally well to great leadership. Match some truly exceptional players with an exceptional leader and look out—think the Michael Jordan championship-era Chicago Bulls and Phil Jackson, or the Jimmy Johnson-coached Dallas Cowboys. But if you read Phil Jackson's book and try applying his Zenlike leadership philosophy to a bunch of ordinary employees, you're in for rough sailing. You may need more than Zen meditation to survive it. More like a few stiff drinks. And, by the way, exceptional people can thrive with bad leadership, mediocre leadership, or no leadership at all, too. Think Barry Switzer "leading" the Cowboys to the Super Bowl.

The majority of the people you'll be trying to win in business with are just not going to be exceptional. Not exceptionally motivated or dedicated or ambitious. Not exceptionally skilled or talented. Not exceptionally intelligent. Not exceptionally anything. They will, at best, be average. And average people don't respond well to the "leadership" that excites exceptional people.

There's still a place for the much-ballyhooed, much-yakked about, much-admired "leadership," but to think it is some elusive but magical potion that if gotten just right, like lightning in a bottle, will transform your collection of average folks into eager-beaver, highly responsible superstars is delusional. People putting on grandiose leadership seminars love to sell this fantasy. A lot of executives and business owners like buying it, too, because it's fun to talk about leadership but not a lot of fun to be armpit deep in the minutiae of systems and their enforcement. It's ego satisfying to view oneself as a great leader dedicated to great leadership and then blame the troops for being such unresponsive mallet heads they don't appreciate you; it's not at all ego satisfying to blame yourself for poor systems and weak enforcement. So the next faddish brand of "leadership hocus-pocus" is being thought up as we speak. But if you really want to get your business producing maximum profits with the people you're really going to have to work with in real-world conditions, you'll skip the seminar.

CHAPTER 16

Marketing the Master,
All Others Servants

"Nothing happens until somebody sells something."
—ATTRIBUTED TO TWO DIFFERENT SALES TRAINERS, ELMER G. LETTERMAN
AND ARTHUR "RED" MOTLEY; WHO SAID IT FIRST IS UNKNOWN

Several years ago, I (foolishly) agreed to personally conduct a "staff training program" for key employees of about a dozen of my clients. They sent them to me as a group for two days. Their employers weren't there. And boy, did I get an earful of things I didn't want to hear. It might seem surprising they'd be as candid with me as they were, but that was due, in large part, to the fact they didn't even realize how damaging and incriminating much of what they were stating was. As example, the majority complained bitterly about two things: 1) having their "real work" and "important work" constantly or unpredictably interrupted by "customers" calling up, emailing, or coming in, and 2) having their "real work" disrupted by their bosses' decisions to quickly implement an extra promotion or sales effort.

If this surprises you, it shouldn't. I can assure you that your thoughts about what the important work is in your business and what their thoughts are on this subject are miles apart.

Further, sound marketing, promotion and sales ideas, initiatives, and projects are constantly sabotaged by operational concerns and employees who view every such thing as "more work."

I have sat in meetings and listened as clients were assaulted by their own employees' barrage of reasons why "we can't do

> Bill Martin, an early Imagineer, said Walt Disney often got irritated with being given limiting information. "I don't care what you *can't* do," Walt would say, "I want to hear what you *can* do."
>
> My own ruthless assessment is that any idiot—or any MBA—can create a long list of reasons something can't be done or can't be funded or afforded. That work deserves minimum wage, at best. Where is the value in it? Why do you need to hear any of it? The genius is in figuring out how something can be done. How something can be financed and made viable. How your business can do what it needs to do to be the best or to grow the fastest or to dominate a market or to launch a bold, new initiative. I urge you, stop signing paychecks for people who busy themselves assembling all the reasons you can't do what you want to do. Instruct your team: Making Can't Lists is a giant waste of time and (hopefully) talent, and you are unwilling to pay for it. If that's what they are best at, it's best they go do it elsewhere. Ideally, in the employ of your competitor.

that." Their businesses are literally being managed by the "can't do" plan.

In one fairly large company, I demonstrated with reasonable certainty that sales could be increased by 50% or more if the prospective customers booked by its telemarketing center to come into showrooms at preset times were accurately accounted for, with hour-by-hour reporting from the remote showrooms back to the corporate headquarters, so a series of follow-up steps including email, direct mail, and telemarketing could occur in quick succession with every prospect who failed to show up as promised. The regional sales managers told the company's president such a thing couldn't be done because the salespeople would never accurately account for who was there and who wasn't, thus accounting for how many presentations they made and thus revealing their true closing percentages. The vice-president of sales said it couldn't be done because of the complexity of handling all that feedback and triggering the proper follow-up steps. The vice-president of finance said it couldn't be done because half the remote sites weren't equipped with internet-connected laptops and there was no budget for them. A manager of its printing department insisted they could never get the customized mailings out on a timely basis. And some other manager insisted that her "entire data processing department would mutiny if asked to do anything this complicated and time sensitive."

I watched the CEO shrink and surrender. A strong, able-bodied 6-foot, 2-inch man with a matching tie and pocket hankie and a management degree from Stanford reduced to a melted puddle of pinstriped mush. His army of can't-doers left triumphant. I was embarrassed for him.

The kindest description of this is "operations controlling marketing." It should always be the other way around. Why? Because marketing is what brings in the money. As the business owner or president or other-titled leader, your paramount job is to figure out what the best, strongest, most powerful, most effective advertising, marketing, and sales strategies are—then demand that they be implemented. If they create a lot of operational challenges, difficulty, and even chaos, so be it. Whatever is required has to happen. If the beautiful full-color charts of how things are done have to be thrown out and redrawn, if job descriptions need to be rewritten, if people with inappropriate skills or resistant attitudes must be replaced by fresh troops, if funds must be diverted from other expenditures, so be it. **Best marketing rules; all others are its servants.**

I no longer tolerate this crap from the clients who pay me. If I determine the best mailing we can do for a client's particular promotion needs to go in a seven-inch-long tube made of neon green plastic, into which we are going to stuff bags of peanuts along with the sales letter that directs people to a new website, my client knows better than to tell me his vendor only stocks four-inch and six-inch tubes or ask if cheaper cardboard can be substituted for the plastic or to tell me that there's a peanut

Recommended Resource #2

You can obtain a FREE subscription to my *No B.S. Marketing Letter* along with a special package of other gifts at www.GKIC.com or by following the instructions on page 379 of this book. This will help you make marketing rule!

shortage in his town due to rampaging elephants or that his website builder has suddenly been stricken blind. My clients know if they tell me anything of the sort, I'll fire *them*!

Presumably they have found ways to impress a certain reality upon their people that the CEO described earlier was unable to convey to his; the job of management, of folks in operations, heck, of everybody around here is to invent solutions, not construct roadblocks; is to support marketing, not sabotage it; is to help a new opportunity rise and walk rather than wrestling it to the ground and clubbing it to death.

You have to very firmly decide what imperative is going to govern your business, the employees in it, and the vendors who serve it. There can be only one number-one imperative. Only one master.

For many businesses, sadly, the number-one imperative is the can't-do crowds' protection of the status quo and avoidance of difficult challenges, heightened pressure to perform, stress of change, and demand for creative thinking. Their number-one imperative is collecting next Friday's paycheck without any disruption of their routines, new learning curves, or "extra" work.

In many other businesses, incredibly, the number-one imperative is keeping peace with the staff. I hear about this from many small-business owners—they shake their heads and say, "It just isn't worth the grief it'll cause me in the office." These owners are *whipped*. The governing imperative is the convenience and comfort of *the staff*. A doctor told me that even though he got lots of requests from new patients for initial appointments on Friday afternoons, he couldn't take them because his staff wanted to leave early on Fridays. Tuesday and Wednesday morning were nearly devoid of patients, and I saw staff members sitting around reading magazines. The week needed to be re-arranged for Monday and Thursday 9:00 to 5:00, Tuesday and Wednesday 11:00 to 5:00, and Friday 10:00 to 6:00 P.M.

In other businesses, in bizarre logic, the number-one imperative is what's cheapest rather than what delivers the best return on investment. In some businesses the governing imperative is entrenched logistics. *We can't do this because the vendor we use . . . the software program we use . . . the delivery service we use won't or can't.* Bye-bye. Next.

Again, you have to very firmly decide what imperative is going to govern your business, the employees in it, and the vendors who serve it. There can be only one number-one imperative. If you want maximum profits, that imperative had better be maximum profits. It won't take much analysis to determine the number-one imperative governing profits. To save you the trouble of looking, it's having the most effective marketing to attract new customers, to optimize the value of customers, and to rescue lost customers.

Again, there can be only one master. Its name is Marketing. All others bow and say: "Yes, Master. How may I serve thee, Master?"

CHAPTER 17

Beware the Bean-Counters

"My money manager's motto was 'I shall manage your money until there's none of your money left to manage.' "

—WOODY ALLEN

At the time I am writing this book, I have an especially prickly bug up my butt about the bean-counter mentality, so in this chapter you're getting a rant and I'm getting catharsis cheaper than therapy or breaking dishes.

If you happen to be a bean-counter—like, say, a Chief Financial Officer, accountant, banker—and have mysteriously gotten this book and made it to this point, please skip ahead to the next chapter. There's nothing here for you. I'd just as soon not offend you for no good purpose, but I want to speak frankly and bluntly to entrepreneurs and business owners about you. Don't let that arouse your curiosity. What kind of candy might be inside the gold box marked candy is a great curiosity if you like pretty much any kind of candy. You can be Forrest Gump. But I'm telling you in advance there's nothing in this box for you but foul-smelling, sour-tasting turds. Don't open the lid. Move on.

Now, just you and I are left. Entrepreneurs. Let's talk.

Don't Let Any of This Happen to You

You know that saying: Friends don't let friends drive drunk. Well, you're a friend, so I'm going to try and prevent you from ever driving your business off a cliff. I'm thankful, with 20/20 hindsight, that I was *not* able to go to college, and I'm wildly thankful I never got an MBA, this gratitude reinforced by the book I've read twice and underlined the heck out of, that I now urge you to read. The book is by Bob Lutz, one of the last real "car guys" at GM. The book is: *Car Guys vs. Bean Counters: The Battle for the Soul of American Business.*

I don't agree with Lutz on *everything* (particularly his enthusiasm for the electric car). But 99% of this book is so on target, I wanted to stand up and applaud a number of times while reading it. I want you to read it all, but I'll point you to key items.

Get the paperback, published 2011. The preface added to the paperback edition is must reading. Don't skip it. And the example of corporate gobbledyspeak on page ix is priceless. Beginning with the last paragraph on page 16 through page 17, and pages 41 and 42, the disregard for vision and creative understanding in business is exposed—a pervasive problem in almost every big company, invading smaller businesses more and more. Lutz describes the disempowering of "the product guys" and transfer of power to the finance guys in painful detail. Bob's insider story reveals a vital truth: When people who don't *love* the product get control of a company or even get key positions in a company, trouble often follows. You see this play out in inherited family businesses but also with big, public corporations. Historically, one of the best stock investment strategies is to short stock in any entity where the CFO becomes the CEO. CFOs love numbers, not products or businesses. They love rigid order, not entrepreneurial chaos or spirit. The very idea that each (successful) business has a soul is simply incomprehensible to them.

Lutz exposes the danger of a fundamentally correct idea, brought to fruition—stubbornly—at the wrong time or raised to priority above other, more important matters on page 61, with the story of GM's acquisition of Opel. Another grievous error I often see: Stripping the "personality," "soul," unique appeal, or unique connection with a customer tribe from a product(s) or company is illustrated by GM's near ruination of Saab. See page 62: "Every effort to expand the appeal of Saab by making it more *mainstream* and less *quirky* ended in failure." The lack of insight into what Saab was all about, and, worse, the lack of *interest* in what Saab was all about by those into whose hands it fell by GM's acquisition is a great cautionary tale. Page 83 describes the common affliction of ignoring the *one* essential and critical key to success or failure for a business—because it is difficult—and instead busying everybody with everything imaginable but that key. Pages 86 and 87 take you inside a "brand strategy" meeting Lutz fingers as "unmitigated hogwash." Page 197 describes why, when, where, and how American business schools went wrong and started pumping out fools. Page 207 zeroes in on the absolute wrong way to cut costs. Page 212 explains succinctly why the best leaders rarely get the opportunity to lead in big business.

There are two specific hazards for you: 1) Successful growth to the point that you begin to doubt your own qualifications to make the vital decisions for your company, and begin setting your own best judgment aside. "Replacement of self" is an entrepreneurial goal, but it is lit dynamite to handle with extreme care. 2) Squeezing out the "life force" when reining in and controlling costs. We face a *shrinking* economy. Many business owners will need to embrace "Less Is More." But again, it's lit dynamite. If the squeezing is delegated to bean-counters, they'll squeeze the wrong stuff.

This book is a laugh-and-cry catalog of every which way a business can be screwed up and sidetracked and put into peril, your list of what never to do, what not to let happen, and what to recognize as B.S. the minute it is presented to you by anybody. When GM's leadership sidelined their "car guys" and put their faith in numbers and spreadsheets, determined to eliminate the "personality worship," cut "waste," and worry less about the customer than about "better management," the seeds of disaster were sown. GM had to bring Bob Lutz out of retirement (much like Apple drug Steve Jobs back) with a mandate to save the company's soul. This story of his battle royal inside GM is a great read.

Many of you reading this have not had easy paths. Like me, you started your climb without a ladder or a leg up. You bumbled, got bloodied, restarted, struggled, scrapped. You sold to eat. You were surrounded by doubters. You have had to teach yourself truths and find other truths by diligent search. As David Sandler, founder of Sandler Selling Systems, said, you can't *really* learn to ride a bicycle in a classroom. You got on it and fell down. As you contemplate things to be thankful for, be thankful for all *that*. It is because of all that, that you *actually know* how to do things. If you are in the middle of such a bruising climb up a steep and rocky path, I know there is little consolation in my telling you that if I could go back and get a free Harvard education and MBA instead of the street battle I got, I would not want it. But that's the truth, and when you make it through, you too will be thankful for your "expensive experience."

We Don't Have a Budget for That

I have a number of Bob Lutz-like stories of my own. This is the saddest.

A number of years back, I did a sizable piece of marketing work for Weight Watchers International before the advent of today's inexpensive smartphones. A problem quickly identified had to do with, in marketing language, unconverted leads. All advertising and marketing drove upwards from a million callers a year into the company phone rooms, where prospects were given information and booked into their choice of several upcoming meetings in their area. There, in the church basement, the public library meeting room, or the Weight Watchers location, a leader ran a meeting and signed up new members.

Not everybody who booked showed up. In fact, less than half. My question had to do with those people whose good intentions faltered—what was done, in what order, at what speed after each meeting to get to those people and rebook them or otherwise sell to them?

I was stunned to discover they had no knowledge of who came and who didn't. That information *never* flowed from the hundreds of meeting leaders back to corporate, let alone got there the next day. When I somewhat sarcastically suggested that there were laptops that could be equipped with antennas, so that lists of

> Herb Ryman, a Disney artist, tells this story about the construction of Walt's personal railroad, in his backyard. "The tunnel of the railroad in Walt's backyard was 120 feet long on a long S-curve, so you couldn't see the other end when you were inside. Walt liked the mystery. The foreman on the job suggested it would be cheaper to build it straight. Walt said, 'It's cheaper not to build it at all.'"

the prospects booked could be checked off and magically transmitted to the home office, triggering mail, email, and outbound call follow-up, the CEO hustled me into his office to explain that *he had no budget for equipping the field force with laptops.* Keeping calm and carrying on, as the saying goes, I said the money should be grabbed by reducing advertising and marketing spends. He patiently explained that 1) laptops aren't advertising or marketing, 2) trying to convince the bean-counters or corporate board that laptops were advertising or marketing would be dangerous to him and futile, 3) he had to spend 100%+ of the ad budget on advertising and the marketing budget on marketing or have those budgets cut for the next year, and 4) I needed to forget about laptops and follow-up on unconverted leads and busy myself creating more direct marketing to pour more new and fresh leads into the bucket with the big hole in its bottom, cash my checks, and be happy.

I am, as of this writing, just ready to turn 59. I have actively worked in marketing and business development for 42 of those years. I started young. I had my first experiences with corporate stupidity and excessively empowered bean-counters in those earliest years. I imagine I have heard the bean-counter motto, "We Don't Have A Budget For That," a gobazillion times in these years. When I hear it, it is restated in my head as "We Have Predetermined Not To Do It Even If It Is Essential To Sustain Life Or Be Enormously Profitable." If you let *that* be your company motto, may I recommend earnest prayer?

When It Comes to Direct Marketing, Budgets Are Bullshit

If your MA-CAC (Maximum Allowable Customer Acquisition Cost) is $100.00 and you find a way that you can buy a customer for $99.50, then you turn around and speed up and buy as many as you can for $99.50, as fast as you possibly can, before the great god of economics changes his mind and demands $105.00. If the opportunity to buy 100,000 of them exists and the capital to do so exists or can be obtained, you do it. It's simple: If I'll give you a bona fide $100.00 bill for every $99.50 you give me, how many times would you like to make that exchange? Ah, but if the bean-counter has imposed a budget for the quarter, year, century, department, etc., you must stop exchanging $99.50 for $100.00 when you hit the budget's ceiling. Incredibly, that happens. A lot. In fact, it *has to* happen if a company is managed by budget.

A lot of business school B.S. teaches people to set advertising and marketing budgets based on a percentage of gross revenues. But I routinely double, triple, quintuple, and ten times businesses at high speed. Impossible if limited by a percentage of the prior year's gross revenues. **Percentages of past revenue are prisons**. This does not mean you *just* spend. Objectives, targets, formulas, very flexible budgets, and careful monitoring of immediate and over-time return on investment is required. But you can't predetermine and prelimit spending, because success or difficulty may call for more. Further, the correct approach to budgeting has to do with maximum allowables—what you can and will spend to buy a new customer, what you can and will spend to retain a customer, what you can and will spend to get a repeat order, and so on. These are numbers you can make investment decisions with. (Read Chapter 46 for a description of more smart money math.)

How Bean-Counters Drain the Life Out of a Business

The second person I ever fired in my life was a bean-counter, officially and pretentiously called a Chief Financial Officer. The company was dancing on the edge of bankruptcy, starved for sales, but he had magnificent spreadsheets and computer print-outs, the product of being locked in his office all day counting a dwindling supply of beans. Outside, the crew is yelling about the giant iceberg. He stays down below, checking the inventory of cocktail napkins. He was the second of 41 to go. (The first was the Human Resources Director.) This bean-counter, by the way, had two assistants. The sales manager had none.

You can actually choke the life out of a business.

Bean-counters are great at this. They kill spirit. "We don't have a budget for that" is just as deadly as "We tried that before" and "That's not the business we're in" and a dozen other poison-tipped harpoons. Of *course* we don't have a budget for that—it's a *new* idea. Just because you f***'ed up something five years ago doesn't mean it can't and shouldn't be done now. And, gee, maybe we *should* be in that business. So take your poison-tipped harpoons, get out of this meeting, go back to your cubicle, and leave those of us who MAKE money alone.

I've been in meetings where you could play the drinking game with "we don't have a budget for that" and be blind drunk just 20 minutes in.

Gradually, everybody with ideas just shuts up. They wilt like plants without water. As they say, and invent, and do less and less and less to the least that can be said and invented and done, a power vacuum grows, filled by—who else—the bean-counters. Whether this is done on purpose or by accident, I can't say. When I used to travel to companies to consult (now everybody comes to me), I could *smell* this as soon as I walked in. There is a sense of death in buildings where bean-counters rule.

When Iacocca told the guys to take blow-torches, cut the roof off a car to make it a convertible, drove it around, had college girls asking about it when he stopped at lights, and returned to the plant and said, "Make these," he had no budget for it,

American-made convertibles had all died out, Chrysler had tried it before and failed, and it needed a 12-month feasibility study and, damn it, a budget. All of which he ignored. See, that's a *real* CEO. And you would never find a CFO on the planet who would do such a thing. Just telling a bean-counter this story can cause the poor guy's ulcer to explode. When power moves from the Iacocca guy to the bean-counter guy, look out.

You'd never see a Trump building look like a Trump building if bean-counters designed them. Read Trump's books and his legal-beagle right-hand man George Ross' books, and you'll realize just how far from bean-counter beliefs and practices their success system is. I've been on programs with Donald Trump, Ivanka Trump, and George Ross as a speaker, and quizzed George particularly about their "odd math." They take into consideration the nearly instant increase in value created by Trump owning it. Trump says that he has "overpaid" for every one of his best deals. If Roy instead of Walt had been in charge, there'd be an ordinary amusement park, an ordinary zoo at best—more probably, nothing.

Some years back, at GKIC, then Glazer-Kennedy Insider's Circle, I had to push Bill Glazer very, very hard to spend triple the historically typical cost for the featured celebrity-entrepreneur speaker at the company's number-one annual event, the Marketing And Moneymaking SuperConferenceSM. It is essentially a multiday convention for our Members, rich with training and networking, but also where we sell membership level upgrades, coaching programs and mastermind groups, new and backlist courses and resources, and future events. That year, we brought in Gene Simmons, at roughly triple what we had spent on anyone in any prior year. A big leap. I'm sure you know, but just in case, Gene Simmons created and fronted the rock band KISS, retained all rights, and has built an amazing licensing business around KISS, and that year was featured in a popular reality-TV show. He was and is iconic. I knew people would be more excited about seeing him, hearing him tell his story, and having a photo opportunity with him than for any other celebrity entrepreneur we'd ever had or could conceive of having.

There was a budget for speakers in total as well as for this speaking position, and we blew it up. Had it been a carved-in-cement budget in an entity ruled by bean-counters, it would never have happened. Had different speaker options and fees been discussed in a boardroom group including bean-counters, the life would have been drained from this daring leap in investment. But the entrepreneurs were still in charge, and to his credit, Bill pulled the trigger. The results were epic. Not only did we get a significant attendance bump, at higher fees with fewer discounts, but the on-site buying mood was supercharged and on-site revenues per head came in at a multiple of prior years, and the buzz surrounding it had good afterlife, raised our star in the industry, and provided other gains. It turned out to be the best bargain ever.

Well, bean-counters crave and love bargains. But they don't know how to *create* a bargain like that.

Beware the Bean-Counter's Magical Illusion

Bean-counters can appear to make money when they are often just sowing the seeds of future destruction. Goes on all the time. Companies get fat and sloppy. The new bean-counters arrive and find and cut the fat and slop. The trouble is they don't know how to do anything but cut. Their entire toolbox consists of knives. And if all you've got is a knife, *everything* looks like something to be cut. And cut some more. They can make themselves look brilliant with their spreadsheets, showing all the fat and slop cut, and the temporarily improved bottom line to their masters in the boardroom or at the bank. But they have no idea where to stop. They serve no purpose but this. If they are left there in power or, worse, gain power, they just keep cutting and cutting and cutting. As if you hired a surgeon, gave him only one patient—ever—and evaluated him monthly on how much surgery he'd performed. Soon, a small bag of bones.

Saving a dollar has a lot of merit. Recapturing a truly wasted dollar is a lot better than making one—you may need 10 or 20 or 100 to have one stick to the bottom line. But, when a dollar is saved at the expense of crippling the business's growth, damaging its relationship with and hold on its customers, or killing its spirit, it is a dollar saved with a future cost of 10 or 100. Bean-counters don't grasp these distinctions. To them, a penny saved is a penny earned, *period.*

Anybody who thinks *that* is very dangerous.

If All It Took Was . . .

Often bean-counters are put in charge as managers, commissioned just to "make the trains run on time." This can be okay, for a while, *if* there are a bunch of trains that run every day. But most business aren't that at all. None are, over time. Somebody fires up the trains every day. The tracks move. The engine needs to be painted pink to attract more attention. If you have a chain of shoe stores in decent locations that have been there for a while, you can put a bean-counter atop the empire and people will come in today, tomorrow, and the next day at about the same pace and quantity as the week, month, maybe even the year before, and the bean-counter can count the shoes and boxes and beans and put in lower-watt light bulbs and figure out how to open at 9:30 instead of 9:00 and keep the trains running on time, and probably wind up with more beans in the bucket at the bottom of it all. For a short while. The trouble with this is all the other shoe stores and DSW and Amazon's Zappos and the new barefoot-on-Friday movement. All this is ignored by the busy bean-counter busy counting beans. As fewer customers come through the stores' doors, he just counts fewer beans more furiously. Soon, there's nothing to keep running on time because there's nothing running at all. The cheapest light bill is no lights turned on at all.

If you put a bean-counter in charge, this is what you'll get, and it's what you deserve.

If all it took was this, you'd find all of America's legendary companies started up by bean-counters and trains-on-time bureaucrats, instead of by entrepreneurs and salespeople and hustlers who much, much later bring in the bean-counters and bureaucrats. Old man Gamble said, "Any idiot can make soap. It takes a genius to sell it." He might have said, "Any idiot can make soap. Anybody with an MBA can count the flakes in the soap. It takes a genius to sell it."

A Necessary Evil. Kind of Like Lawyers. And Barn Cats.

I have a stable of racehorses. Even if you aren't a cat person, you need to have a bunch of cats in your barn—unless you like mice and rats. In a barn, cats are necessary. Personally, I've had a long and happy business career with fewer than five times needing a lawyer. I have friends, clients, coaching members who are attorneys, but as a breed, I'm definitely more fond of cats and it's a toss-up with rats. I acknowledge, however, that they are necessary. Similarly, you need bean-counters. But . . .

- They must be confined and controlled.
- They must be made to count beans in a way you—the creative leader and entrepreneur—want them counted (see Chapter 46).

- They must NEVER be given power or authority—that has to pass through you.

Am I being overly simplistic, harsh, and disrespectful? Yes to the second, with deliberate intent. No to the first. This is a simple matter. Different creatures have different purposes. You do not saddle a cow to race in the Kentucky Derby nor milk a racehorse. You do not attempt using a hot air balloon to go 20,000 leagues under the sea. You don't hire blind people as jet pilots. Bean-counters are on this earth to count beans. Not to exercise control over how beans are brought in to be counted.

I favor their isolation. They talk to you; you talk to everybody else. They do NOT talk to everybody else. They belong in quarantine. And you must steel yourself to mine them for information but stay immune to their opinions about all subjects they don't know anything about, like how we make beans. It is the nature of bean-counters to try and assert influence and authority rather than just provide information. Beware.

There *are* people who shouldn't be allowed to talk directly to one another within companies.

I learned very quickly, in the manufacturing company I took over very early in my career, that nobody in production could be allowed to talk to anybody in sales. The Production Manager and his tribe view each sale as "ugh—more work" and any sale requiring even the slightest tweak from the standard and off the shelf as a "foul ball." They are quick to regale the Sales Manager and his tribe with a long list of pain and suffering to be absorbed in the filling of the order. The rule should be: Don't tell me about the labor pains, just birth the baby. But it's the opposite. On top of that, production folk do not understand and therefore hate sales folk. The production folk believe they are working hard every minute 9 to 5 (which they damn sure aren't) while they see the sales folk goofing off, going to two-hour lunches, and polishing their pinkie rings. Production folk can't grasp that five minutes of productivity from a great salesperson can provide everybody's payroll for the week. Conversely, the Sales Manager has zero interest in or sympathy for the Production Manager. He sees him as an obstacle to maximizing sales, and knows him to be a liar—he has been told "impossible" too many times only to then, under pressure, have the impossible deadline grudgingly met or the impossible product modification unhappily made. These two managers and their respective tribes are just not going to hold hands at the campfire and sing the company song. I separated them and installed an intermediary through whom communication flowed and, usually, was translated and restated in nonincendiary language and terms. He could negotiate or dictate as he saw fit.

Similarly, I think having the bean-counter speak directly to the sales troops or the production troops is a big mistake, and ever letting the bean-counter speak to a client or customer is flat-out insane. With the first 10 words, the bean-counter sets the sales folk's teeth on edge and has bile forming in their bellies, and raises the hackles of the production folk. The sales folk despise the bean-counter. They see him as 1) head of the Sales Prevention Department and 2) as somebody incapable of making money. He equally despises the sales folk. He, too, resents their lounging about between appointments or calls, their long, expense account lunches, and their pinkie rings. The production folk also hate the bean-counter, because he is constantly forcing them to sacrifice quality for short-term gains—as Bob Lutz describes in painful detail in his book *Car Guys vs. Bean-Counters*. And they hate him because he is worrying over how much toilet paper they use. They know he wouldn't last doing real work in their job for a day. He has disdain for them, too. They are, after all, comparatively uneducated, lazy, wasteful, and their expense grows on his pages month by month. Do you really want these people trying to co-exist? It's the old Wild West problem. As soon as the white guy in charge of the fort sits down with the Indian chief and says, "Okay, red man" and the chief says, "Well, pale-face," you can toss the peace pipe off the cliff.

How To Ruin a Top Performer

Maybe the worst negative effect of excessively empowered bean-counters let loose on everybody else is the loss of the best and most valuable people. Mediocre salespeople, lousy managers, and utterly uncreative executives are all people who fear they can do no better and will suffer just about any indignity to keep their jobs—they stay. It's the good ones and definitely the great ones, who know they can go elsewhere and keep moving until they find an environment that doesn't suck all the life out of them, who leave. You wind up with the dregs.

On a terrible team losing every game, coached by a complete nincompoop, who never asks to be traded? The player who's certain no other team would pick him up. Who's out of there at the first opportunity? The superstar. LeBron James couldn't wait a minute to escape the Cleveland Cavaliers*. The feckless coach who came because LeBron was there didn't up and quit. The benchwarmers stayed and clung hard to the bench, just hoping for one more paycheck. Trouble is, you can't win a championship with a team absent any champions. You will, of course, see bad coaches in the NFL and NBA, but no owner has yet been goofy enough to make his chief bean-counter the new head coach. Imagine that game. *What, you need to rewrap that bad ankle? We didn't budget for more than one roll of tape this week.* Thus, the Pro Bowl running back would sit on the bench,

*Four years later, LeBron returned from the Miami Heat to the Cleveland Cavaliers, much of the city forgave his defection and new expectation of championships filled the air. As of this writing, we shall see. But it's worth noting he only made a two-year commitment.

plotting murder or getting traded, while the third-string scrub with tortoise-like speed but no need for ankle taping would be sent into the game.

Top performers must be allowed to be and encouraged to be top performers. Drones do their jobs at a consistently mediocre level regardless of motivation or demotivation. They do enough for their paychecks not to be fired. But top performers require motivation and respond very badly to demotivation. Anybody can manage mediocre people, even a bean-counter. Get the door open and the lights on. The drones will go to work. Watch over them some, and they'll do some work. It takes a totally different mindset and skill set to get top performance out of top performers.

How do I know this?

I have been a top performer, a lot, my entire life. In my first sales job, with a five-state territory in disarray, I rose to number-one in the national sales force by my fourth month, opened more new accounts and locations than anybody month after month, and even delivered higher net margin than anybody else. But I quit. Not because I didn't like the work or the products or the customers (I did). Not because of the compensation (tt was fine). There were three reasons, and the biggest was that the National Sales Manager refused to keep his beady-eyed bean-counter from pestering me. My expense account ran low vs. other reps, yet I was badgered to justify this or that expense, and about not having a receipt for some piddly thing. I was harangued about gifting free freight to certain accounts, mostly ones neglected or abused by the previous rep, despite my overall net profit exceeding that of the other reps. A straw breaking this camel's back was the bean-counter sending me a detailed written analysis of my movement throughout my territory for a month and advising me on how I could route myself more efficiently and less expensively—this while he sat in sunny Los Angeles while I navigated snow, ice, and locust attacks on the Midwest's frozen tundra. Both the bean-counter and the sales manager needed Jimmy Johnson's advice (Chapter 28). I grew to hate them.

Were I a mediocre or poor salesperson, their bottom or near-to-bottom guy, knowing I dare not leave or lose this job and the base pay and the company car, I would have suffered in silence and tolerated the bean-counter's crapping in my sandbox, maybe forever. Their two lowest producing guys were still there ten years after I left. One routinely sat at the bar at day's end, with a glass of Scotch, a glass of water, and a glass of Maalox®, sipping from each in order, 1, 2, 3, 1, 2, 3, to dull his emotional pain without firing up his ulcer.

Why and When This Big Mouth Goes Silent

As a consultant and a coach, in one-to-one and in-group settings, I am paid a whole lot of money to hear questions and provide answers, either solutions or opportunities. Occasionally, someone will respond to my advice by telling me they've tried it before, it doesn't work in their unique business, the 51 reasons it can't work, or, God forbid, that they have no budget for it. I immediately shift into three strikes and they're out. When they do this three times, I clam up and shut down. For the remainder of their time, I only appear engaged. I nod. I grunt. I ask them what they think their options are. I volunteer nothing. I create nothing. I count the minutes until it's all over. They get nothing for their money, and I have zero regret about that outcome. It is, apparently, what they wanted. It's definitely what they deserve. Because they are clueless about how to manage a top-performing advisor, they get my alter ego, a nonperforming advisor.

Were I a barely adequate consultant, I would simply plod along with my standard routine regardless of good or poor response, resistance or creative interest, intelligence or stubborn stupidity of any given client. Plod.

These days, I'm even more dangerous. I have no need to make any money. I have squirreled away more than enough nuts for an endless winter decades long, to my most optimistic life expectancy. I am also at my most valuable. I have 40-plus years of experience, I have perspective, I have wisdom, I am at the peak of my powers in my chief competencies. I can make it rain money. If I am sufficiently demotivated to be uninterested, whoever I am working for loses in a very big way. When I nap, fortunes ebb. And nap I do, when annoyed enough. I can just go through the motions, meet the minimums contractually required of me, give no extra thought to doing any of it better or smarter or more effectively. I can and I will. You might question the ethics of dogging it like this. You might have a just criticism. Doesn't matter. Like 95% of the population, I make up my own ethics, situation by situation. (Refer to Chapter 21.) If you want the highest value out of me, you have to manage me as I am, not as you think I should be based on your ideas of morality, ethics, or fairness. I don't operate by your code. I operate by mine.

Since I know this about me, I know it about other top performers. Others confess it, too. Bob Lutz did in his book. In sports, it is said that the coach has "lost the locker room." That means top performers are unofficially on strike. A very famous actor I won't name once told me, of his last year in a TV series, that he started "just phoning it in" and "didn't give a damn" because he couldn't stand the new director's pinhead assistant, who was always bothering him about being five minutes late or ordering too many bottles of his favorite water. And the series went from popular to dead in a year, and the small-minded bean-counter worrying over water woke up with no beans to count. Better to have bought the damn water.

There is the foolish notion that only poor performers need to be motivated, that top performers are self-motivated. Actually, the more capable, successful, and secure someone is, the more they need to be cleverly motivated. Their tolerance for being annoyed or disrespected goes to zero. Read the part of Jerry Weintraub's fabulous book, *When I Stop Talking, You'll Know I'm Dead*, about his handling of a difficult Sinatra. This is what it takes. If a bean-counter would dare to question Sinatra, Frank would have smacked him in the nose and quit—the movie, the TV show, the concert tour. In a heartbeat. Leaving the bean-counter with a busted nose and no beans to count.

What To Do About This

Now, about you. It's *your* business. No one else's. So you must ruthlessly rein in and manage *your* bean-counter(s). Whether they benefit or harm your business is your responsibility. You cannot and dare not expect them to manage themselves in a way that produces the best results for your company. They don't even know how to do that, even if they were so inclined. *They know how to count beans.* **That's it.** Get this through your head. They have little sense of and less concern over consequences beyond the edges of the ledger page. They have no creative vision. Left to their own devices, they will wreak havoc and ruin if need be to wind up with a perfect spreadsheet or a nifty looking bar graph. This does not make them evil or stupid. It only makes them what they are: bean-counters. It is up to you to use them wisely, to enable them to be valuable, to prevent them from doing damage. You must be able to differentiate between information they can provide vs. opinion they're not entitled to. Ultimately, you must lead.

I have nothing against bean-counters per se. In fact, I have a client I admire, Lisa Miller, the founder and CEO of VIE Partners, the best expense reduction and control consultancy in the health-care industry. Time after time, she and her team move in and work their way through different departments in hospitals small and large, uncovering overpayments to vendors that can be recovered, fraud and embezzlement to be stopped, sloppy expense management to be reined in, and they are paid millions of dollars entirely based on their success at this. Their consistent success is surprising and impressive, as they must navigate politically charged waters, dealing with at-odds constituencies of the top administrators, the threatened internal finance people, department heads, doctors, vendors, occasionally incompetent people, occasionally thieves. In about a dozen years, they've created hundreds of millions of dollars in recoveries and expense reductions. To her credit, Lisa is a marketing-oriented person, helming a team of expert bean-counters. She takes great pains not to throw monkey wrenches into the engine that gives one hospital competitive edge over another, brings in patients, attracts top doctors. In fact, she and I have been toe-in-the-water collaborating on ways to improve hospital marketing (most of which simply sucks and is mind-blowingly stupid). Her kind of bean-counting is necessary. Spending creep, spending slop, and spending larceny are all inevitable in complex institutions, and yes, somebody *does* have to count and recount the paper clips. But make no mistake: Lisa is very, very careful about her bean-counters' communications with the staffs, executives, and doctors. She is the chief intermediary, playing a role quite similar to the intermediary I put in place between sales and production in my little manufacturing company all those years ago. Because she is savvy and expert at handling the explosives, she routinely gets cooperation and positive results as an outsider, when the parties within are unable to do so on their own.

The bottom line, a favorite bean-counter cliché, is that these guys are as essential to a company as those barn cats are at the stable, where, without them, we'd be overrun by mice and rats. We do not, however, put the cats in charge of the care or training or motivation of the racehorses.

CHAPTER 18

Mice at Play

REGULATION #22: Loafing, loitering, visiting or unauthorized absence from work will result in disciplinary action, and may result in loss of your job, and withholding of a good time.

—INSTITUTION RULES AND REGULATIONS, ALCATRAZ

My friend Lee Milteer checked "History" on one of her employees' computers in the office. The most recent 30 stops were at Facebook, Pinterest, Match.com, and Amazon. Given that there had been previous incidents of on-the-job theft, the employee was fired.

Yes, it's theft, and it's rampant and epic. It's time theft, which you need to look at exactly the same way as cash theft—or you haven't got a fighting chance.

Online community businesses like Facebook and ecommerce giants from Amazon.com to eBay would be starving shadows of themselves were it not for all the daytime use by employees at work, effectively stealing from their employers while playing on the internet. In fact, these companies don't really, truly *make* the lion's share of their money at all. They merely are the beneficiaries of a theft and transfer of productivity from other businesses, including yours. If every employer in America suddenly did what they should do and stopped all workplace access to these sites, and these sites were totally dependent on use by their customers on their own time instead of their employers' time, many of these online entertainment and shopping businesses would dry up and disappear.

As an author, I selfishly love Amazon.com, B&N.com, and other online booksellers. As an Amazon.com stockholder, I've done well. But make no mistake: Facebook, eHarmony.com, Amazon.com, Buy.com, etc., etc., etc., are your mortal enemies in your battle to get a just, fair, and full day's work for a full day's pay. And make no mistake: While the cat's not watching, the mice are at play at these websites, playing computer games, doing their personal banking online, sending email greeting cards, text-messaging friends, watching movies, while your business phones go unanswered, your customers get treated as annoying interruptions, paperwork gets hidden and buried.

Many of my clients are entrepreneurs with small offices, with one to several employees. These cats work mostly from home and often travel, leaving the mice unsupervised for days on end. Were they able to snoop on their offices, they'd be horrified. When, at my urging, they pull surprise visits or send in someone else unannounced and unknown to the staffs, they are horrified at what they discover. When they do as I urge and run weekend raids, snooping in desk drawers, file cabinets, appointment books, and computers, they are amazed and, again, horrified at what they find. Spending the workday making friends at Facebook is mild, in the grand scheme of things. The mice are doing much worse.

Other clients have professional practices, retail stores, or open-to-public offices like insurance agencies or real estate offices. These cats are also often absent, in the back room drilling teeth or in the car driving to and from appointments. When we have their businesses mystery-shopped by phone or in-person visitors, we uncover mice not only at play, but mice actually, quite deliberately, sabotaging the business. For example, it's a common and frequent "catch" in professional offices any day the cat's out to find the mice putting all the phones on hold for hours at a time while they play on the computer, or talk to boyfriends, girlfriends, and spouses on cell phones. Frustrated callers take their business elsewhere.

Oh, and you don't need to take my word for it. ABC's *20/20* did an outstanding show on this, where it hired people to do on-the-street surveys and then secretly watched their work. They let employees in an ice-cream shop believe the owner was going out of town for the entire day, then observed their work with hidden cameras and sent in mystery shoppers. And so on. Of all the employees we saw on this show, only one actually did the work she was supposed to do without goofing off and cheating to cover it up—and she was urged by the other employees to stop. The survey takers met the ridiculously low, easy quota by filling out many surveys themselves, then one took a nap on a park bench, another went shopping, several took lunch breaks much longer than allowed. They falsified their work, defeating its purpose, skewing the results. When shown they were caught, *they were unashamed.* They each had an excuse, from shyness to feeling demeaned having to do the work. But they all took the money. The ice-cream store employees sat talking to each other while the phone rang endlessly. None of this was rigged. It was and is reality.

Of course, everybody says "Not MY employees."

Sorry. Mice are mice.

So.

What I suggest is to first of all create a "productivity-only workplace," with distractions removed. Second, the cat must never be away. I'll explain what I mean.

It's Called a "Workplace" for a Reason

Idea #1: Employees Have Lockers

On arrival at Work, Betty and Bobby are required to put all their personal stuff in their lockers. That includes, in most cases, cell phones or any other personal communication devices (including Star Trek™ walkie-talkies), video game doohickeys, lipstick, toenail clippers, snacks, and every other damned thing not used for Work in their Workplace. This means, for example, that the sales clerk at the jewelry counter in Kohls'® won't be yakking away on her cell phone while a customer is standing there waiting. This means your employee won't be text-messaging or gaming or eating when they are supposed to be—what? Say it with me in unison: W-O-R-K-I-N-G.

On breaks, they can go to their lockers, get their personal stuff and do all the personal things they want, in the break area, employee lounge, parking lot (for the smokers), or wherever else you have for them to go when not working. You might want to set up a really nice space for their personal times, too. A couple 52" flat screen TVs. Some computers they can use to do their banking, buy shoes, play games. You might even want to give slightly longer breaks. That'd be a great trade-off to keep personal stuff in personal time and place and out of work time and place. If you do all that nice stuff, that's nice. But it's really not necessary. After all, you didn't bring them in to play, did you? You brought them into your business for the day to do what? Say it with me in unison: W-O-R-K.

Oh, and by the way, the speed and pace and demand of W-O-R-K are supposed to make you tired. At the end of a workday, you should actually feel like you worked. As I mentioned previously, I own harness racing horses, and I drive professionally, too. Nothing's more irritating to me than sitting in that sulky going back to the barn after a race we didn't win, behind a horse that isn't really, really tired.

Of course, there have to be modifications made for different folks in different jobs. But you ought to very carefully consider them and reluctantly make them. Every exception weakens your rule. Through every loophole leaks productivity and, thus, profit.

Idea #2: Everybody Doesn't Need to be Hooked Up to the Internet

Here's a shocker. The brilliant investment analyst and money manager Charles Payne, in one of his appearances on the FOX Financial Network, told of taking desktop computers and pads and smartphones away from many of his employees for at least some of their work hours. These are all analysts and clerks you would think must be connected to the internet every minute. He reported a sharp increase in his company's revenues by making people think and work, disconnected.

People who read my *No B.S. Time Management for Entrepreneurs* and otherwise hear of my personal work life find it hard to believe that I am 100% disconnected. A consulting client visiting my home asked for my wifi password. We have wifi at the home because my wife uses it. I have no idea what the password is. My three computers have no internet connection. I use them as typewriters and file cabinets. As a writer, I do not need distractions. I get financial news during a lunch break and world, national, and local news at night, and twice a day is plenty. If I worked in an ad agency instead of at home in isolation, I imagine I'd be the only one there not fully connected, and giving more minutes of each day to things other than writing copy, accessible through the box, and being interrupted hundreds of times a day by others intruding through the box. I make a seven-figure income from writing, and I am not a bestselling novelist or a Hollywood movie writer. So there. My income from my kind of work is exceedingly rare, as is my disconnection. I don't believe in coincidence. And if I had others in my direct employ, I, like

Charles Payne, would forcibly disconnect them. This would be about as popular as Jeff Bezos' outlawing of prepared PowerPoint presentations at Amazon's internal meetings or Marissa Mayer's radical demand at Yahoo! that people actually report to work at the workplace—something probably slashing Starbucks' sales significantly. But I would not care about popularity. Only about productivity.

If Betty and Bobby use their desktop computers to enter data or do accounting work, they need computers. They don't need email and access to YouTube, their NFL Fantasy Team sites, or Twitter. In a decent-sized office with a number of employees, were it me, there'd be one computer hooked up to send and receive email, in a Communications Room that you went and logged onto and used only when you actually needed to send a message. Think of it like a fax machine. If Betty does a lot of research online, OK, maybe Betty needs to be hooked up. But just because Betty does, Bobby doesn't. And no, your people do not need to be emailing and text-messaging each other every other minute all day long either. They can learn to "clump" the items they need to discuss with each other, and actually talk, like once a day. Although, of course, you can have an intranet without having everybody hooked to the internet.

You have to teach people how to manage their time, access to them, and communication with others in a productive way. You have to teach it, then require it. They do not know how to do this. They won't like it either. Most people prefer frequent interruptions and distractions to nose-to-the-grindstone work. Most people prefer casual communication over organized communication. You dare not leave them to their own devices about this. Get a copy of the novel *Lord of the Flies* for a chilling reminder of what happens when children are left to their own devices.

No university teaches people how to be productive. To the contrary. No one's former employer will have taught it. You'll be all alone in this. You can't presume anybody you have or bring into your business has the faintest idea or, for that matter, passionate ambition about being as productive and profitable an employee as possible. You should assume the exact opposite.

Taking away or restricting use of toys is part of the management for productivity and profit equation.

Idea #3: The Cat Never Leaves

I am not at all in favor of Big Brother watching me in my private affairs and personal life, so I certainly understand other people objecting to such invasion of their privacy. Heck, I still refuse to use grocery store discount thingamajigs because it irks me they have a record of what sinus remedy or magazine I buy. Politically, I'm as close to a Libertarian as you can be without simply abandoning any practical participation in politics. But note the words: *personal life*. Personal life occurs during personal time in personal space. In public places, people need to grasp that they have no right to privacy, and we should have surveillance cameras in public places like busy streets, so we can prevent terrorist incidents and quickly apprehend terrorists, just like they do in London—and did, for example, in July 2007. In the workplace, people need to grasp that they are there to work; they have no right to expect privacy. *Whatever* they're doing is *your* business as long as they are doing it at *your* business on *your* business's clock.

According to a study reported at Salary.com, American companies spend over $750 billion (that's *billion* with a *b*) paying people for work they're *not* doing. Add to that your best guess for the amount paid to people for work they are doing that's not in compliance with the employers' standards, policies, and procedures. Whatever share of that is coming out of your pocket is too much.

In the workplace, Big Brother has to watch. The cat must never be away.

There are several ways to accomplish this.

One is with technology. A technoboob myself, I'll keep this short, sweet, and in plain English. Just know there are plenty of service and software and equipment providers you can find to implement every suggestion I'm about to make. Find them and use them.

Specific to computers, you can zip in to any of your employees' computers at any time from any location and monitor what's being done with it at that precise moment in real time. You can also access recorded histories of where the computer's user has traveled, the sites he visited, and emails sent. Such things can even be resurrected after they've been deleted. Better, they can be harvested all day long. Even the most computer illiterate of bosses can accurately track the internet usage in his company by location, by office, by department, by individual employee, by day, by hour, by minute.

Specific to workplaces, you can install video and audio surveillance systems, which can record everything and that you can access from any remote location via your laptop and watch and listen in real time. (I've written more about this in Chapter 19.)

Washington State University researchers found that workers who knew they were being watched got more done, but weren't as happy! Gee, I wonder why. Could it be because they were actually having to—say it with me in unison—W-O-R-K? Well, here's a secret: Your really good, honest, productive employees, few by ratio, hate the bad, dishonest, unproductive slugs. The good ones are thrilled when real enforcement with real teeth occurs. It doesn't make the good ones unhappy. Only the bad ones.

Specific to salespeople, installers, delivery drivers, and the like out in the field, there are GPS tracking devices.

And there's more. The point is, if you choose to, you can know who's doing what, when, where, and how . . . whether or not they're complying with your policies, procedures, sales scripts, installation instructions . . . how they are using your assets and your time minute by minute. If you don't choose to, sorry, but you're a chump.

Another way to watch the mice is with human snooping. There are legendary stories of Martha Stewart suddenly, unexpectedly swooping into a Kmart store to inspect the display of the Martha Stewart-brand merchandise, and raising hell if it wasn't done properly. Good for her. But the more practical approach is organized, consistent "mystery shopping."

There are professionals to mystery shop your stores, offices, practices, or showrooms; trade show exhibits; or any other place of business. They'll play prospect and call in, they'll visit, they'll pose as customers and buy. Such services are available simple and cheap, or sophisticated and expensive but worth it. You need to determine what level of expertise is appropriate for your business, how in-depth the mystery shopping investigations need be for your purposes, what the frequency ought to be, and whether or not you want to have the same experts provide or assist with employee training or just use their findings and do the (constant) training yourself. You need to intelligently assess the values of lost customers, to arrive at how much to invest in this. Then you NEED to put a comprehensive, ongoing program in place, integrating your *program* (what's supposed to be done and how it's supposed to be done), training, mystery shopping, enforcement, rewards, and firings.

You also need to "raid" your employees' work spaces when they aren't there. At least once a month, invest a Saturday morning in carefully searching some of your employees' work spaces. In doing this myself, I've found hidden, long-overdue work, resumes made on my copier and being sent out with my postage (initiative that surprised me), and unanswered complaints from customers. Others have found much worse.

Like the client who discovered he had an extremely sympathetic clerk in his employ, who believed any sob story provided by a customer, and was taking customers out of the monthly billing system for months on end but still letting the company fulfill the prescheduled monthly shipments of product—to the tune of $236,700.00 of unprocessed credit card charges. When confronted, she was enraged at the invasion of her privacy! And she made it clear she thought her employer sold overpriced, ineffective goods, didn't deserve to be making all the money he was making, and that she was the victim here, being penalized for being a good person giving these customers a break. The fact that she essentially robbed her employer's son of his college fund notwithstanding.

A third way to keep tabs on things is to let good mice, pardon the pun, rat out the bad mice. At my suggestion, a client of mine with several offices, several stores, and several restaurants set up a toll-free number for employees to rat out underperforming or badly performing employees anonymously and safely. They were promised no attempts would be made to determine who called the number. In just the first six months, reports to this anonymous tip line led to catching one employee stealing merchandise from the store on an almost daily basis, another spitting and even putting dirt from the floor in customers' meals, a receptionist putting all the phones on hold while she—honest to Mick—used a little vibrator to pleasure herself . . . for an hour every day, and finally in this hit parade, a clerical employee who was copying the office's customer and lead files every week and selling them to a competitor for cash. To be fair, the owner had to sort through bogus reports of misconduct left on the recording by spiteful employees just seeking revenge against others for various slights. But what he discovered is that good, honest, hard-working employees deeply resent bad employees' bad behavior, want to see them caught and removed from the workplace, and will eagerly rat 'em out if they can do so in secrecy.

Finally, a fourth strategy is to actually be there and manage your business, these days something of a radical concept. A lot of business owners seem more interested in being on the golf course, at the beach, at home, playing with their kids, hanging out at Starbucks®, and everywhere else but at their business, doing everything else but managing it. Well, I'm all for fun in the sun, and I urge business owners to organize their businesses as servants not masters. I also urge business owners to stay away from the business some of the time, to do important, high-value work—like creating advertising or marketing plans—in a more conducive, interruption- and distraction-free environment. But. A very big *but.* I'll keep saying it over and over and over again: If you insist on having employees at all, then you have to accept the responsibilities that come with them. Leadership, management, AND SUPERVISION. Further, it's impossible to really know what's going on in a business if you're never or rarely there. You just can't beat what Tom Peters called MBWA: management by walking around. Listening in. Joining in and doing. Seeing and being seen.

Michael Gerber, the famous E-Myth guy, says most business owners spend way too much time working *in* their business rather than *on* their business. A decade ago, I agreed with him 100%. Now I don't. His observation is sometimes true. It's a sin many business owners do commit. However, there are just as many who sin by not working in their businesses at all. Some even avoid working in OR on their businesses! Suggestion: If you dislike your business so much or are interested in it so little that you avoid being there, working in it, working on it, then sell it, give it away, or burn it down. Now, not later.

The right balance varies business by business. But as a big-thumb rule, I'd say the ratio ought to be about 75% working on the business, 25% working in the business.

To define, working *on* your business means doing big things, strategic things, creative things. Examples would be developing a new product line's advertising campaign, or attending my kind of mastermind and coaching group meetings for exchange of information and ideas with other carefully chosen entrepreneurs, or plotting pre-show, at-show, and post-show marketing strategies related to your industry's annual trade show. Many of these things are often better done away from the office, plant, store, at home, or walking around the zoo.

In means hands-on, waist deep in the nitty-gritty of implementation and execution. Examples include face-to-face meetings with individual employees and groups of employees to work on specific projects or problems, taking calls from key clients or vendors, or even actually doing work: serving customers, making sales, stocking shelves, potting plants. In some small businesses, the owner has no reasonable economic option but doing some of the work. In all businesses, it's useful for the owner to at least occasionally do a bit of all the work, so he knows what it takes, can't be easily fooled, and everybody knows he knows. "In" time is also wisely and profitably used for more human snooping, too. For example, every owner should randomly and periodically snatch all the incoming mail and open and examine it himself before anybody else gets to it. Same with a day's emails. Or randomly take an hour or two and answer the phones and actually hear from customers. This is how you keep tabs on what's really going on. No, actually, this is the only way to keep tabs on what's really going on!

Now that I put it that way, it seems eminently reasonable, doesn't it? Well, it's not going to happen by putting some "success posters" up on the wall, holding hands, singing "Kumbaya" together.

The Goals Are . . .

- To have a workplace that is a place of work.

- To have a workplace that is a "productivity only" workplace.

- To get a fair, just, full day's work for the agreed-upon day's pay. From every employee being paid. Every day.

- To get compliant work, meaning work done as you intend it to be done.

- To quickly and ruthlessly identify, eliminate, and replace those employees who refuse to deliver a fair, just, full day of compliant work every day.

- To effectively support the employees who do deliver a fair, just, full day of compliant work, by not saddling them with also having to pick up the slack of the bad employees.

CHAPTER 19

Out Smoking a Cigarette

"Trust. But cut the cards."

—President Ronald Reagan

I n an upscale shopping area near the Outer Banks in Virginia, my colleague Lee Milteer wandered into a luxury women's wear shop—to find it deserted. On the counter, a person's open purse and a cell phone. She called out; she looked in the back room. She shopped for more than ten minutes and did find a couple things she would have purchased, had there been anyone there to ring up the sales. Periodically, the store's phone rang, 10, 20 rings, and went unanswered. At the 15-minute mark, Lee gave up and left, actually a little worried—had the staff been kidnapped? Were they tied up in the basement?

As she exited, somebody called out to her from across the street. A woman, seated at a patio table with two other women, yelled to her: "Is there something in the store you'd like to see?"

Lee walked over to find the women smoking and drinking coffee. She asked the one who yelled if she was the owner. She said no; she just "ran the place." At which point Lee gave her a brief "motivational" speech: "If I knew the owner, I'd have your posterior fired. You saw me enter the store and still stayed over here smoking. You're so dumb you left your purse, wallet, and cell phone on the counter. And the store's phone has been ringing off the hook. You *need* fired."

Odds are, had Lee succumbed to the fleeting temptation to answer the store's phone on the 20th ring, she could have talked to the owner. Later, if the owner asks her employee why she didn't answer the phone, the employee most likely lied and said she was with a customer.

The store lost more than $500.00 in sales. Its owner will never know of the loss. It is just the same as that employee stealing $500.00 in cash from the cash register.

And your immediate response to this is:

Not In MY Business

Not MY Employees

And if that is your reaction, you are either so hopelessly naïve and delusional you need to be put away somewhere safe for your own protection, or you are willfully stupid, to avoid all the ugly work of really, properly managing a business. I find the latter true more often than the former.

It is in damn near EVERY business, including yours, and should you care to place a large wager on whether or not I can catch *your* employees goofing off, driving away customers, ignoring customers, lying and stealing, contact me personally. I like gambling when my win is certain.

This sort of thing is a national epidemic.

Which brings me to my next suggestion.

My Case for Surveillance

My (mostly accurate, yet unwelcome) advice to clients who own stores, restaurants, offices, professional practices, and pretty much any and every kind of business is to install and use full, wall-to-wall video and audio surveillance equipment that can be monitored real time via a laptop from anywhere. With such a system in place, you can "drop in" many times, at random, from anywhere you may be, without even a warning footstep. Now you can watch and listen to your salesperson's actual sales presentation, watch and listen to the patient being greeted at the counter. In most businesses, it currently costs from $4,000.00 to $10,000.00 to have this sort of system custom installed and internet-hosted, and at that, it's the bargain of the century. A small price to give your walls eyes and ears.

Grant Miller owns Sun Your Buns Tanning Salons. There is a prescribed way of doing the tour of different tanning rooms, booths, and options, and a script for it. There is a prescribed way of taking care of the customer at check-out, including scripted next booking, upsells, and promotion of the month. It should be no surprise that his employees are much more likely to follow these procedures now that they know they are under video and audio surveillance than they were when they could not be monitored. That compliance produced a significant increase in and steadying of sales revenue, as well as higher customer satisfaction, and better bonuses for the employees. It is a win-win for winners.

This sort of surveillance serves five purposes.

1. Maximum Deterrent Effect

Whenever there's an execution, a bunch of "experts" are trotted out who claim that the death penalty is not a deterrent to criminals. It may not be for people committing crime-of-passion murders.

But you'll never convince me that having and promoting the use of the death penalty for an expanded array of heinous crimes and publicly televising the executions wouldn't slow down *somebody*. Professional burglars say that a loudly barking dog is enough to deter them—there are, after all, other houses. Regardless of this theoretical argument, the facts are in regarding workplace surveillance. A number of studies, including one by Washington State University, prove that more work gets done when workers know they are being watched. Years back, when I worked with a top theft control expert in the retail industry, he had a client suffering nearly a 30% employee theft problem from the warehouses. It dropped overnight to under 8% with the installation and monitoring of wall-to-wall video surveillance equipment. I doubt Lee would have found an empty store with its employee parked on her butt at the patio table across the street if said employee knew she and the entire inside of the store were being continuously videotaped and the owner might look in via her laptop at any moment.

2. Employee Security and Legal Liability Protections

You can worry a lot less about sexual harassment or hostile workplace environment litigation if every inch of the workplace is under video and audio surveillance every minute of the time. In a small chain of convenience stores in very bad sections of town, violent acts against employees during robberies dropped from "frequent" to "almost never" as soon as full surveillance systems were installed, were very visible, and signage boldly announced their existence. Unfortunately, the frequency of robberies didn't drop much. But the employees themselves were in less danger.

3. Better Compliance

This is the biggie. If you're a dentist, chiropractor, or cosmetic surgeon, you have a certain way you want the phone answered, a script you want followed when answering callers' questions about fees and other matters, and a prescribed way of greeting people when they enter. But you're in the back drilling teeth or stretching spines or sucking fat out of fannies and installing it in lips, and you can't see or hear what's going on out there. If you own five auto repair shops or oil change shops or tire stores, you have similar procedures for the phone, for greeting customers, for offering upsells ("If we go ahead and change your oil filter now with your oil change, sir, I can give you free windshield wipers"), for shaking hands with customers when they leave. But you own five shops. You can only be in one at a time.

If you own a mail-order company, you have instructed your employees in shipping to pack your packages of whatever carefully, put plenty of bubble-pack around them, fill the carton to the top with packing material so when the top, bottom or sides of the box get pushed on or have other boxes piled on top in transit they don't collapse or crumple and wind up with your whatevers getting there all smooshed. You've told them to put your envelope full of bounce-back offers and catalogs inside every box, right on top. But I got a box from you yesterday without enough packing, with the side smashed in, with my whatever smooshed, and no catalog inside. I'm not going to call you up and give you the bad news. It's not my job as a customer to supervise your employees and run your quality control operations. I just won't order from you again.

Ah, but, if you had a video surveillance system in your shipping room then you could peek in anytime you liked in real time or pay your son with the MBA you bought who has moved back into the house and is contemplating his navel all day to review the video tapes and give him a $10.00 bonus for each violation he spots and brings to your attention. There won't be as many violations as there most certainly are absent the surveillance equipment because the folks packing those boxes know they're being watched. If you add audio surveillance, you won't have one sexually harassing the other, or trying to inveigle the other two in a scheme to steal, or trying to talk one of the others into punching his time card in for him so he can sneak out early.

Now here's another biggie: These surveillance systems have been relatively common in manufacturing areas to control theft or foster compliance with health and safety rules. In fast-food restaurants, for example, video surveillance of food prep areas is now common. But, in the future, smart business owners will be using video and audio surveillance to compel compliance by their salespeople with their scripts and prescribed sales practices. This is new. And I am an early screaming advocate and champion.

Years ago, I was hired to do an extensive sales training seminar for a company that owned and operated retirement communities throughout the state of Florida. Beforehand, I did two things. First, I found out how the salespeople were supposed to be selling these properties. Second, I rented a little old lady to "play" as my grandmother and went around to the communities to personally experience the sales presentations. I spent two days schlepping my rented grandmother around central Florida. Suffering through the tour by golf cart and sales presentation again and again and again, by different sales reps at each site. Once we saw an alligator at the edge of the golf course lake and that livened things up a little bit. But guess what we never saw or heard? Right. The sales presentation delivered as it was supposed to be. Not once. Not even close. And a critical "step down sale technique" crafted personally by the company President, for moving the person not ready to buy a lot down to an open, first right of refusal deposit, and finally to a $250.00 deposit by credit card, was *never* used.

Sure, of course, you fire them all. Or feed 'em to the alligators. But then, what do you replace them with? You just are not going to find a small army of *voluntarily compliant* salespeople. The only way to get compliance is to compel it. I know you instantly think otherwise. You think: *Well, if I show them that my way works best and makes them the most commissions, they'll do it voluntarily.* You're wrong. They won't. They'll think you're a buffoon. They'll freelance. They'll wander off the reservation. You think: *Well, if I tell them it's my way or the highway and I'll fire anybody caught not doing it my way, they'll comply to keep their jobs.* Not a chance unless they are certain they can and will be caught and fired.

What I would advise if I were working with this client today is that every salesperson must bring every prospect into the "closing room" in the office to make the actual presentation, and it be under video and audio surveillance. In addition, I'd add frequent and random human mystery shopping. But I'd be running *Candid Camera* in there all the time.

4. Better Compliance = Better Profits

Here's the next biggie: assuming your prescribed sales methods, your telephone and in-person sales scripts, your upsells, your customer service policies, etc., are well designed and profitable if complied with, then better compliance equals more appointments from every x number of calls, more closed sales from every x number of presentations, happier customers, better retention, more referrals, more orders from catalogs inserted in every well-packed box, lower costs with less waste, and a host of other outcomes that add up to better profits. In fact, the surest and best way to boost profits in your business is compelling compliance with your best practices. This is almost always a greater profit improvement opportunity than any kind of bean-counterish cost cutting. It's usually a better profit improvement opportunity than a sales and marketing breakthrough producing more customers.

5. *Personal Freedom*

A lot of small-business owners strive for compliance by being on premises, looking over everybody's shoulders in person. If that's you, my sympathies. Your business has you chained to it, like a big, dumb elephant ankle-chained to a stake driven into the ground. You're in prison. Hey, I think your paranoia is well justified; I just think you're treating it with the wrong medicine. Implement a full-scale surveillance program and learn how to use a laptop, and you can oversee your operations from anywhere. You can go somewhere free of interruptions to work *on* your business or spend a pleasant afternoon at the lake on your fishing boat yet still, simultaneously, be supervising *in* your business. You are at once liberated and multiplied.

Is This Ethical?

Morality is often used as protection for a lot of immoral activity, and people taking money from you to work, produce a certain amount of work, or to do work in a certain way, who don't do so, are thieves. Using morality as a shield for noncompliant, negligent, or poor performance is like justifying child rape with a piece of scripture or categorizing the most vile and vicious racism as humor. It's false. Just because we don't like being ruthlessly managed does not mean it's immoral. It is what it is.

Nobody likes being snooped on.

But people are, increasingly, volunteering. Auto insurers have convinced customers to voluntarily install devices that record their driving behavior in exchange for purportedly lower rates. Soon, it will be mandatory. If people are foolish enough to let Obamacare take root and then lead as it is designed to do to single payer, government-provided health care, a device monitoring your eating and exercise by the payor won't be far behind. In exchange for protection against terrorism, we have permitted our access to commercial air travel to require unprecedented snooping. People are voluntarily trading away privacy, apathetically trading away more privacy, and—under pressure—surrendering even more privacy by the day. I personally abhor and fear much of it, and I personally avoid a good bit of it. I do not own or use a cell phone or smartphone, for example. But despite my personal misgivings, individuals and society as a whole have the right to agree to or accept these exchanges of privacy for discounts, for conveniences, for subsidies and "goodies" from the government, for security or illusion thereof, for whatever reasons. Now, given that so many are willing to make so many of these trades, why is it unreasonable or unethical for you, the employer paying the bills, to ask for a trade of employee privacy?

It is unethical, in my opinion, if undisclosed and secretive. But if properly disclosed and transparent, and used for legitimate data mining, management, best practices enforcement, and coaching purposes, there's nothing unethical about it at all. No one is ever forced to accept any such conditions. They can go work somewhere else or, thanks to redistribution of wealth by government gun, even choose not to work at all. If they are told they are going to be spied on, i.e., remotely and constantly supervised, and they find it objectionable, there's a door with a sign above, required by law to be visible and lit, that reads: EXIT. You bear a cost for that sign. They get to use it, free of charge. This MUST be your ruthless manager attitude.

The most common and most asinine argument against this is that there must be trust between employers and employees, bosses and subordinates. Oh my, the hand-wringers whine, this breaks all the bonds of trust. This is asinine because *critical and essential* job functions are simply not left to trust. Your plane's pilot must log in and log out, diary his hours, and let his smartphone be tracked to evidence he has the mandated amount of rest between flights. The airline doesn't just take his word for it, and you can be glad they don't—because some still cheat and do fall asleep up there. If it were on the honor system, who knows? Surgeons operate under observation and surveillance. Be glad. Police officers are now surveiled by dash cams, in part to reduce use of unnecessary force to protect your rights. I drive professionally in harness horse races a couple hundred times a year. It's not just my safety at stake, but seven or eight other drivers—so I must check in and blow the Breathalyzer before being permitted to race. They don't take my word for my sobriety. We are also randomly urine tested, for drug use. I suppose there's a lot of distrust in all of this. But trust and *don't* verify just doesn't work very well.

If you want to argue that the employer should operate on trust, please argue that all his employees do the same in their everyday lives. Leave their cars and homes unlocked. Never check a restaurant or grocery receipt for accuracy. I would imagine your employees would prefer that the preschool workers entrusted with their toddler or the nursing home workers entrusted with grandma are not blindly trusted at all. I imagine your employees favor criminal background checks, drug testing, and surveillance for *those* employees.

The moral argument against oversight is a rhubarb. This was long, long, long ago settled. There is only argument, now, about methodology, and there is more opposition for it from employees toward employers than by those same people in all other aspects of their lives. There is no moral case here at all. If someone agrees to do certain work a certain way for you in exchange for your money, you have every right to every kind of oversight available to verify that you are getting that certain work done that certain way. You arguably even have a moral *responsibility* to do so, for it is immoral for you to waste money—there is Biblical instruction about good stewardship, and theft is immoral, so facilitating it when you could prevent it must also be immoral. If you and your business take money from consumers in exchange for certain products and services and customer service delivered in a certain way, it is your moral responsibility to exercise every possible oversight to ensure that they get what they are paying for. Otherwise, you are stealing. If you have shareholders or others dependent on the profitability of your business, it is your moral responsibility to do everything possible to foster that profit.

The fact is, success very, very rarely occurs on the honor system.

CHAPTER 20

The Holiday Inn Telephone Warning System

"Elementary, my dear Watson!"

—The Famous Quote Never Actually Spoken
by Sherlock Holmes in any Arthur Conan Doyle Novel or Story

For a couple years, during our family's "poor dad years," my father had a second job as a banquet manager, room service guy, and handyman at the local Holiday Inn. Holiday Inn periodically put an executive or team of executives on the road to pull surprise inspections on properties in different areas. Turned out, it wasn't much of a surprise. There were seven Holiday Inns ringing Cleveland at the time. Whichever one the inspectors arrived at first immediately called the other six to warn them.

Employees often cover for each other. This is how you wind up with the culture of corruption that permeates the U.S. Congress or might infect a police precinct. They're in their own private club. You aren't in their club. Push to shove, they'll side with each other more often than with you. At the very least, they look the other way while those around them behave badly. At worst, they'll be enticed to join in.

I was waiting in the reception area of a professional's office. He comes in and out through the back door. The door inexplicably has a door chime on it, which can be heard whenever it is opened. When it chimed, I watched his front-desk staff put away the Avon catalog, pull up work on the computer, and hastily get very busy. Two minutes later when he arrived at the front of the office to welcome me, his front office was a beehive of important looking activity. "Looks like they'll need overtime again this week," he said, "just to keep up with everything. I'm advertising right now to add a sixth employee."

I said, "It'd be cheaper to disconnect the door chime."

CHAPTER 21

Thieves Like Us

"All the children in Lake Wobegon are above average."

—GARRISON KEILLOR

I learned a lot in the several years I spent working with, then, America's number-one expert in employee and deliveryman theft control, in the supermarket, convenience store, and drugstore categories. Virtually every major national and regional supermarket and convenience store chain had him training their managers and providing "human systems," meaning strict procedures to be used in the stores. He knew his stuff in part because he himself was a former deliveryman thief who had not only robbed the stores he delivered bread and baked goods to himself but also had collaborated with the stores' employees on much of the theft.

I learned, for example, that there are over 152 ways that store employees and the deliverymen steal from store owners

every single day. I learned that shoplifting is trivial compared to all the internal theft, contrary to what most companies and business owners insist on believing. I learned how to walk into any cashier's area and instantly tell you whether or not she's stealing—and often, how much. I learned how to beat bar codes. I learned how to spot a lot of the deliveryman thieves with one simple observation, from a distance. Mostly, I learned that every business has thieves. But, beyond those specifics, here's how this applies to every single reader of this book with any kind of a business and employees:

You will start out vehemently denying it, but you *now* have employee theft occurring in your business. The only questions are type, quantity, and frequency, not if. In all probability, it's a big hole through which your profits are disappearing that can and should be plugged. It's a way to immediately increase profits without investing a plugged nickel in more advertising, marketing, products, customers, or staff. To begin moving from your vehement denial to plugging your profit holes, we need to recognize that your employees are thieves like us!

Now you're in denial *and insulted.*

Give me five minutes to change your mind, change the way you manage your business and all your relationships forever, and empower you to make a lot more money from now on.

The Secret of Situational Ethics

You are at the grocery store as a customer. You get out to your car and there realize the clerk gave you $8.00 too much in change. Do you go back into the store to return the $8.00? Almost everyone would.

You are at the grocery store with your twin six-year-old boys, who are overdue for a nap. You parked your car way far away from the busy store. You get out to your car and there realize the clerk gave you $8.00 too much in change. Do you go back into the store to return the $8.00?

You are at the grocery store with your twin six-year-old boys, who are overdue for a nap. You parked your car way far away from the busy store. It's pouring rain. One of the bags rips as you lift it out of the shopping cart, spilling several items into a puddle. When you finally get into your car, you then realize the clerk gave you $8.00 too much in change. Do you go back into the store to return the $8.00?

You are at the grocery store with your twin six-year-old boys, who are overdue for a nap. You parked your car way far away from the busy store. It's pouring rain. One of the bags rips as you lift it out of the shopping cart, spilling several items into a puddle. And the cashier was rude to you. And you are already a half hour late getting home to get ready for the twins' birthday party. When you finally get into your car, you then realize the clerk gave you $8.00 too much in change. Do you go back into the store to return the $8.00?

At what point do you begin thinking, "Hey, it's not MY job to count change for her. And eight bucks is no big deal to that store. And geez, I spend a lot of money there, I'm a good customer, I deserve a break."

I'm sure you consider yourself an honest, ethical, moral person, yet in this example, you just stole money and justified it in a way that—until I ruined it—let you continue thinking of yourself as an honest, ethical, moral person. And that's a big part of the problem; anybody can find a way to justify all kinds of really bad behavior without ever looking in the mirror and calling himself a liar, cheat, or thief.

So, here's how humanity divides. There are 5% of the people who are hardwired never to lie, cheat, or steal. They can't. Starving, if they see a loaf of bread fall out of a bread truck, they'll pick it up and chase the truck to give it back. You can try and only hire such people, and in fact, there are tests predictive of honesty you might want to use in hiring. But the likelihood of you being able to meet all your employee and vendor needs with people in this unique 5% is, well, at best 95 to 5. Terrible odds. These people also tend to be useless in most jobs because most jobs *require* situational ethics! Your secretary has to lie and say you're out when you're in. Your dental assistant has to pretend to be interested in Mrs. Persimmons' long-winded story of her grandchild's wrapping the neighbor's cat in aluminum foil. Your ad copywriter better use some "poetic license" in romancing whatever stone you sell. Further, truly sanctimonious, rigid, and unbending saints are no fun to be around.

Oh, and just for the record, there are no obvious guarantees somebody's in this unwaveringly, perfectly honest category. I actually had a client who would only hire professed evangelical Christians who matched his faith, and I observed them stealing him blind. Bad idea to rely on religiosity. The Catholic Church's leaders lied and schemed to cover up a massive problem with pedophile priests, then mercilessly stonewalled the victims, then wound up having to steal millions put in collection plates by well-meaning parishioners eager to support the church's "good works" in order to pay off victims and lawyers. There are technical terms for this: *racketeering* and *organized crime.* Over in the evangelical community, we've had Jim and Tammy Faye blithely selling the same time share for 860% use, and Jimmy Swaggert, and the guy with the homosexual prostitute. And the happy hit list reaches far back in history and will keep reoccurring in the future. I could go on and insult every organized religion. If yours wasn't named, don't feel smug. The point is: The badge of spirituality worn on the lapel is absolutely not a warranty of good or honest behavior. Be a bad idea to rely on position of trust either—say, lawyers and judges sworn to uphold the law, or elected officials from your local mayor to

Presidents of the United States, plural. *"I am not a crook." "I did not have sexual relations with that woman."*

Pretty much anybody who presents himself as being in the 5% who will never lie to you or steal from you is lying. Odds are 95 to 5.

There are also 5% who are hardwired to lie, cheat, and steal at all times, in every situation, even when it doesn't benefit them. They can't NOT steal. They are often detectable with tests and reference checks. However, your odds of encountering such incorrigible characters are also 95-to-5 against.

It's the 90% in between, where you and I live, that causes all the trouble.

For us, there are three things necessary to steal: 1) perceived or real need, 2) ability to rationalize the acts, and 3) belief we can go undetected.

Now we get to the crux of this matter: how you plug the theft holes in your business.

Quickly, we have to define *theft*. In the grocery store there's some obvious theft, like eating food and not paying for it—it's called "grazing." One hundred employees each eat one package of Twinkies®, one bag of chips, one candy bar, and drink one Coke® each day, call that $3.00 hard cost; $300.00 a day; $109,500.00 a year. But at their profit margins, they need to sell about $1,000,000.00 to equal that. So it is like stealing One Million Dollars. Or the bigger, more brazen stealing steaks to take home. Or 80 or so other thefts. There and in most businesses, there's a lot of known and shrugged-off theft, like running off her kid's homework project on the company copier using a ream of your paper, your toner, your electricity, and a half hour of your paid-for time. Finally, maybe most dangerous, is all the unobvious, nonsanctioned theft, from stealing toilet paper (about which I have an amusing story) to stealing time (a lot; more about this in a minute) to theft by sabotage of your advertising, marketing, and promotions (examples coming up).

There's Only One Way to Plug the Holes

You cannot control somebody's needs or perceived needs. Martha Stewart had no need to make or avoid losing $10,000.00 when she foolishly risked her brand, personal reputation, and entire empire by impulsively engaging in insider trading, then lying about it, then getting nailed for obstruction of justice and being sent to the clink. If you put 100 billionaires in the room and ask how many need more money, all the hands go up. Whether psychotic need or real need, the effect's the same. If you aren't safe with billionaires in your employ (yes, they'd eat the Twinkies® without paying for them, too), imagine just how unsafe you are with your people given the wages you pay and their bad financial habits. A lot of inside theft and embezzlement starts, by the way, when a situationally ethical person is confronted with a new and dramatic ethical dilemma, like discovering her husband has not been making the mortgage payments and now there's $20,000.00 needed in 30 days to avoid foreclosure or the favorite grandson gets arrested for driving around with a car full of prescription drugs for which he has no prescriptions and needs $5,000.00 nobody has for a lawyer. The first problem occurs in roughly 1,000 households a week, peaking right around the time the damned Cowboys fail to cover the spread three weeks in a row. The second problem or variation thereof happens with comparable frequency, even in the best of families—think Al Gore's. So, your normally nearly honest, situationally ethical employee is suddenly faced with a choice: you or her house, you or her grandson. You cannot control need or perceived need with pay, pay raises, bonuses, motivational seminars, employee-of-the-month parking spaces, long relationships, membership in the same church. You can NOT.

Next, the ability to rationalize the theft. You cannot control a person's inner thoughts and twisted logic. Consider:

- There's a room full of copy paper here. What's one ream?
- There's a store full of Twinkies® here. What's one package?
- I'm stuck here working my ass off while he (the owner) is off cavorting with his girlfriend at the beach, hanging with buddies at the golf course, at some trade show in Las Vegas—where I never get to go/etc.—and the cheap bastard hasn't given me a raise in a year . . . I deserve this . . .
- Suzie, Carol, and Ted are all doing it. Why should I be the only sap? . . .
- He charges outrageous fees. He can certainly spare . . .

You get the idea.

And combining real need with such rationalizations, now you've got something. When I was a young kid, our family was very well off. In my teens, we were very poor. My father went from "rich dad" to "poor dad" almost overnight. For a number of years he worked a number of bad, low-wage jobs, usually two at a time. One was in a window factory, one at a gas station, one at the local Holiday Inn, handling meeting and banquet room setup and room service deliveries. In contrast to where he'd been, it was demeaning and discouraging. But he always did his job well, never shirked, never let his disappointment and frustration adversely affect his work. He was a "good employee." Also, my father was, usually, one of the most honest people ever to walk the planet. He would never dream of actually stealing from anybody. But at this time, we were really, really, really broke, and it wasn't a secret. He was driving to work in my beater car I'd bought for $25.00 because his bad car was broke down and needed several hundred dollars of repairs that could not be paid for and the gas station was already carrying a hefty tab for the gasoline put in the car to get to and from work. So when my father found a big package of frozen hamburgers and box of buns on the seat of his car after work, he asked no questions and brought home what he called his "tip." It was, of course, stolen from the kitchen by the chef and put in the car. And my father was not a stupid man. This occurred not once but with regularity for months. Overall, you couldn't find a better employee than my father. Always there, always on time, competent, pretty good attitude, self-disciplined, and requiring little supervision, with a good ethic about quality and getting things done right. However he was also a co-conspirator in continual theft. It's a safe bet that the charitable chef was putting a few goodies in his own car, too.

My father, of course, had a terrific collection of rationalizations for what was going on that I need not list here. I can remember a dozen or so he voiced when I questioned this. He was poorly paid; the hotel's owner was a big corporation owned by rich people and they would certainly never miss a package of pork chops or ten pounds of beefsteak; his boss was a moron; etc., etc., plus the fact that we really, really, really needed the food. And we even shared some of it with a family friend also in dire financial difficulty at the time. Robin Hood.

Truth be told, were you to find yourself in the same circumstances, you would probably behave in exactly the same way. That's important to understand—they are thieves *like us*. Some worse than us, some engaging in theft behavior we would

That leaves only the belief the thief can get away with it undetected. This is the only thing you can control, and control it you must. Unless you're happy seeing your profits carted off by thieves.

not. But many engaging in theft behavior we would. It's just not as simple as "good people" and "bad people." This has to do with 90% of the people.

Okay, so you can't control need and you can't control the ability to rationalize.

In the aforementioned retail categories where my theft control expert client worked, the net profit margins are so thin that the employee and deliveryman thieves combined get a higher percentage of store sales for themselves—with no capital investment, no risk, no leases, no equipment, and, hey, no employees!—than the stores' owners do! Your situation is probably less dramatic. Still, it won't take much theft of cash, goods, time, or sabotage per employee per day to add up to the difference between you retiring wealthy or not. I realize that idea isn't enough to motivate most business owners to do much about this. For some reason, business owners who would be enraged at an employee stealing cash from the register or embezzling from the checking account take a much more casual attitude about all other kinds of theft. So I'll finish with a brief look into the other thefts that might get your blood boiling enough to act.

Here's a great case history. A large tax preparation office's owner devised and ran a big gift-with-appointment promotion. When a new customer came in to meet with the tax preparer, he got to choose a free gift: a set of steak and carving knives, a leather duffel bag, a cubic zirconia tennis bracelet, or a nifty little camera. Each item carried a price tag and retail value of $50.00 to $99.00. And he got to enter a drawing for a Las Vegas vacation, where, presumably, he could blow his tax refund. In marketing lingo, that's called a *relevant premium*. Anyway, this business owner spent a lot of his valuable time planning the promotion, writing the ads and newspaper inserts and fliers, placing ads, and coordinating the mailing (investment 1). Then he spent about $10,000.00 on advertising space, printing, and postage (investment 2). He also staffed up for the two weeks of the promotion (investment 3). One day he entered his private office through its back door so his receptionist didn't realize he was there and overheard her telling a new customer presenting his coupons:

> *You know this is a scam, don't you? My boss is buying that junk dirt cheap from some closeout place and you're paying for it anyway 'cuz you can get your tax work done cheaper at H & R Block. And I'm betting a relative wins that trip.*

And off went the customer.

As bad as that is, with freshly motivated investigation, he found seven of his ten tax preparers failing (refusing) to have the "upsell conversations" with the customers about the other financial services offered. One of the preparers was undercharging for work being performed and pocketing $10.00 bills under the table from the customers getting the big discount.

In short, his office was a den of thieves.

Let's say his investments, $10,000.00 in advertising and another $10,000.00 in time, brought in 400 new customers, at a cost of $50.00 each. Harriet The Not-On-Board Receptionist stole $50.00 by driving off that customer, right? Wrong. We don't know how many customers she was telling her truth to, but that number is more than one. Based on the ad results, some snooping, he figured at least 50. Now we're up to $2,500.00. But that doesn't include the lost profits, on their business plus expected referrals of family members and co-workers. And the lost business due to their spreading the word to others. Harriet stole at least $50,000.00. Theft by sabotage.

Incredibly, after confronting her, he defended her to me. *She was having a bad day. She might be right about it being too carnival-like and unprofessional of a promotion. She'd been with him a long time.*

She swore she'd never do it again. Harriet ought to be in sales. She's wasting her talent.

By the way, he earns about $200,000.00 net from his business. She stole 25% of his pay.

Of course, you can't imagine this going on in *your* office. Doesn't mean it isn't. Just means you lack imagination.

Doesn't need to be this blatant either. Can just be your grizzled, cynical salesman who poisons the attitudes of your new recruits, telling them you don't know what you're talking about, that your lead-generation ads pull in mooches who just want the free stuff and can't be closed, and that using your presentation is a waste of time. He's stealing from you. Could just be your staff person who's supposed to be doing patient recalls on the phone when not needed at the front desk but is, instead, playing on Facebook or doing her Christmas shopping at eBay (or running her side business on eBay) and simply falsifying the call reports. She's stealing.

There's only one way to plug all these holes and control all this theft. Here's my theft expert's "cookie lecture":

Mom and little Johnny are at home during the day. No one else is there. Mom bakes a dozen fresh chocolate chip cookies. Mom then decides to walk out to the mailbox at the end of the driveway and get the mail. If she expects there to still be a dozen cookies there when she returns, she must call Johnny into the kitchen and say: "Johnny, we are saving these 12 cookies until your father gets home. You are not to eat any while I go out to the mailbox, get the mail, and come back. If you do, you will be punished. Now, Johnny, there's no one here but you and me. Not your father. Not the dog. Nobody. You and me. Together we will count the cookies—1, 2, 3, 4, 5, 6, 7, 8, 9, 10, 11, and 12. I am now going to the mailbox. You will be the only one here. The minute I get back, you and I will again count the cookies. If there are not 12 there, your ass is grass."

You'd Better Start Counting All the Cookies—and Never Stop

In some cases that means *literally* counting the cookies. It's called inventory control. If you're a dentist and you give a tube of special toothpaste and a bottle of mouthwash to every new patient, and you start out on the first of the month with 36 of each in stock, and see 30 new patients, there damn well better be 6 of each left at the end of the month. Instead, most dentists have the same person in charge of inventory control and purchasing all the supplies. She's counting her own cookies. Won't be long before it occurs to her she can take some home with no risk of ever being caught.

In most cases, it's not as simple as actually counting cookies. Time theft and theft by sabotage, trickier. But still manageable. In Chapter 19 I talk about how to control the computers and internet use, use of cell phones with built-in movie, music, text messaging, games, even pornography in the workplace, and time and tasks. I talk about the use of video and audio surveillance as well as human mystery shopping and snooping to detect theft by sabotage and noncompliance. I didn't put that in this book for fun.

I can't end without my toilet paper story. Years ago, I took over an audio cassette production company, manufacturing multicassette programs for authors, speakers, consultants, and training companies, on sales, management, motivation, and self-improvement topics. We had a large warehouse full of inventory of these products, behind a chain-link wall and a cage door with a giant lock. Anybody going in or out had to get one of the two supervisors with a key to let them through.

After a few months there, I noticed that we were buying truckloads of toilet paper, paper towels, soap, and similar sundries. This was all stored in a closet conveniently near the factory exit, with no lock. I called my plant manager in and said,

"I have figured out why our productivity is so low. To use the quantity of toilet paper we are using, every employee is sitting in the bathroom 6.8 hours a day." I told him to take the motivational tapes out of the cage and lock up the toilet paper. There was no risk of the employees stealing self-improvement tapes. But toilet paper—you betcha!

DO YOU PRACTICE SITUATIONAL ETHICS?

"Honey, does this dress make me look fat?"

CHAPTER 22

Broken Windows, Broken Business

"Little hinges swing big doors."

—W. CLEMENT STONE, AUTHOR, *SUCCESS SYSTEM THAT NEVER FAILS*

I am a clicker. At times, I click from channel to channel to channel, stopping briefly, here and there, as something catches my eye or interests my ear. This is how I landed on Bill Maher's show on HBO to hear him deliver a rant that was shocking to hear from him. It was conservative, and Bill is a wild-eyed liberal with a smidgen of Libertarian thrown in. He finds the "traditional values crowd" offensive. Yet this night he was sarcastically, with visual aids, assigning blame for the societal and economic mess we find ourselves in to the sacrifice of class and civility—specifically to the embarrassingly sloppy way in which people now dress when leaving the house and showing themselves in public. He said that most people are slobs. He noted that he was an atheist and still found the way a lot of people dress to go to church offensive. He showed a photo of a 1950s family, with Dad in a shirt, tie, and jacket, and Mom in a dress, and suggested we'd all be better off with more of that formality. This is Bill Maher, not Sean Hannity. This is hip, cool, snarky, liberal Bill Maher lecturing like a grumpy old man. He sounded like me.

Maher then referred to the clean-up and restoration of New York City via the broken windows, broken city concept, and he specifically mentioned Michael Levine's book on the subject. The same one that is referenced here, as it was in the original edition of this book back in 2008. Bill is catching up.

The best, most truthful, most useful business management book I have read—out of more than 300—is Levine's book *Broken Windows, Broken Business,* and I urge getting it, reading it, and taking it seriously. Its core, the so-called "broken windows theory," was first enunciated by two criminologists in a magazine article in 1982. Their idea was that aggressively policing even the pettiest criminal acts, such as graffiti or loitering, could clean up a neighborhood and reduce all crime, because of the message it sent. Conversely, that petty crime ignored equaled broken windows in a building; an invitation to further decay. They said that a building with one broken window left unrepaired would soon have all its windows broken, and a neighborhood with such buildings would soon be consumed by crime and decay. The broken windows communicate that property owners and community leaders do not care. **Little things shrugged off invite anarchy.**

This theory, scoffed at by many in law enforcement, was the basis for Rudy Giuliani's zero tolerance policy for all crime that led to a true renaissance of New York City while he was mayor. During his tenure, the numbers of murders, assaults, other violent crimes went down, a generally unlivable city became livable, landmark areas like Times Square went from prostitute

and drug dealer territories to welcoming areas for tourists—
and it all started with an insistence on cleaning up graffiti on
subway cars. The Giuliani cleanup of New York is explained in
considerable detail in Levine's book, as the basis for business
applications. Levine says that in business,

> . . . *a broken window can be a sloppy counter, a poorly located*
> *sale item, a randomly organized menu, or an employee with*
> *a bad attitude. It can be physical, like a faded, flaking paint*
> *job, or symbolic, like a policy that requires consumers to*
> *pay for customer service. When a call for help in assembling*
> *a bicycle results in a 20-minute hold on the phone, that's a*
> *broken window. When a consumer asks why she can't return*
> *her blouse at the counter and is told "Because that's the rule,"*
> *that's a broken window.*

In short, tiny things sabotage big things. Not long ago I was
in a dentist's "Taj Mahal office" with luxury décor throughout,
coffee latte and biscotti, a fountain, a floor-to-ceiling aquarium
on one wall. Friendly, personable staff in crisp uniforms.
Above the dental chair, a 42-inch flat screen TV. Everything
was in deliberate harmony with this dentist's positioning as
"the best" and his way-above-average fees. But in the corner
of the operatory, just above that TV, a little cobweb. In another
corner the wall covering was torn and scuffed. And the window
was a little dirty. Those three defects stuck in my mind and
pushed everything else about the office's designed-to-impress
environment out of my mind. I later found myself commenting
about the three defects to a friend.

A leading Thoroughbred breeding and boarding farm
in Kentucky where, for several years, I had Thoroughbred
broodmares has a long, long, long approach road with white
three-rail fences on both sides, horses with shiny coats in the
pastures. The owners of the farm have full-time employees who

do nothing but paint those fences. They start at one end, paint to the other, turn around and paint back in the other direction. Day in, day out. Why? "Because," the owners told me, **"we are judged by our fences."** Implicit in this answer is that it would not matter how good their core services were, how professionally and perfectly they cared for the boarded horses, how many winners their studs begot, if people's perception of the place was "second class." Levine says that perception is something that happens in the blink of an eye. I would add: or in one poorly chosen sentence said, one brusque or rude response, one too-long wait or delay. Any broken window is one broken window too many.

Magnificent Obsession

Simply put, you not only have to decide to have zero tolerance for broken windows in your business, but you have to be *obsessed* with it. Decide that nothing is insignificant. Nothing is to be shrugged off. Nobody excused from ruining a customer's perceptions of your business as "just having a bad day." Of course, most business owners will insist this is totally unreasonable. After all, who can afford to have somebody doing nothing but painting fences, washing windows, immediately repairing a wallpaper tear, policing the message conveyed by the physical facility? Wrong question. You can't afford not to. That cost is nothing compared to your losses racked up in wasted ad and marketing dollars to bring people through your doors only to leave with a negative impression. But, hey, everybody has a bad day once in a while, right? No such permission can be given. Your people need to show up ready to play, or you'd be better off if they stayed home and had their bad day with only their family as victims. This is all top down, just as it was in New York City. Just as it is for Trump, known for his obsessive-compulsive behavior and temper tantrums over a lone cigarette butt left on his property's men's room's floor or any other appearance defect. You need to be obsessed, compulsive, eagle-eyed, eagle-eared, intolerant, constantly leading and coaching, and disciplining on these issues.

No B.S. Ruthless Management Truth #5

Any broken window is one too many.

A big part of your "zero tolerance for broken windows policy" must govern your personnel. Again quoting Levine (capitalizing mine): "When an employee—ANY employee— becomes a detriment to the company for ANY reason, that employee has become a broken window, and the ripple effect from his or her FAILURE, however slight, can be DEVASTATING to your business."

What about reasonable tolerance for human frailty, human error, human inconsistency? Levine:

> There is a significant tendency in business today to forgive more than is rational . . . . Employees, even those on minimum wage, can no longer be allowed to sleepwalk through a day's work when dealing with the clientele. They can't be putting in their time at work and failing to uphold the integrity of the company with each and every encounter they have. They can no longer be allowed to consider their jobs a distraction from their lives . . . businesses these days are far too slow to fire people. More employees should be getting fired. Often

they should be fired immediately. Why? Because they are not performing the jobs for which they were hired in the first place.

Amen, brother.

A Word About Moral Authority

Years ago, I did a favor for a client, a doctor with a large chiropractic clinic. He was frustrated by his employees routinely arriving late for work, returning tardy from lunch, and, to use Levine's term, sleepwalking through their jobs on Mondays and Fridays. He asked me to come in and conduct a little class on "peak personal productivity," with the secret intent of encouraging more responsible behavior. My little class was scheduled for 9:00 A.M. to 11:00 A.M. on a Saturday, to be followed by a light lunch. He was to pick me up at the hotel close to his office at 8:30 A.M. He arrived at 9:05 A.M.—with me standing outside, fuming. We got to his office at 9:20 A.M. I did not give the presentation he'd asked for or expected. I did "Dan lite" and entertained them. Afterward I told him that I had diagnosed the real problem and it wasn't his staff, and that neither he nor I by proxy had any moral authority for a lecture on time management and responsible behavior. He was his own broken window.

CHAPTER 23

On the Other Hand, Good Enough Is Good Enough

"The physician can bury his mistakes but the architect can only advise his client to plant vines."

—Frank Lloyd Wright

I am constantly haranguing my clients not to be **perfectionists.** Perfectionism is paralysis. Perfectionism is costly. Perfectionism is a distraction from the reality of winning and losing in business. It is often promoted in management books and seminars as some sort of holy grail to endlessly pursue, yet it's the wrong mission altogether if our chief goal is maximum profit.

I'm a huge believer in "good enough is good enough." I personally practice it to the greatest extent possible. For example, this book will have been picked at by editors and proofreaders over months, attempting to force me into perfect grammar and syntax, doing battle over politically incorrect and insensitive statements that might offend even one easily offended pygmy, and, of course, striving for certain prevention of even one typographical error. Consequently, it takes six months to a year for this publisher and most traditional publishers to get a book to the shelf after it's been written. In my own businesses, I write five newsletters each month, several books each year, a weekly fax, dozens of home study courses every year, and shove them all out the door so full of typographical and grammatical errors they can keep a widowed, sexless schoolmarm occupied for months on end. That flawed product output satisfies well over 100,000 happy, repeat, frequent customers and fuels a thriving business that includes the largest circulation and fastest growing paid subscription newsletter of its kind. It also facilitates rapid speed to market. But how can all this flawed output be so wildly successful? Because its consumers care far, far more about the value of my advice, my prolific output, and my speed of providing it to them than they do about dotted *i*'s and crossed *t*'s. And because I deliberately attract such sane customers. And because I manage their expectations carefully, and overdeliver against what's promised and expected. (Not against some false god of perfection. Against what's promised and expected.) For me and for them, my good enough is more than good enough!

So, there is no existential conflict between the "no broken windows allowed" and "good enough is good enough" concepts. None at all. They're perfectly compatible. The bridge between the two is "standards."

Establish the Best Standards for Your Business

General Norman Schwarzkopf, who brilliantly prosecuted Gulf War I to a quick and successful conclusion, appeared immediately before me as a speaker in about 30 or 40 large public seminar events over a period of two years. We waited in the Green Room backstage together for an hour or so on each of those occasions, so we got to know each other reasonably well. My take on Schwarzkopf is that what you see is what you get, no pretending. So his speech about leadership given by his onstage persona accurately reflected how he actually led his troops offstage and out of sight of any audience. And unlike most of the nincompoops writing books about leadership, he actually practiced his principles in real-life situations. In his speech he pointed out that, in most cases, if people screw up in business only money is lost, but out there on the battlefield, lives are lost. He said the key to keeping as many people alive as possible while successfully waging and winning war was "standards." When I asked him about his comments privately, he said, paraphrased, that nuances are nice for whiskey-and-cigar conversation and flexibility is a synonym for enough rope to hang yourself with. In battlefield conditions it is most useful for everyone to have been brought up on and conditioned to perform within absolutely rigid standards. It is my contention the very same thing is true in business. Casual can get you killed.

Only you (and your customers) can decide what your standards should be, to facilitate your optimum success in the marketplace. But decide you should.

Consider the food service business. McDonalds® has a vast, successful, even dominant empire built on the solid foundation of *mediocre* food. Everybody with the brain of a flea, the life experience of a ten-year-old, and any taste buds at all knows full well there are better-tasting burgers readily accessible to them at any number of places. It's not a secret. The standards that McDonalds® and their customers have wound up in agreement on have to do with consistent and reliable mediocre quality, cheap prices, and fast service. For McDonalds® to invest time or money in making their burgers taste better or taste fresher would be a giant waste and a form of perfectionism as paralysis. Doing so would undoubtedly raise prices or slow service and would likely never be appropriately rewarded. However, The Palm® or Smith & Wollensky® steakhouses have very different covenants with their customers and must meet much more exacting standards concerning food excellence, although slow service is not a problem. The servers have to be knowledgeable, friendly, conversational, attentive, but *slow* service is expected. Oh, and these places are noisier than hell and that's expected, too. (If you want quiet, you go to Flemings®.) We can go through the restaurant industry chain by chain, Starbucks®, Dunkin' Donuts®, Denny's®, Dominos®, on and on. Each has a different covenant with its customers mandating certain standards. In very few cases are those standards "perfect" or even "excellent" in every category of fulfillment. And achieving "excellent" in ways outside the covenant would rarely be financially rewarding. However, failing to meet the standards dictated by the particular business's covenant with its customers, in even the tiniest of broken-window ways, will very, very quickly rot and ruin the business.

Finding the Magic GE-Spot

What I'm about to describe is enormously rewarding and admittedly difficult, but finding the GE-Spot isn't half as maddening as trying to find the G-spot!

The GE-Spot is "the Good Enough Spot."

Your leadership role here is to figure out exactly what your customers value most vs. value least in a relationship with a business like yours. Not what's important to you. Not what you think *should* be important to them. What IS important to them. To figure out what aspects of your business offer opportunity to "wow" your customers and give you some sort of competitive advantage—without undue cost, without the paralysis of perfectionism. To be able to communicate this clearly to others.

You must arrive at a comprehensive understanding of the "Good Enough Spot" in every aspect of your business. Determining this is magic of the highest order. This is how you finally quantify what so few business owners can ever quantify. How you clear away the fog of uncertainty, confusion, and vague ideas from your own thinking, your employees', your suppliers', and your customers'. Having a clear and definitive "Good Enough Spot" for every aspect of your business is *the* most empowering management breakthrough possible—and itself worth 100,000 times the little price paid for this book.

To be sure I've conveyed this accurately, consider these examples of the "Good Enough Spot" concerning when and how quickly the telephone is answered in a business. For the criminal defense attorney, bail bondsman, or "fixer-type" publicist serving celebrity clients, the GE-Spot is probably 24/7, first ring. For the flower shop, it might be 9:00 to 5:00, five days a week, third or fourth ring OK, except on the two days immediately prior to and the day of a major holiday like Mother's Day or Valentine's Day, when it probably should be 7:00 A.M. to 7:00 P.M., first ring. For a service business that gets a lot of its business from Yellow Pages ads, like plumbers or chiropractors, we have ironclad empirical evidence that huge, invisible losses are suffered by businesses not answering 24/7, third ring or faster—consumers with immediate need or interest will not leave messages and wait; they'll just call the next ad and the next until they reach somebody. (Switching these office phones to staff members' cell phones in rotation or to an outside "live" answering service equipped with good scripts and the ability to set appointments or at least guarantee return calls within a set time has proven to be immensely profitable vs. voice mail. And many of these kinds of offices have their phones going to voice mail 30% of the time during regular business hours plus off hours.) Businesses that get their clients by direct marketing means, establish themselves as expert providers, and offer services purchased more deliberately, such as financial advisory practices, can typically operate successfully with no "live" answering of phones at all; messages invited with a promised and kept time frame for response. At my office, we haven't taken incoming calls for years, and I'm never accessible to clients or prospective clients without a prescheduled telephone appointment, often after a two- to three-week wait. At the GKIC™ offices, the customers have been trained to communicate predominately by fax and email, and, if calling, do not get "live" answering. As you can see, every business's GE-Spot about the telephone is located in a different place! So it is with *every* GE-Spot.

It is up to you to locate these GE-Spots and assemble them into a list of specifics that supports the overall positioning of your business.

Your marketing role is to turn that into a clear, clearly understood and embraced covenant with your customers. Your positioning, advertising, marketing, public relations, publicity, sales, physical environments—your entire presentation of your business to the marketplace—have to manage customers' expectations.

A very visible secret about companies that really prosper is that they have clearly understood covenants with their customers. Southwest Airlines is a great example. I'd describe its covenant as no food, no frills, kind of an ugly boarding process (if you're not early, you're probably stuck in a middle seat), basically a bus on wings; but we're kicking butt to take off on time, get you there on time, and our people will ease your pain with good humor. Disney's theme parks' covenant is Walt's original "The Happiest Place on Earth®." There's something going on constantly to make everybody happy. Characters signing autographs, parades, happy music, and every employee—right down to the store clerks trading collectible pins with kids and the street sweepers who initiate helpful conversation with anybody looking confused—authorized and empowered to turn unhappy folks into happy folks by instantly making things right. The last time I was there, I saw a little kid waiting in line to see Pluto drop his ice-cream bar on the ground and burst into tears. A Disney employee rushed over, told the kid to wait and he'd bring him a new one, rushed off to the ice-cream stand, and returned with a new ice-cream bar. Each highly successful company has a different kind of clearly understood covenant with its customers. The people running the company and the customers all know where the business's GE-Spot is. They share a common understanding.

Your management role is to translate that covenant into clearly defined standards for how your business operates, how your products are made, packaged, and delivered, how your employees perform, how your salespeople sell. You need to come to grips with both the need to meet your standards 100% of the time without fail, without deviation, but also not to waste time, energy, or money in seeking perfectionism or excellence outside or beyond those standards. I know, I know, this contradicts so much of what you read and hear from all the happy-thought theorists in creativity, leadership, and excellence bailiwicks. The most famous of all "excellence books" featured companies that went bankrupt or were otherwise marketplace losers in years following its glorifying them, in part because these companies wasted resources pursuing, and in some cases achieving, celebrated standards of excellence incongruent with their covenant with their customers and their customers' prime directives, at high cost, with poor reward from the investments. Aspiring to unmitigated excellence is a lovely theory. But the reality is that *all* the most successful, sustained successful, dominant, and profitable companies in every category of goods or services find their way to the place I've described. They establish

FIGURE 23.1: The Four Responsibilities of Business Owners in Dealing with Employees

Leadership (Motivation)	**Management** (Implementation)

• 1, 3, 5, 10 Year
• Big Ideas
• Visionary Viewpoints—seeing what others can't yet see
• Defining Purpose, Mission—"What is this business *about*?"
• Setting Major Objectives and Directions—never losing sight of the profit imperative
• Influencing Culture:
  – by example and moral authority
  – by strategic plans
	• Year, Quarter, Month
	• Translating the Big Ideas into:
	  – Practical action plans and projects—including plans designed to ensure maximum profit
	  – Assembling and allocating resources to support plans
	  – The Program—how things are supposed to be done around here
	  – Incentive, recognition, reward, enforcement, and punishment policies
	  – Measurement and accountability systems
	• Integrating the Program with the Promises Made by Marketing
	• SERVING Marketing in Every Way Possible

Supervision (Enforcement)	**Marketing** (Customer Acquisition, Value Optimization, Retention)
• Minute, Hour, Day, Week; Individual Acts • Police Work • Getting Compliance with the Program • ESPECIALLY Getting Compliance with the Marketing-to-Sales Program • Police Work • Disciplining and, when Necessary, Eliminating the Noncompliant • Police Work • Making the Trains Run on Time • Police Work • Creating an Environment Supportive of Maximum Productivity • Police Work • Meeting Profit Targets	• Years, Year, Quarter, Month, Week, Day/Campaign, Project, Event • Translating the Big Ideas into a "Position" in the Marketplace • Leveraging What the Business Does Best into Covenants with Customers • Attracting Customers Most Appropriate and Most Profitable for the Business • Repelling Customers Inappropriate and Least Profitable for the Business • Seamlessly Integrating Advertising, Marketing, Sales and Fulfillment • Integration with MANAGEMENT and SUPERVISION to Successfully Honor Covenants with Customers

a complex matrix of exact standards and meet them. They don't bother trying to "outexcel" the standards they've established. If you will now examine and analyze highly successful companies through this prism, you'll quickly see just how right I am.

Finally, your supervisory role is to enforce your standards. No exceptions, no excuses, no creative deviation, no improv. And I mean "enforce" in every sense of the word. Not just teach (although you must teach), not just reward (although you must reward). Enforce.

This is the responsibility nobody likes; just about everybody neglects it and desperately rationalizes the neglect, ardently defends the neglect.

Unfortunately, there is more B.S. in management theory books and promulgated by lecturers about this than any other of the responsibilities of business ownership. Combined, it delivers a giant guilt trip. There's the "if you don't trust your people, how do you expect them to trust you," the "you can't run a business like a prison," the "these are old, outdated ideas that won't work with the new worker," and another hundred or more anti-enforcement themes woven through the books, the articles, the seminars. For the business owner already uncomfortable with police work, desperate to be liked, deluded about the actual nature of employer-employee relationships, and eager to avoid enforcement, this blather is cocaine. And it is at least as dangerous.

The problem is, *everything* else you might do right and get right is sabotaged by lack of supervision and enforcement. Every investment you make reduced in value. Every customer you acquire at constant, high risk of loss. Every grand idea, every noble policy, every clever marketing strategy castrated.

CHAPTER 24

"But My Business Is Different . . ."

Thought for the Day:
Every morning, all the stupid people you know get together and
plan ways to make your life more difficult.

Everybody has some excuse for being unable to
manage properly for profit as we're discussing in this
book or for being unable to use the highly effective
marketing strategies I discuss in the other books in the *No B.S.*
series. Their letting-themselves-off-the-hook escape route from
reality often starts with "I totally agree with you" and always
features "but my business is different."

I hear this so often it's become an inside joke with my
private clients and the business owners in my coaching groups
and attending my seminars. One client presented me with a big
yellow banner with the five dumb words on it, to hang up in my
conference room.

There are just two things you need to know about this.

One: No, it's not.
Your business isn't different.
Nor is anybody else's.

All businesses succeed or fail, prosper or struggle based on the same short list of critical factors. The only possible exception lies within companies that only make and sell things to the U.S. government. They can make billion-dollar space shuttles that have to be repaired by space-walking astronauts with staple guns and duct tape and still get paid in full with our tax dollars. But excepting them, all—repeat: *all*—other businesses win or lose based on executing or failing to execute the same basic game plans. The sooner you get over the limiting and erroneous belief that your business is different, the sooner you'll be able to "borrow" best practices wherever you find them, from diverse businesses outside your own tiny little world, and use them to improve your business. This gives you a big competitive edge because all your competitors have the same narrow perspective. When you broaden yours, you can see what they can't, embrace what they automatically reject, and improve in ways they bar themselves from using.

Two: People who are good at making excuses
are never very good at making money.

The two skill sets are in mortal conflict. The "but my business is different" whine is nothing more or less than an excuse for lazily staying stuck with the status quo. No matter how bitterly you complain about it, you are the one unwilling to change it, so shut up. As a matter of fact, if you happen to be dissatisfied with your income, you might investigate all the excuses you own. People in poverty usually have a wealth of excuses.

As an aside, this is first about you, but then it is also about the people around you—your associates, your employees, and your vendors. Having people around you who are good at

> # No B.S. Ruthless Management Truth #6
>
> Excuses and profits are incompatible.

making excuses for themselves or for others creates an entire culture of missed deadlines, unkept promises, lost customers, missed sales, waste, and inefficiency. At the end of each game, there is a winner and there is a loser. The score is posted on the scoreboard. The list of losers' excuses is never put up there in lights next to the score. There's a reason for that—it doesn't matter. That's the culture you need in your business.

CHAPTER 25

How To Make Every Employee's
Job a Profit Center

"There are two ways of making yourself stand out . . . one is by having a job so big you can go home before the bell rings if you want to. The other is by finding so much to do that you must stay after the others have gone. The one who enjoys the former once took advantage of the latter."

—Henry Ford

Susan has to answer the phone. You have to have your phone answered. But what can Susan do while answering the phone to convert that required cost of doing business to a profitable opportunity?

She could ask a few survey questions to collect information permitting better segmentation of your list. She could tell everybody about your special of the month or direct them to your website for the article of the week. If taking orders, she can upsell and cross-sell. If taking calls from prospects, she can capture full and complete contact information for follow-up and to build your mailing list. She can do more than answer the phone.

In your hotel, the maids have to clean the rooms. But they can also place your product catalog in a very visible place (as is done in Westin® properties). She can have a scripted conversation with any guests she encounters in person, inviting them to the hotel's sports bar that night for the big game and free appetizers.

At your restaurant, the waitstaff sell food and beverages, take orders, deliver meals. But they can conversationally urge customers to join the birthday club or VIP club, get those cards filled out. (There is no more valuable asset a restaurant can own than a customer list with birthdays.)

In a dental office, dental hygienists can deliver hygiene. Or they can be taught, coached, and supervised to sell dentistry while delivering hygiene. The difference to a dental practice can be a cost of about $40,000.00 a year to a terrific profit center worth over $100,000.00 a year.

Everything I've named so far can be quantified, measured, and, if you choose, incentivized and rewarded. Which I encourage. I like to see every employee have some opportunity to earn bonus money above base pay, at least based on behavior, but at best connected to their direct contribution to profits.

One of the greatest breakthroughs that can ever occur in a business is the realization by everyone involved that everything is marketing, and that everyone ought to be involved in marketing. There's a natural inclination to separate "marketing" from "operations," which leads inevitably to viewing some jobs and the employees who perform them as costs, and as necessary evils, rather than profit centers and opportunities.

CHAPTER 26

Create Better Jobs
So You Can Demand More
(and Fire Faster)

"Companies that grow people, grow profits. Companies that shrink people, shrink profits . . . Look at the investment in human assets to make sure it's enough."

—Tom Connellan, *Inside the Magic Kingdom*

Make all your important jobs better jobs. Make every position that involves any contact with your customers at all a really, really good job. Pay better than average wages; pay to have employees' uniforms cleaned for them; provide a good working environment; offer significant behavior-, performance-, and results-based bonuses as well as spontaneous, unexpected, varied rewards and recognition. Create jobs people really want and that good people won't want to lose.

Why should you do all this?

Not to be a generous soul. Not to be liked. Not to win some award.

So that your bloody axe is feared and you can be fearless in swinging it.

CHAPTER 27

Exceptions to All
the Rules

"Never eat at a place called Mom's. Never play cards with a man
called Doc. Never go to bed with a woman whose troubles
are greater than your own."

—NELSON ALGREN, NOVELIST

"If only I'd been given those rules when I was starting out in life!"

—DAN KENNEDY

Anybody who has very many employees pass
through their portals over time will have a few truly
exceptional people—usually they come and go, but
sometimes stay.

One of my clients has five inside sales positions he must
keep filled with profitable employees at all times. One woman
has been there, in her position, for nearly ten years. She is
extraordinary. She loves her job. She likes the high income. She
appreciates her autonomy, flexible hours, nominal supervision,
and ability to schedule her own vacation time. She meets or
exceeds the minimum quota necessary for her to be profitable
100% of the time. And she cheerfully chips in from time to time
to help train the new ones going in and out of the other four

chairs at a speed close to that of Ex-Lax® through a diarrheic duck. To keep the other four positions functioning, each at about 70% of the profit she produces, requires hiring and having quit or firing 16 to 24 reps a year. A revolving door. This with extensive work on my part devising a recruiting system to find clones of her, not just doing ordinary "sales help wanted" activity, and using two highly respected hiring assessment tools in the interviewing process. My client suffers slumps in profitability from time to time because he wearies of the revolving-door hiring and firing task, but there's no solution to it. It is what it is. And to make the several-million-dollar-a-year net income he makes from his business, it's an acceptable "ugly"—because no exceptionally profitable business is ever entirely free of "uglies." His management job is as much about managing his own emotions about this "ugly" as it is about managing these people. The exceptional one needs virtually no management. The other four aren't around long enough to manage.

Personally, in my entire career, I believe I've gone through a grand total of 56 or 57 employees in different types of jobs and positions of importance. I have employed family at different times, and my mother and my father were both exceptional employees. Not perfect mind you; *exceptional* is not a synonym for *perfect*. Exceptional really means more profitable and less trouble than others you've had in the same position. It's a comparative term, not a definitive one. Anyway, my wife ran my office for a number of years and was exceptional. And I'm fortunate to now be in the fifth or sixth year with my current single employee, personal assistant, office manager, major domo, etc., running my little office all by herself at the opposite end of the country from my two homes. I never go there. We communicate by fax, a brief phone call three times a week, and every Friday I receive a nicely organized big box of bills to pay, mail, faxes, notes for upcoming coaching calls or meetings, checks received, etc. She is exceptional. As is the arrangement, as it violates a number of strong recommendations made in this book, notably having only one. I, however, am cross-trained, and my own business is these days a very, very simple one. GKIC™ is another story altogether, with offices located in Chicago, Illinois. I visit there but once or twice a year and have regularly scheduled calls with the CEO, but am divorced from all management matters.

Two other exceptional-in-their-own-way employees I had working for me for a handful of years were a Hispanic husband-and-wife couple. At the manufacturing company where I first had them as employees, they were a problem—they simply could not get to work on time even for a few days in a row. He had nonexistent communication skills, was uncomfortable around people. In these and other ways, they were a disruption to the orderly way that army needed run. When I left that company, I took them with me to my newer, smaller, leaner business and struck a new deal with them: salary rather than hourly wages, no time clock, a workspace all theirs alone to do with as they saw fit, and only one imperative: The required work had to be done and every order fulfilled and shipped by the end of each week. Some weeks they might work a lot, other weeks little. They outfitted their space with a refrigerator and microwave; she brought food and cooked meals. Some days they were invisible but came in at night, with their young toddler, and worked into the wee hours. Essentially, they job-shared. I paid them above-average wages and left them alone. They were happy and performed. In reality, it was a thin line away from outsourcing. The important thing is that it worked.

Often, working with my clients, I find that when they do wind up with a truly exceptional person, they need to make exceptional (i.e., out of the ordinary) arrangements to keep that person. When they can be, why not make them? I could not have let that Hispanic couple function as they did in a bigger operation with 40 other employees. But in my smaller business, I could, I did, and I'd do it again in a heartbeat.

I do not believe in equality at all. Paying by the job is about the only way you can handle ordinary, commoditized jobs and a bevy of people doing them. At the factory-job level, you're forced into universal pay, universal incentives. But with more important jobs and exceptional people, it's better to structure the job and the compensation to fit the person. Sometimes force-fitting an exceptional person into a "hole" drilled out for ordinary people either ruins or drives off the exceptional person, who could be the most profitable person you ever had.

CHAPTER 28

Fairness Be Damned

"All animals are equal.
Some are more equal than others."

—GEORGE ORWELL, *ANIMAL FARM*

Two-time Super Bowl coach Jimmy Johnson told me this: "If Emmitt Smith puts his head down on his desk and dozes off in a team meeting, we get him a pillow and have somebody stand next to him, to be sure he doesn't fall out of his chair if he wakes up suddenly. If a third-string lineman who missed four blocks in last week's game dozes off, he wakes up traded to Buffalo."

CHAPTER 29

To the Winners,
the Spoils

REGULATION #5: You are entitled to food, clothing, shelter, and medical attention. Anything else you get is a privilege.

—Institution Rules and Regulations, Alcatraz

Lest you think I'm some sort of Snidely Whiplash character, a boss with a whip and a chair, a trap door in front of my desk to drop the out-of-favor employee through to hungry sharks below, there's another side to me and my belief system about managing people for profit. That side is as generous as ol' Saint Nick with the good little boys and girls. I believe in big stockings overflowing with toys. I also believe in lumps of coal.

There's a very good restaurant near one of my homes in northeastern Ohio, in a semirural area between two cities. Its manager conducts a training class for waitstaff titled "How To Make $100,000.00 a Year Here," and she fully expects her full-time waitpersons to break six figures. The owner wants the top-performing people to enjoy top pay. That sums up my idea of how things ought to work in any business. Employees who excel should have an opportunity to outearn less-effective employees and to earn considerably more than employees in comparable jobs in comparable businesses. You should be the highest-paying employer of your kind to top-performing people.

Years ago, one of the chiropractors attending my marketing seminars for that profession leased shiny new convertibles for each of his five staff people. The cars were theirs to drive as their own, free, as long as they met their described job performance standards, and referred two new patients a month in from outside the clinic, from their own circles of influence. From his standpoint, that would guarantee at least ten new patients a month at a lower cost than he could get them from advertising, and he correctly believed that a staff person who wasn't enthusiastic and articulate enough about his practice to bring in two patients a month from all her friends, neighbors, acquaintances, and family shouldn't be let loose talking to his patients in the clinic either. He also presumed this would boost staff morale. And he gave them a grace period of one month per half year they could miss quota without losing the car. Fail any two months out of six, you lost the car for six before you could get it back. The idea's brilliant, and the results are instructive.

One of the five staff persons loved this deal, never missed a month, usually brought in more than two patients, and was terrific in the office as well. She was appreciative of her nifty little convertible, cheerful, happy to take on extra work, and always supportive of anything the doctor wanted to do to promote his practice. Two met the minimum consistently and were satisfactory employees in every respect. A fourth hung on by a thread. She was still late getting to work from time to time (a failure in meeting minimum standards), and over three years I know of, she lost the car and got it back twice. She was often grumpy and barely worth having in the office. Finally, she quit. The fifth lost the car immediately and was underperforming in every other way, and as soon as she lost the car, she became bitter, irritable, and uncooperative and had to be fired. So it all worked out perfectly. It forced him to fire the bottom 20% (1 out of 5) again and again and again, every 6 to 12 months like clockwork. It caused the next worst to quit. And it rewarded the best performers.

At a simpler level, when I took over a very troubled company with 47 employees, the absenteeism and tardiness stats among the factory and clerical workers were high comedy. I instituted a very simple bonus plan, featuring $100.00 a month for perfect attendance. Whammo. A whole lot of people who had been consistently unable to get to work on time and had more grandmothers dying than there are idiots in Congress were suddenly able to show up every single day right on time, buffed 'n shined and ready to work. Amazing. There were four, however, who just couldn't get with the program. Two of them were fired shortly into my tenure. But the other two stood in the back of the room every month, frowning and shuffling their feet, as I handed out $100.00 bills to the others. Not surprisingly, one of those two could really have used the extra $100.00. Her need did not interest me in the slightest. I was very happy to leave her wage low and reward the others who excelled. (Sad commentary that showing up on time every day constituted excellence, but you've got to start somewhere.)

A friend of mine at the time owned a fairly large assembly plant. He divided the workers into two teams, each with a captain. Each week, the team with the fewest quality control errors and best on-time completion rate was declared the winner. Its captain got $100.00; every team member got $50.00. In the late '70s, to minimum wage assembly workers, this meant something. And every two weeks, he switched captains, so each captain got the other one's team. Every so often he shuffled up the teams. It shouldn't surprise you that, in 48 workweeks, one of the captains won 36 times—75%. It reminded me of the old quote attributed to the great college football coach Bear Bryant: "I'll beat you with my team in the first half, then we can switch, and I'll beat you with your team in the second half." Something close to that anyway. I'm not a Bear historian, and I'm not going to the trouble to hunt down the precise quote. Point made. Winners win, losers lose. In this case, the best-performing supervisor made an extra $3,600.00 for the year; the, uh, runner-up made an extra $1,200.00. As it should be.

I have, over the years, personally had individual employees who I've paid yearly bonuses to—by formula—as large as 300% of their base salaries. Happily. I've also had employees who got the cursory minimum, a $25 gift card and a "Ho, ho, ho."

CHAPTER 30

When Bonuses Become
Obligations

"Alimony is like buying oats for a dead horse."

—BUGS BAER, NEWSPAPER COLUMNIST

I was hanging around in a client's office one Friday, right before lunch, waiting for him. I heard his staff talking about "pizza Friday"—for hitting the office's sales quota for the week, he sprung for pizza, sub sandwiches, and soft drinks for everybody. Apparently this happened frequently. One staff person told the others: "And the cheap bastard orders from whatever place he has coupons for!"

I made this kind of mistake myself years back, when I had a lot of employees. Confusing "bonuses" with "being nice." If bonuses become routine, then they become expected, then they become a valueless expense. Maybe you remember the Christmas movie starring Chevy Chase, in which he and his entire family are so expectant of his Christmas bonus that, when it isn't forthcoming, all manner of mayhem ensues including, as I recall, a kidnapping of the boss.

We should begin with a philosophical position. Many people view bonuses as rewards for jobs generally done well or, in my opinion, worse, a requisite sharing of the wealth from the business's prosperity. I strongly disagree with this premise. Just throwing money around without securing measurable return on investment is in violation of your chief responsibility as CEO: to maximize profits for invested shareholders. You may be CEO and sole shareholder. Doesn't alter your mandate. And, as my "cheap bastard" anecdote illustrates, you can't buy morale or compliance this way. My position is that bonuses should buy something of value that you can clearly and definitively measure. Bonuses may be used to correct unprofitable behavior, encourage profitable behavior, encourage education and self-improvement, encourage doing difficult or uncomfortable things. They are not gifts or obligations; they are tools.

No B.S. Ruthless Management Truth #7

Bonuses should buy something of value.

Let's also clarify the difference between "bonuses" and "recognition." Getting the employee-of-the-month parking space, for example, is recognition. It is not a bonus. A bonus is money, extra time off, or things money buys, like vacations or merchandise. Recognition is pins, plaques, newsletter articles, parking spaces.

Bonuses are very troublesome things, and team or group bonuses are the most difficult. Frankly, I'm not convinced there are any good answers to this conundrum, although some seem worse than others. I've had many business owners and smart consultants show me their "plans" for bonus compensation, and I've found them all flawed, one way or another.

I'm not a fan of group bonuses tied to sales, because far too much of that outcome is outside the control of the employees, and the reward is almost always overly generous to some and miserly to others. The best results seem to come from very targeted, behavior-based, individual bonus plans. These are usually engineered to get an employee to do something he tends to avoid, neglect, or find uncomfortable or difficult, often connected to making that employee and his job function more profitable for the company. Such bonuses do, however, become obligations. If you take away the bonus compensation, the bought-and-paid-for compliance also goes away. Such institutionalized bonuses can be perfectly OK and profitable, but you need to realize what you're getting into before you start. Undoing any is ugly.

Even on a group level, it's best to narrow the focus of the result rewarded by bonuses to what's very much in the control of the people in that employee group. Consider an office or showroom where prospects come by appointment to meet with a salesperson. The three people fielding the phone calls from prospects responding to advertising have near total control over how many such calls convert to kept appointments, but they have little if any control over how many convert to customers or how much they buy. Tying their bonuses to sales can be "demotivating," especially if the sales reps are having a slump. Or consider a service business like a restaurant or a dry cleaner. The counter clerk, cleaning folks in the back room, chef and cooks, concierge and car valets have little or no control over total sales, as that depends a lot on the effectiveness of the business's advertising and marketing, pricing, and possibly even physical location. But they all have considerable impact on customer retention and repeat business.

How To Assemble Your Bonus Plans

In developing bonus opportunities for individual employees or groups of employees, you have to think about what "extra effort" behavior you want to try and buy, what it's worth to you, and what you are willing to pay for it.

Next, you have to figure out what will be most motivating to the person or people you are trying to buy extra effort behavior from with your bonuses. Money may or may not be the right answer, all or part of the time. For example, in a marketing test I conducted for a client, offering $100.00 cash or a choice of a $100.00 Walmart®, Olive Garden® Restaurants, or Bed, Bath & Beyond® Gift Card, three times as many people opted for the gift card. Why? Given cash they would feel compelled to pay bills with it. Given a gift card they feel free to go and splurge and buy themselves something they want. If given $750.00 cash, they might feel compelled to pay off a big credit card balance—and certainly not to run off to Atlantic City for the weekend. But being given a weekend at an Atlantic City hotel, room, meals, a show, and $100.00 cash to gamble with might be much more inspiring. You also have to decide whether to rotate different incentives and bonuses during the year, tied to the same behavior being purchased and rewarded or to lock in the same bonus every month. You should also consider the frequency of bonuses or at least the frequency of measuring progress toward them.

Finally you have to decide whether to institutionalize the bonus plan or to set it up as temporary and short term, then to go away and be replaced with a different one.

The last thing about this I'd like to say is that bonus plans shouldn't be considered out of context of your entire compensation scheme. Most employers act as if they are paying people to show up. In reality, you are attempting to purchase certain behaviors and results connected to those behaviors, cooperative and even enthusiastic compliance with your Program. So, all compensation should be tied as clearly and directly as possible to those objectives. Woody Allen was probably right when he said that one-third of success is just showing up. But in managing people, it's the other two-thirds we really have to worry about!

CHAPTER 31

Is a Happy Workplace a Productive Workplace?

"We have to pursue this subject of 'fun' very seriously if we want to stay competitive in the 21st century."

—GEORGE YEO, THEN SINGAPORE MINISTER OF STATE FOR FINANCE AND WORLD AFFAIRS

"Happy" is such a subjective idea.

I know one employee, who is extremely productive and a real nose-to-the-grindstone gal, who detests all distractions. She hates birthday celebrations, radios playing in cubicles, people hanging around engaged in casual conversation. She wants everybody to leave her the hell alone so she can work. She prefers hearing 5 words to 50. This makes her happy. I visited another client's company with nearly 100 employees and found something that looked more like *Animal House* than *Workplace*. Wildly, individualistically decorated work areas, people zipping through the office on skateboards, impromptu meetings left and right, three people shooting baskets at the end of the hall while discussing solutions to a key account's unhappiness, and lunch extended that day by a half hour to watch somebody, I forget who, on *The View*. He insists his crew is infinitely more productive if happy and happiest if free to have fun. It ain't your daddy's Buick® factory. I suspect somewhere between the extremes lies the sweet spot for your business.

You don't want your people living the life of the doughnut shop manager in the old Dunkin' Donuts® commercial, seen slowly dragging himself from bed and sadly mumbling, "Time to make the doughnuts" as he shuffled off to work. You don't want "the gray man syndrome": a business populated with people gray of pallor, gray of dress, gray of mind. But I am pretty certain you don't want a perpetual Chuck E. Cheese® party going on either.

I hear of—and occasionally see—these happy 'n fun workplaces from time to time, often glorified and celebrated in business media, and I am skeptical.

At the very beginning of my career, when I entered the advertising business, I had a picture in my mind of incredibly creative people sitting around smoking funny stuff and batting about ideas. The real development of effective advertising looks nothing like that at all. I have since discovered that no business is much like what it seems to outsiders. Most businesses' success has a whole lot more to do with organized, disciplined, machine-like work than with fun. As a professional speaker, for example, I made over a million dollars a year for the ten years I chose to hopscotch the country working every week. I did it with a precision-crafted, scripted presentation that drove people in stampedes to buy my books and audio programs delivered with such robot-like consistency I came to understand it as very highly paid factory labor, and, frankly, it wasn't much fun. That's not to say I didn't enjoy the camaraderie of the other speakers and the audiovisual team or some of the people I met or some of the places I went; I did. But the fun was "around" the work, not in the work itself. The work was high stress, high pressure, and mind numbing. I've been an insider of sorts in over 150 different kinds of businesses. The successful ones all have this in common: work that isn't much fun.

There's a profound difference between enjoying your work and the people you work with, doing work you're confident at, good at, and proud of, feeling rewarded by work . . . and trying to turn work into *fun*.

Fun

You might, at this point, think I'm opposed to people enjoying their jobs, let alone having fun at work. Actually, nothing could be further from the truth. In fact, the company I admire above all others, marvel endlessly at, and study constantly (and own stock in) is Disney®. Southwest Airlines® with its happy, singing, joking flight attendants and consistently sky-high levels of customer satisfaction also merits a spot on "The Most Interesting Companies" list.

Many business owners inspired by examples like these, and eager to emulate them, misunderstand what they are observing.

The two companies I just named—and many others celebrated for their wildly creative workplaces and people having so much fun at work it's play—are actually in the entertainment business. Their workplace is a stage for performers and performance. The much used example of Pike's Place Fish Market in Seattle is in this category. An entire popular "have fun at work" training and consulting company, bestselling books, badges, hats—named FISH—was built around this singular example. Southwest Airlines® created its "goofy culture" to entertain passengers, to substitute its low level of service—early on, all it could afford—for competing airlines' reserved seating, available first class, meals, and movies. These companies' strategies do not necessarily transfer wholesale to businesses not in the entertainment business.

On the other hand, there's nothing wrong with people enjoying their jobs and the people they work with and the environment they work in, so some aspects of the "happy place" ideal can transfer to just about any business—with caveats. So . . .

Beneath the happy, fun veneer of these companies lies a comprehensive, microdetailed and aggressively enforced collection of policies that keep tight control over what seems to be footloose and fancy-free employees . . . and that focus on, measure, and manage profits. To the casual observer, it may seem improvisational. To the insiders, it is rigidly choreographed. And beware: Most books lauding these highly "creative" companies delight in telling anecdotes that further the legends, that strengthen the idea easiest to sell—that just creating a happy place and letting happy people loose in it will somehow create profits. These books devote little or no attention to the rigid choreography.

At Disney®, for example, I took a group of my clients to a private luncheon with two Imagineers. When questioned by my smart group, they were loathe to discuss anything about the "management by numbers" that goes on in the parks, at a microscopic level. Pressed, they admitted that everything and everybody is intently measured. For example, the cheerful store clerks wearing all the little collectible pins on sashes who seem to be having just boatloads of FUN trading pins with kids are each monitored for pin sales, by location, by shift, by person, by same day prior year, and by other factors that determine whether that person continues as a pin trader or not. The clerks who do the best at selling a lot of pins this way obviously do enjoy it and have fun doing it, but their fun is managed for profit.

Disney® is also an intensely hierarchal environment, with managers on top of managers on top of managers, supervisors on top of supervisors, enforcing very rigid Programs. Disney® is all about tightly scripted performances, from the answering of a phone to the handling of a frustrated customer. All the FUN you see going on around you is occurring within some very tight and narrow parameters—kind of like watching a couple dogs playing in a small yard confined by the Invisible Fence®. You can't see that fence with the naked eye. But it's there.

At Southwest, its profits depend on "the ten-minute turn"; its unique, never replicated ability to consistently land, empty, clean, and fill up an airplane in just ten minutes. That puts massive pressure on the crews to perform. It is a microchoreographed process administered with zero tolerance for deviations and not even a millisecond for people to tell each other jokes. The checklist is carved in cement, the race is on, and woe be to the employee who derails this process—whether he's having FUN or not.

In short, all the "fun stuff" only works if paired with several other essential elements, none of which are "fun" to talk about or implement. If you try replicating just the fun stuff without these other essentials, you'll be a crying clown seated on a hard bench in a very unfunny place: bankruptcy court.

CHAPTER 32

Hire the Thick-Skinned

"Immense power is acquired by assuring yourself in your secret
reveries that you were born to control affairs."

—ANDREW CARNEGIE

I find Donald Trump fascinating. There is a very negative, critical book about him written by an obviously bitter ex-employee. Included in its criticism is a portrayal built by anecdotes of Trump as a belligerent, bellicose, outrageously demanding, harshly critical boss from hell. I've talked with Bill Rancic, the first year's *Apprentice* winner, about working for Trump. Bill jokingly said the person who finished second and didn't get the job might have really been the winner. I'm quite sure working for Trump is no Sunday picnic.

Actually, every highly successful entrepreneur I've ever been around is a boss from hell by many of their employees' and ex-employees' definitions. To paraphrase a line from a famous President, "Give 'em Hell" Harry Truman: Bosses of high-profit companies don't give 'em hell. The employees just think it's hell.

In her book *Ballsy*, the very talented and clever author Karen Salamansohn writes: "There are no wishy-washy rock stars. No wishy-washy astronauts. No wishy-washy Nobel Prize winners. No wishy-washy CEOs." As a matter of fact, everybody in the super-high achiever category is pushy, demanding, impatient, intolerant, prone to losing their cool, screaming, throwing things, and sending the weak-minded and weak-willed scurrying for cover. Most of us simply have no time to be gentle.

Steve Jobs was and Jeff Bezos is famous, or if you prefer, infamous for their extreme impatience. In his book *The Everything Store: Jeff Bezos and The Age of Amazon*, Brad Stone notes that intensity and volatility are not at all unique to Jobs or Bezos, and cites Steve Ballmer, Bill Gates' successor at Microsoft—famous for throwing chairs, coach Bobby Knight style. Andy Grove, the longtime CEO of Intel, was legendary for vicious conversations with underperforming executives. A subordinate once fainted during a particularly harsh performance review. Bezos largely ignored new-style leadership ideas like consensus building; he was as autocratic as can be, and known for melodramatic temper tantrums. Ex-employees described Amazon as having a "gladiator culture."

Amazon began as an idea in 1994. With it, Jeff Bezos has created more than 90,000 jobs and built one of the best known, most respected—and feared—companies on the planet. I freely confess that I was initially skeptical of Amazon, but, at a certain point in time, and a fortuitous one, I came around, acquired a sizable block of stock, and have seen it more than quadruple. I remain anxious and uncomfortable about Amazon's negligible profitability, but I recognized and recognize Bezos as a winner. My own personal investment strategy—not that I'm dispensing investment advice for you—is to focus on the person at the helm. I look for a management approach that is likely to be perceived as ruthless by underperforming people in the organization and by outside observers, but that has proved itself again and again.

One of the disgruntled employee's criticisms of Trump was about his unreasonable fetish for pristine cleanliness in his hotels. I'll tell you something I told Donald Trump personally, when we were speaking at the same event: I have stayed in thousands of hotels and put on meetings and conferences of all sizes in hundreds of hotels. I have spent fortunes in the highest regarded hotels including Ritz-Carltons® and Four Seasons®. When I took a small client group to the Trump Plaza® in Atlantic City for a two-day mastermind meeting, I had low expectations. I realize that Atlantic City isn't Las Vegas. My pre-conception of the property was as a gingerbreaded-up Motel 6® with slot machines. I even warned my group not to be grumpy about accommodations or service. To my pleasant surprise, I can say that I have never been treated as professionally, courteously, and cooperatively by every single member of a hotel's staff anywhere else. I never once heard the word *no*. Even though ours was a tiny group of little apparent economic importance to the hotel, our every request was greeted with pleasant, prompt response. The service was, for example, infinitely better than that at the much-hyped Bellagio in Vegas. The facility was clean and well attended to. The food, terrific. Somebody running this joint is doing a whole lot of things right. If that's out of abject fear of hearing Trump scream "You're Fired!" well, I'm all for it.

I work mostly with entrepreneurs, not corporate executives. My advice to entrepreneurs is: Hire the thick-skinned. Hire people who can perform under pressure, be unfazed by your outbursts and tantrums, be responsive to sudden and urgent demands, turn on a dime, give as good as they get, play tough. Do *not* hire the gentle or fragile of disposition to work anywhere in close proximity to you or direct relationship with you.

If you are a highly charged, hard driving, highly successful entrepreneur, then, quite a bit of the time, you aren't going to be a lot of fun to be around, especially for the thin-skinned. **But you should *not* change.** I've come to appreciate that the successful entrepreneur is a unique and delicately balanced combination of dysfunctions, bad habits, and personality defects as well as incredible genius, daring, and drive. You don't want to tinker with that. What works for you works, and you need people around you who can adapt to the strange creature in their midst; *you* shouldn't be adapting to suit *them*.

Let's assume we have an extremely fast, rocket-fueled, high-performance racing car with more than enough speed to win every race of the year. But it's damnably hard to handle. Its raw speed and brute power makes it hard to control and intimidating to drive. It is stripped of all comforts, so driving it at maximum speed strains every muscle, jostles every body organ, and, with most people, would bring up breakfast every time. It has no air conditioning; it generates furnace-like heat. It is ultra-responsive, so even the slightest, tiniest false move with hand or foot can send it into a screaming tailspin. What do we do with this machine? Do we re-engineer it so Granny can handle it without soiling her girdle? Or do we find a driver

---

No B.S. Ruthless Management Truth #8

Be wary of fixing yourself to suit "them."
Remember, they work for you!

---

made of all the right stuff who's a match for this machine, who can win with this machine, and then support him and it with the fastest, smartest, toughest pit crew available on the planet? You, my friend, are this machine. You need to be surrounded by and supported by people who appreciate what you are, can handle your most challenging characteristics, and can work with you to obtain optimum performance.

CHAPTER 33

Managing the Sales Process

"The ultimate disease of our time is vagueness of expectations."

—JOE D. BATTEN, AUTHOR OF THE CLASSIC
TOUGH-MINDED MANAGEMENT

I n most businesses, sadly, selling is an act, not a process. The mistakes made here are many. Everything is separated and isolated. Advertising. Marketing. They deliver a prospect to Sales, where, typically, the entire outcome is placed in the hands of very fallible Salespeople permitted to freelance at will, committing random acts of Selling. Afterward, the customer is dumped off to Operations, where the promises made may or may not be fulfilled.

Examine just about any business with more than one person doing the selling, and you'll find each salesperson doing things differently than the others. Over in accounting, everybody's using the very same bookkeeping ledgers and 2 + 2 = 4, period. But in sales, for some crazy rationale, everybody's allowed to "wing it."

If you want maximum profits, you'll figure out what the best sales presentation is, and everybody will use it. You need a program for selling that all your salespeople comply with and use.

Wrapped around the human salespersons adhering to your program, you need a complete system for selling, for moving each prospect neatly along a path—or, as the marketing wiz behind BluBlockers® and author of a terrific sales and marketing book, *Triggers,* Joe Sugarman, calls it, a "greased chute"—that connects advertising to marketing to selling, that qualifies and prepares prospects to buy before they consume the time and talent of your salespeople, and that both supports and helps control the efforts of the salespeople. One of the best quotes about all this is from a highly respected sales trainer, David Sandler, founder of the Sandler Selling System®, now with trainers and offices nationwide. David said: "If you don't have a system for selling, you are at the mercy of the customer's system for buying." I would add: and for not buying.

Such a system has to be built at the macro and micro levels.

The macro parts link all your advertising, marketing, publicity, sales, and operations pieces together with common themes, a clearly understood covenant with customers, and, as I said, a process for moving the customer smoothly along the path, from first expression of interest to completed purchase. Think of this as an exercise in control over the prospect and the process. The micro parts have to do with all of the human interaction between the prospect and receptionists, clerks, and, most of all, salespeople. Think of it as an exercise in control over the actual selling and the people doing the selling.

There's a lot of nonsense spewed about leaving salespeople to their own devices to preserve spontaneity, encourage creativity, and so on. It's all B.S. Selling is a scientific and mechanical process, not something you should make up as you go along. The person widely judged as America's number-one sales trainer, Tom

Hopkins, and I are both strong advocates of scripts. As a direct-response copywriter paid upwards of $50,000.00 plus royalties to write advertisements, sales letters, and websites, I can assure you that choice of words, that is, language, matters. What I do in writing is "salesmanship in print." If it matters there, it matters in "salesmanship live," too. But "live," not only do words chosen, scripted, and used matter, so also does appearance, dress, physical movement and body language, the selling environment, the actual movement of the prospect from place to place, seating choices, props used, and much more. My colleague Sydney Biddle Barrows and I call this Sales Choreography®. We believe that everything should be choreographed, from the first step the prospect takes into the selling environment, moment by moment, movement by movement, sentence by sentence. There's quite a bit of resistance to this idea, of course, because it requires a lot of thought, discipline, and practice by the salespeople and other staff members and a lot of supervisory enforcement by management. I can assure you that, for the few who embrace it, the payoff is enormous.

Recommended Resource #3

Information about Sydney Biddle Barrows' Sales Design®/Sales Choreography® consulting services, on-site sales and customer service training, and availability for speaking engagements can be obtained at www.SydneyBarrows.com.

Incidentally, I push my readers, newsletter subscribers, coaching members, and clients toward a "whole approach." Most of my work has to do with everything leading up to the sale. I devise the systems as well as write the copy that gets ideal prospects to raise their hands, step forward, and step onto the path constructed to then move them through qualifying and preparation, so by the time they face a salesperson or a buying decision, they view the salesperson as an expert and trusted advisor, see the company as unique, and are predisposed to do business with them. And I teach business owners how to do this for themselves. I have consultants and service providers I recommend if intense work on driving traffic online to websites or renting mailing lists or the handling of inbound calls or software systems to manage lead flow (see next chapter) are needed. At the point that the prospect begins engaging humans and will be face-to-face with staff and salespeople, there are resources and a telecoaching program on Sales Design® that I've developed with Sydney Biddle Barrows, and Sydney does go on-site as well. Sales Design® is about mapping out step-by-step-by-step everything that is to occur with and be said to the prospect, every if-he-says-this, you-say-that movement forward toward purchase. You can get much better acquainted with all of this by accepting my offer of two months' Membership in GKIC™, including my *No B.S. Marketing Letter* and audio CDs—*free*—on Page 379 of this book.

The Biggest Improvement You Can Make as Manager and as Sales Manager: Stop Accepting Less Than You Should Get

If you get nothing else from this book, do nothing else as a result of this book, you ought to at least take a fresh, analytical, tough-minded look at what you are getting from your people as a whole and individually for the money you are spending.

Most business owners accept shockingly poor sales results
as if they make sense. In the hearing aid industry, the "close
rate"—people who come to the store, get a hearing test, and get
a full sales presentation—ranges from as poor as 25% to as good
as 40%. Out of every 100 people, 60 to 75 who come in suffering
from hearing difficulties and in need of a hearing aid do NOT
buy! How can anyone managing this business accept such a
thing? In the automobile business, roughly 20% of the people
who come into a showroom buy a car there. That means 80 of the
100 left their homes, got in their cars, drove across town to the
car dealership, braved the selling environment, looked at, asked
questions about, even test-drove cars that interested them, but
then were not sold a car. To me, incredible. Awful. Embarrassing.
Yet car sales managers confronted about this shrug and tell me,
"That's about right." No. It isn't. In a dental practice, chiropractic
practice, or the like, patients coming in for consultation and exam
are subsequently given a sales presentation. Here I see wildly
differing results. One doctor will close 70%, another a pathetic
30%. Why the difference?

In the last comparable, completely controlled selling
environment I managed myself, we brought doctors into a small
meeting of several hours to group sell a product. We had one
employee doing these meetings in about 25 cities a month and I
did them in five a month. In three years, his close rate was never—
never—below 85%. Mine hovered at 80%. Most of the time, he
closed all but one person, called him the next day and closed him
after the fact. I have been told by many others trying to replicate
this model or with experience in this type of selling that such
numbers are "impossible" and that he and I must be "freaks of
nature." They're wrong. Not only are such results possible, but
they should be expected, normal, and customary. We achieved
them for reasons anyone *can* replicate in *any* business: at the
macro level, we had a system delivering interested, qualified,

prepared prospects to our selling environment; at the micro level, we had a precisely crafted presentation delivered perfectly.

If people come to buy, they ALL should buy. If that's not happening, you should be racking your brain to figure out what you are doing wrong.

The Human Factor: If You Are Going to Have Salespeople in Your Employ, Pick Carefully and Manage Tough

It's not just "Can they sell?" It's "Will they sell?" and "Will they sell here?" I learned this from a top sales management consultant, Bill Brooks, and it is profound. It's not just limited to salespeople either; it really applies to every type of employee in every type of job. Reality is, somebody who might be a good employee at Company A may be a lousy employee in the same job at Company B.

This is what makes hiring by resume so flawed.

But how can this be? After all, auto sales is auto sales, so a guy who was successful at the Cadillac dealer in Chicago ought to succeed at the Cadillac dealership in Cleveland, or the guy who was successful at the Cadillac dealership in Chicago should thrive at the Lexus dealership in Chicago. And the person who was a super receptionist at one financial planner's office will surely be just as super at another financial planner's office, right? Wrong.

Different people flourish or flunk in different environments.

Let's start back at the first question: Can he sell? If you are hiring experienced salespeople, then you can answer this question by looking at their experience to date, checking their references, seeing proof of their commissions earned. If you are hiring inexperienced people and making them into salespeople, then you might rely on much more in-depth interviews including discussing what they think is the right thing to do in different selling situations. You might utilize an aptitude test purchased from one of the many companies that provide assessment tests. And you'll be looking for nonsales experience that evidences the attitudes necessary for success in selling. For example, one client of mine with a very successful sales organization, who hires only people with no prior selling experience, asks, "Have you been successful in anything?" and "Have you struggled and found something so difficult you almost quit but then stuck with it and succeeded?"

The second question: Will he sell? Again, if recruiting experienced salespeople, you can look into their historical track record. If they had peaks and slumps and inconsistent results where they were, you'd need a good reason to believe they aren't going to import their inconsistency into your business. If they increased their sales and earnings year to year, you could hope for that same pattern in your employ. If they stagnated, you'd need good reason to expect otherwise. Sometimes just the change of scenery will revitalize a bored or complacent experienced pro, but that will usually be brief. If he got complacent there, he'll get complacent here. When considering "Will he sell?" you're trying to solve the mystery of motivation, and that's not easy. But self-motivation leaves clues. The most recent sales book he's read, most recent sales seminar he's been to, most interesting technique he's introduced to his repertoire in the past year. What he can tell you about his goals. If hiring inexperienced people for sales, again, you have no specific history to consider, but you do have nonspecific history, basically the person's whole story. Did he work two jobs to get through school or did mommy pay his way? Has he worked in any job dealing with the public, like waiting tables? Is he really interested in a sales career or settling for it because he can't find what he wants? If he's interested, he'll already be reading books, listening to CDs, and educating and preparing himself.

The third question is the trickiest. Just because he can and will sell does not mean he'll excel at selling in your employ. Your company culture may be very different than ones he's previously experienced. You may require him to present things in a way he feels is deceptive, dishonest, or unethical, or he may feel hamstrung and neutered by the ethical restraints you impose on the way he presents things. You may have a better-defined program you insist be complied with than his prior employers. He may welcome the organization and discipline, or he may chafe at it. These matters need to be explored in lengthy, frank, and detailed discussions once you get serious about a candidate. There is no point in hiring a sales professional without full disclosure of your program and how tough you are about compliance with it.

Right Sales System + Right Salespeople = Outstanding Success

Almost. The other missing link has to do with lost but viable prospects. Most systems controlling everything leading up to the sale give up on prospects too soon and too easily, or leave ongoing follow-up to the human salespeople. Doing that can be a huge mistake. Salespeople really adept at selling are usually incredibly inept and irresponsible at follow-up. They are called "salespeople," not follow-up people. The next chapter talks quite a bit about plugging the leaky holes of poor follow-up. Its author is a client of mine, and I also endorse his company's unique software system. It's the one we use at GKIC™, and most of my clients use it as well. In interest of full disclosure, I am a stockholder in this company as well.

However you accomplish it, here's what's important: Once someone has raised their hand and expressed interest in your products, services, solution, or information and you put them on your path, they should be moved forward toward the sale at a prescribed yet flexible pace, with a lot of nudges by mail, email, fax, drives to different websites, teleseminars, webinars—a primary sequence but for those who fail to move at its pace, a continuing, patient sequence. Most businesses waste the lion's share of all the money spent on advertising by, first, not using it to create and capture interested prospects and then by poor or insufficient follow-up.

Beyond that, follow-up after the sale shouldn't be left in the hands of salespeople either. They will instinctively focus on their next hunt and kill, the next prospect, the next sale. But, hopefully, you are interested in creating, measuring, and maximizing long-term customer value. To do that, you have to wow 'em after the sale and continually, frequently "arrive" to keep the relationship alive.

So, finally, you have to *manage the relationships* with your prospects and your customers.

CHAPTER 34

Maximizing the Value
of Your Sales and
Marketing Personnel

By Clate Mask

I want to talk to you candidly, from one entrepreneur to another. You have a great product or service. You have big dreams and aspirations for your business—it doesn't feel like a small business to you. You're going to make something of it. You're passionate about what you're doing. You're confident, you're working hard, and you're enjoying some success.

But you sure wish there were more of YOU to go around.

You've probably learned that effective management of your people and resources has everything to do with your bottom line. And nowhere does that ring more true than in the sales and marketing functions of your business. If you could only get more out of your sales and marketing efforts, you know your profits would soar.

If this strikes a chord with you, then this chapter will be one of the most important and exciting messages you will ever read. Because this chapter is all about the ONE thing that is sure to dramatically improve your sales.

It's all about follow-up. Follow-up, follow-up, follow-up, follow-up.

Let me start from the beginning . . .

Many years ago, my software company was providing customized software to small businesses wanting to use the power of automation to grow their companies. We built all sorts of custom software applications. Most of them had a customer management component to them.

Then one day, a guy came to us and asked us to help him more effectively manage his leads and customers. He was trying to follow up with his prospects and customers, but he was making lots of mistakes. He was having a heck of a time keeping leads, prospects, and customers organized. He couldn't track things properly and the follow-up was hit or miss.

So he hired us to write a software program that would help him *automatically* follow up with prospects and customers, track the communications, organize prospects and customers into groups, and run the whole follow-up function of his business. He was thrilled with what we created for him, and he went away very happy.

But then he came back. Turns out, he had a bunch of mortgage-broker clients who realized what his software was doing for *his* business . . . and they wanted it for *their* businesses. So, we "productized" the software program and provided it to a few dozen mortgage brokers, who began to rave about the product.

Things were going so well with our mortgage-broker clients that we moved away from the custom software business and began selling our "follow-up machine" exclusively to mortgage brokers. I was doing the selling, talking to prospects, following up with leads, educating people on the benefits of our software, and so on.

And then something amazing happened.

We began to use the follow-up features of the software in our own sales and marketing efforts. Suddenly, prospects I had never talked to were calling me up saying they were ready to buy. I was having conversations with people who had heard from me several months earlier and had been receiving my follow-ups.

Streams of prospects were literally coming out of the woodwork, calling me, emailing me. They were hot and ready to buy.

That's when I knew we were on to something.

And our business hasn't been the same since. Today tens of thousands of people use our software every day to follow up, educate their prospects and customers, cultivate lasting relationships, and maximize the value of their prospect and customer lists. The software does many things for small businesses that want to grow fast, but "autopilot follow-up" is at the heart of it all.

What does this all mean for you? How does it apply to your management of the sales and marketing personnel in your business? Well, you don't need an army of telemarketers to do this. You DO need to know the proven secrets to mastering follow-up. And I promise you that when you put them in play, it will change the way you do business. It will supercharge your marketing and sales in ways you never believed possible. And it will enable you to get much more productivity out of your all-critical sales and marketing personnel.

It will put your marketing on autopilot, which is the best way to get the most out of your prospect and customer lists without hiring that army of telemarketers to do your follow-up for you.

OK, so now that you know where I'm coming from, let me ask you a potentially painful question:

Are you consistently, religiously, and effectively follow-ing up with ALL of your prospects and customers?

I have asked this question to literally tens of thousands of entrepreneurs, marketers, and successful small businesses. And you know what?

Nine hundred ninety-nine times out of 1,000 the answer is a big, fat, painful NO!

My guess is that you're no exception. No matter how well your business is doing right now, so-so, good, or GREAT, you *know* you're leaving a *ton* of money on the table.

Now let me ask you a less painful question:

What would happen to your business if you consistently, religiously, and effectively followed up with all of your prospects and customers?

Now that I think about it, maybe that question is sort of painful.

I mean, just imagine for a second how much more cold, hard cash you could have stuffed into *your* personal bank account last year if you had managed to consistently, religiously, and effectively follow up with your prospects and customers.

Five Foolproof Secrets to Follow-Up Mastery!

Here's the promise: If you'll apply these secrets to YOUR marketing, you'll get two to four times the number of sales or customers from the same batch of leads you'd normally be spending the long hours of night worrying yourself into an ulcer about.

An outrageous claim, I know . . . but let me be even more outrageous. Not only will you close a lot more sales from your leads, but you'll also do it in less time, your margins will be higher, and your job satisfaction will be greater than ever because you'll be selling your product or service from a position of respected authority!

Secret #1: "Cherry-Picking" and the Three Types of Leads

Every time you run a marketing campaign, the leads you get can be divided into three categories:

1. Leads ready NOW (hot);
2. Leads not ready now but will be ready soon (warm—these leads are CRITICAL to your success); and,
3. Leads that may never be ready (cold or bad leads).

The problem is, you can't divide the leads into categories because you don't know which leads go into which categories.

So you or your staff members or salespeople call every lead once or twice and then you spend the time with the leads that look like they're going to close.

Every smart salesperson that works on commission does this—they go for the low-hanging fruit!

That's right. They basically cherry-pick! Cherry-picking is the natural result here because

1. Sales reps are paid high commissions for a sale;
2. Sales reps can't tell the difference between warm leads and bad leads until they reach them;
3. If your sales rep does reach the prospect and the timing isn't right, the sales rep doesn't have the time or patience to constantly follow up.

There's nothing wrong with your salespeople spending their time with hot leads. The problem of cherry-picking comes when they neglect all those warm leads!

Of course, everyone *says* they're going to follow up with the other leads *"one of these days,"* but the fact is, they don't do it.

Or, if they do follow up, they don't do it consistently, religiously, and effectively because, quite frankly, it's a royal pain in the neck.

Instead of doing the tedious follow-up grunt work, sales reps usually wait for a new batch of leads to come in. In the meantime, the warm leads from the last batch get cold, and they are soon forgotten. Simply put, they slip through the cracks.

It's important to remember that, with your advertising and marketing expenditures, you did not just buy hot, ready-to-buy, easy-to-convert leads! You paid plenty for the warm leads and even for the cold leads, some of which will warm up over time.

Your follow-up doesn't have to be hit-or-miss, but it will be if you leave it up to your salespeople. You can get more out of your leads than you're getting right now. You need to get more out of your leads. And when you do, your profitability will soar.

Secret #2: Timing Is Everything!

Here is a very important truth: People buy when *they* are ready to buy, *not* when *you* are ready to sell.

And this means, by definition, **you have to be in front of folks when they're ready to buy.**

In other words, you have to follow up with them . . . religiously!

But truly effective follow-up is a gut-wrenching, time-consuming, tedious, and labor-intensive task that is almost impossible for the human mind to keep straight—so sales professionals simply won't do it. So:

1. You need to follow up with warm and even cold-that-may-warm prospects consistently and frequently for an extended period of time.

2. You cannot afford to leave this in the hands of your sales-people.
3. You need a system for follow-up and tools to implement the system.

Secret #3: Integrate Sales and Marketing

In most companies, the marketing department's job is to get the leads and the sales department's job is to call on the leads and close the sale. But in between "getting the lead" and "closing the sale" there's a huge gap. If you close the gap, your profits will *skyrocket.*

To close the gap, you need to recognize that

1. Marketing's job doesn't begin and end when the lead is acquired;
2. The sales job doesn't begin and end with a "heat check" phone call to each lead; *and,* most important,
3. *Someone* (either marketing or sales) has to be in charge of "warming the leads" that aren't hot right now but will be hot down the road.

Otherwise, your marketing department is flushing money down the toilet on leads that aren't hot right now. Literally tearing up $100.00 bills and flushing them away.

Then, your sales department is wasting time *and* money trying to close sales with prospects who aren't ready.

To sum up this problem of the gap between marketing and sales, think of it this way: Every business has a lead generation department (marketing) and a lead closing department (sales), but they're lacking a *lead warming* department. To bridge the gap between marketing and sales, you need a lead warming department. Simple as that.

So, now that you understand the task at hand, let me give you five tips on how you can make the shift:

1. Send relevant, valuable information to every prospect regularly, relentlessly, and frequently. You need to be doing this until they buy, die, or beg you for mercy!
2. Communicate with prospects efficiently, aside from the normal, time-consuming, one-on-one methods.
3. Log all communications between your office and the prospect in an organized fashion.
4. Arm yourself and your sales reps with an arsenal of specific information you can send to prospects on request.
5. Track the progress of each lead through the sales pipeline, so you always know where every lead stands.

Secret #4: You Must Have a Living, Breathing Customer Database

If you're like most small-business owners, you want to build a business that doesn't rely heavily on outside marketing efforts. You want to maximize referrals and repeat business so that you don't have to spend your time chasing down leads and convincing folks that they should do business with you.

I talk to entrepreneurs every day who dream of having a mature customer base that provides them with lots of repeat business.

But when I ask them what they're doing to make that dream a reality, too often they answer with something like: *"Well, Clate, the longer I'm in business, the more customers I work with and the more I'll get repeat business and referrals."*

There's a lot of profit to be had by being more proactive.

This stance also assumes that your longevity in business translates to top-of-consciousness positioning with your past customers and prospects. It doesn't.

As months go by, your past customers and prospects just aren't thinking about you anymore! That's the cold, hard truth. And no matter how great your product or service is, your customers are busy living their lives. Chances are, they won't remember you. And they definitely won't mention your name at the next family picnic when Uncle Jack starts talking about the pains your product or service fixes.

If you want the strongest possible customer base, you must actively, systematically, and methodically *build your customer base.*

Your "living, breathing, customer base" is much more than the prospect and customer records in your spreadsheets or file cabinet. It must be organized in a way that enables you to execute effective follow-up.

You need to actively build your customer database—every day, every week, every month! All of your contact, prospect, and customer data, order and billing information—everything—needs to be entered and stored in the database.

You need these people organized into meaningful groups. And you need the flexibility to sort through the database so that at a moment's notice you can pull up prospects or customers who might bring you more business.

For example, you might want to pull up a list of all customers who purchased product x within the past 12 months but did not purchase product y. Or, you may want to look at all prospects you worked with over the past six months who didn't do business with you because of a specific reason.

When you combine a solid customer database with the power of consistent, religious, effective follow-up, you are finally able to optimize the value of each and every customer.

Secret #5: Education, Repetition, and Variety

I've repeated the phrase "consistent, religious, and effective follow-up" over and over. This Secret is about what that means. But first, let's talk about what NOT to do.

Most small businesses market their products and services like this:

Step 1. Buy a bunch of leads or generate leads with a mailer or other campaign.

Step 2. Distribute leads to sales reps.

Step 3. The sales reps call on the leads to find the "hot" ones, who are ready now.

Step 4. Sales reps work with hot leads to close a quick deal.

Step 5. Sales reps throw away, postpone, or neglect the leads that aren't "hot."

Step 6. Repeat the process.

Instead, your follow-up must take a combined approach that incorporates these three elements:

1. *Education.* Your follow-ups must inform your prospects and customers. You need to provide valuable information. If you're showing up with no value, you'll wear out your welcome fast. You need to communicate that you are on *their* side and deserve to be trusted. You'll accomplish this if you provide them with accurate, insightful information. Fact is, the sales process is confusing and intimidating for your customers. They *want* to trust you. Give them the information they need and you'll earn their trust. Help them. Serve them. Provide information, and they'll appreciate you for it.

2. *Repetition.* It's a proven fact that human beings have to hear the same thing over and over before it sinks in. Marketing and sales is no different. You know your products and services like the back of your hand, but your customers don't "get it" the first time they hear the message. Don't make the mistake of thinking that if a prospect heard the pitch once, he understood it. Chances are, he didn't. Tell him again and again and again.

3. *Variety.* This doesn't mean you vary your message! You need to consistently tell your message, but your follow-up

delivery needs variety. To maximize your sales, **you must use multistep follow-up sequences that incorporate and orchestrate direct mail, phone, email, fax, voice, and other media!** Some prospects will respond to your call, others to your email or letters, and others to more innovative options, such as invitations to teleseminars or webinars.

The Five Secrets Combined Have the Strength of 500

If you combine all five of the not-so-secret secrets in this chapter into one cohesive, automated, fail-safe system, you won't just see incremental sales improvements—you'll see revolutionary transformation.

CLATE MASK, CEO of Infusion Software, actively works with businesses of all types and sizes to support their sales systems. Infusion CRM (Customer Relationship Management) was built specifically to handle multistep, multimedia follow-up campaigns easily and effortlessly for a small business or a sales team of thousands. Visit www.infusionsoft.com/kennedy for information.

CHAPTER 35

Three Strategies for Managing Salespeople for Maximum Results

"When work goes out of style, we may expect to see civilization totter and fall."

—JOHN D. ROCKEFELLER

This is not an exhaustive explanation of managing salespeople. For one thing, there are many different kinds of salespeople in many different selling environments. It warrants its own book. But, there are three strategies that I have used and bring into clients' companies that never fail to boost results.

Strategy #1: Proper Investment

In most businesses, the investment in salespeople is either democratized, i.e., the same for all, or weighted in an entirely unproductive way.

I have a very crude story to tell, that until now I've only told behind closed doors, most selectively. It includes a memorable image. A very successful, very rich owner of a sales organization said he had gathered his team of sales managers together for what they believed would be a daylong meeting to discuss the sagging sales in a number of areas. They were expecting a sales management master class from their fearless leader, who had once been where they were, and who had built a $50 million business from the ground up, by recruiting and managing independent salespeople. At the time, he was the youngest to achieve his status and income level, in a global organization of more than 10,000 dealers. He invited me along to watch him deliver what he called his Two-Step Sales Management Seminar. He said we'd be in and out in 20 minutes and could go somewhere and have a good breakfast.

In the room, about 15, maybe 16 anxious men were seated boardroom style around a big conference table. Most had flown in from various cities. He walked in, climbed up onto the table, and said, as best I can remember, "There are two steps to successful sales management. You are not adhering to them. I never want you to forget them." From his pocket, he took a book of matches, handed it to one of the guys, and told him to hold it back away from the table. Then he unzipped his fly, took out his penis, and urinated all over the table. Then he said: "Step 1: If and when someone shows a flicker of initiative and capability, get matches and gasoline, and invest yourself in fanning his fire. Step 2: Piss on everybody else. Most sales managers do the opposite."

He zipped up, climbed down, wiped his feet on the carpet, gestured at me to leave with him, and we went to breakfast.

Many of you won't like this story, but you probably won't forget it for a while. And you shouldn't. Most business owners and sales managers invest entirely too much time and money into trying to lift the performance of losers while leaving their winners entirely to their own devices. You will profit to a far, far greater extent by doing exactly the opposite. By supporting, working closely with, and giving more resources and opportunities to champion performers, you will get a lot more sales. If you give that same support, attention, and resources to your poor performers, you may get a little more sales. Do you want a lot or a little?

It begs the question—can you turn a poor performer into a top performer? Yes. That is what sales legend stories are made of. But it is difficult, painful, time-consuming, costly work with low odds of success. It is social work you will more likely be rewarded for in the afterlife than in this quarter's revenues. It is more certainly profitable to ruthlessly discard the weak and recruit and then facilitate the success of the strong. If you now have a sales team, you should carefully analyze who is in the top one-third of its pyramid and who is in the bottom two-thirds, fire at least half those at the bottom, and sit down with those at the top to explore and discuss what you and the company might do to aid them in being even more successful.

Strategy #2: Proper Use

Highly skilled, successful sales pros should be spending as much of their work hours as you can engineer for them—selling. Not cold prospecting, not otherwise prospecting, not stuffing envelopes, not filling out forms. *Selling.*

That means relieving them of as much of everything else as you can.

Prospecting, for example, should be replaced with marketing, and the manual labor of prospecting replaced with media. If you have a sales professional making a cold call to try and create interest from scratch, in this day and age, you are a fool. I also tell salespeople if they work for such a fool, quit and go elsewhere. Prospects can be found or created, brought forward, made to ask for information, and then to ask for a conversation or meeting with a sales pro by any number of means cheaper in net terms than hours of a sales professional's time. My book *No B.S. Direct Marketing for NON-Direct Marketing Businesses, 2nd Edition* is the primer on this. Behind it, read *No B.S. Guide to Trust-Based Marketing.* I have routinely cut the number of salespeople at a business while increasing the productivity and personal incomes of the retained ones, simultaneously increasing the business's revenue, with the methods laid out in these books.

You also want your salespeople selling to the best and highest value, highest probability prospects—not just anyone. Putting good salespeople in front of poor prospects is pretty dumb, but that's what happens when they are left on their own to prospect or when there is no management and qualifying of leads. Consider this example: A financial services firm had three representatives, each producing about $20,000.00 a month in net revenue for the firm, at little expense to the firm but commissions, for they were charged with creating their own leads and getting their own sales appointments. In my work with the firm over six months, the least effective of the three representatives was eliminated, a new direct-marketing system costing the company about $25,000.00 a month to fund and operate was put in place; it generated 80% of the leads needed to keep the two reps fully booked with meetings and—most importantly—it put them in front of prospective clients with nearly twice the investable assets of the prospects previously dug up by the reps, and it put them in front of prospects predisposed to accept the reps as expert and trustworthy advisors. The result: each rep generated more than $60,000.00 a month in net revenue—thus the firm's number went from $60,000.00 to $120,000.00. Simplistically, if you deduct the $25,000.00 marketing cost, the firm's still ahead by $35,000.00 a month; $420,000.00 a year. There's more. By developing this kind of marketing system, a second office, it with two representatives, was possible. Better reps could be recruited and retained, because they were relieved of prospecting, could use their highest and best skill more of the time, and make more money for themselves.

Strategy #3: Proper Accountability

"If the guy meets quota and produces enough revenue, I don't care what he's doing or how he's doing it." I've heard that from business owners and sales managers a lot. Incredibly, I heard Steve Forbes utter it—on TV—about the ad reps working for *Forbes*. I respect Steve Forbes. He's smart about money. But he's dumb as a rock about this.

This is why 90% of prospects actually requesting follow-up at trade show booths never get it. This is how lead flow gets "creamed," and if the rep makes enough money to be happy by the third week of the month, he plays golf and lets unconverted leads and prospects who failed to buy at first opportunity die. You just cannot leave salespeople on their own to decide how they'll use or waste your resources and opportunities. I was largely left on my own in my first sales job, as a territory rep assigned five Midwest states, for a California-based book publisher. I excelled. I outsold all the other reps. I opened more new accounts. But I also, in a year, never went to two of those states! My success masked, and sloppy management missed noticing, that I didn't open a single account in two of my five states, and that the reorder activity in those states all came through mailed or faxed-in orders. In truth, six months in or sooner, my territory should have been cut into two, and a second sales rep assigned to half of it. Since the company advertised nationally, exhibited at national shows, and otherwise reached out to the industry on a nationwide basis, those two neglected states had a cost attached to them but nothing being done to get return on that investment. That's my answer to leaving the rep alone, with *what* he's doing.

You can't leave him alone with *how* he's doing it either. Your business's reputation and long-term sustainability and equity are all put at risk by every spoken or written or emailed or tweeted word and by every action of your representatives. Salespeople need a lot of oversight.

I work with companies that have sales speakers out on the road, delivering two- to three-hour introductory seminars in different cities, days and evenings. These speakers must record every one and send that recording in with the orders and paperwork. Obviously, every recording isn't checked. But enough are, at random, to strongly encourage every speaker stays on script. Deviations can 1) violate laws and put the company in serious trouble, 2) overpromise, setting up under-delivery, customer dissatisfaction, refunds, and online smearing, or 3) sabotage sales. The best and most profitable client I've ever had with sales reps making one-to-one, in-person presentations had a quality-control monitor who called and talked with at least one out of every eight nonbuyers, giving them a gift card for their time, to question them about what they had and hadn't been told, what they liked and didn't like about the presentation and the salesperson, and why they didn't purchase. His salary was easily covered by rescued sales, but he was worth a lot more because the salespeople knew of his meddling and knew they'd be called on anything out of order. This company's nationwide average conversion rate was double that of their industry's.

People who are given a good opportunity, who want to excel, respond reasonably well to accountability that aids them in staying on track and improving. People who resist and resent this kind of accountability are best sent packing.

CHAPTER 36

The Top-Secret
Mission

"We have met the enemy and they is us."

—Walt Kelly's Pogo

P lease don't mistake this book as a giant exercise in blaming the employees.

A lot of employees won't perform and need to be replaced. But a lot of employees who would perform don't, largely because nobody has ever defined what they're supposed to be doing, taken the time to explain why, and provided enough initial and ongoing training so they're able to perform if willing. Business owners who spend fortunes on advertising, fortunes building and decorating their facilities, fortunes on equipment, balk at spending any money on training, and are too busy to bother with it themselves. It's an epidemic: top-secret missions understood only by management.

In his book *The 8th Habit*, Stephen Covey describes a poll taken of 23,000 employees drawn from a mix of companies and industries. Only 37% of these employees said they had a clear understanding of what their organization is trying to achieve. Only 20% could enunciate the direct relationship between their tasks and the business goals. And, understandably, only 20% were "enthusiastic" about their company's goals. Covey equated it to a soccer team where only 4 of the 11 players on the field knew which goal is theirs, only 2 of 11 cared, and only 2 of 11 knew what position they played and what they were supposed to do.

I had a client with a relatively large company run this exercise: He wrote out, from his mind not from a manual, job descriptions for each of his people and ranked in importance what he believed they were doing. He had them do the same. We compared the notes. No matches. Zero. Not even close. For example, for his clerks at the cash registers, he had getting customers to sign up for the email newsletter as Job #1. Of five such employees in his flagship store used for this test, only two had it on their list at all!

That particular glitch was easily fixed with quick, specific training, establishing expectations and incentives, rewarding effective performance, and summarily firing the one nonperformer. Within two weeks, the email capture count went from an average of 3 per day to 30 a day, 18 to 180 a week, 936 to 9,360 a year. We had already determined that the customers receiving his biweekly emails were worth $20.00 more per year than customers not getting the emails, so this was worth $187,200.00 in the one store. He has eight stores. That's $1,497,600.00.

The loss of that dough, entirely, 100% his fault. Not the employees' fault. His. Of course, he protested that. After all, he *had* told them he wanted them asking for and collecting those emails. As if that discharged his responsibility. What he hadn't done was make sure they understood what he expected, how he viewed it as their most important responsibility, trained them in the script for asking for the information, paid attention to it, tracked performance by person by day, and made the comparative performance known to all, policed to be sure it was being done 100% of the time via mystery shopping and surveillance at the counters, incentivized and specifically rewarded successful performance, and quickly fired and replaced nonperformers. *His* fault. *His* fault. *His* fault.

He came to me, by the way, to have me write more effective direct-mail campaigns and ads to bring a lot more new customers through his doors. My fees for the projects he wanted would have topped $150,000.00. Increased advertising and direct-mail budgets by about $200,000.00. And still not returned $1.4 million in additional revenues. But investing a little time in training and enforcement, and paying a $1.00 bonus for each valid email captured—$74,880.00 for the year—could.

This is but one little micro-example of the losses and opportunities that exists in just about all businesses, with their root cause in the existence of top-secret missions.

CHAPTER 37

Ruthless Management of
Word of Mouth

"Not only are the hitching posts repainted every night, the starting time
is based on the temperature and humidity, so the paint will be dry
when the park opens the next day."

- A DISNEY® EXECUTIVE EXPLAINING AN EXAMPLE OF DISNEY'S
FANATICAL ATTENTION TO DETAIL, FROM
INSIDE THE MAGIC KINGDOM BY TOM CONNELLAN

W hat your customers and your prospects tell others
about their experiences with your business is infinitely
more powerful than anything you can say, especially
through traditional, paid advertising. You can drive the sales
of goods, including bad goods supported by lousy service, with
advertising in the short term. But there's not enough money
and ad media and cleverness in the world to sustain a business
against the forces of negative, critical customer buzz.

I was told this story by a Disney® Imagineer:

*Suppose we leave a piece of gum on the sidewalk there, in the
hot Florida sun, and you step on it. It gets all up in the rubber
tread of your walking shoe. Tonight in your hotel, you have to*

pick it out of there with a ballpoint pen. It ruins your day. At home, instead of telling eight people about the great time you had at Disney, you tell them about your miserable battle with the filthy chewing gum. That's eight people who might have gone home after hearing about your great vacation, logged on to our website, let us send them a free DVD and ultimately booked a vacation. Each one worth maybe $2,000.00, $3,000.00, or $4,000.00. And each of them could bring us eight more but now won't. And each of them eight. That's 512 guest families at, say, $3,000.00 each, totaling $1,536,000.00. Even more, though, since each one represents the start of another endless chain of referred guests. So, that piece of gum left there a moment too long costs us more than a million dollars.

Sure, I know what you're thinking. You're thinking that the example's ridiculous and doesn't apply to your business because everybody doesn't refer eight people or your customer value isn't $3,000.00. Or you're thinking: "Well, that's Disney, and I'm not Disney. I can't afford to have a maintenance worker in a crisp, clean, starched uniform every six feet leaping on every dropped piece of litter." And that is why Disney is Disney and you are not.

Think small, stay small; think cheap, be forever doomed to *needing* to be cheap.

That's not to say you need Disney's extreme cleanliness as one of your business's standards. I don't know whether that's true in your case or not. Elsewhere I discuss the fact that different standards are best for different businesses, and that one-size-fits-all excellence aspirations do more harm than good. It is to say that when you figure out what parts of your customers' and prospects' experiences with your business matter most to them and are most likely to lead to negative word of mouth if messed up, you need to ruthlessly manage to make certain these specific things aren't messed up.

When I bought a heavily advertised whiz-bang, high-tech bed, I had the single worst customer service experience of my life. The salesman, the delivery dispatcher, other employees, all liars. I can't recall ever being as enraged as a consumer. Ultimately, I had a vice-president of the company on the phone. He and I have much in common, both direct-marketing professionals. I knew the owner of the company he'd been with previously. He knew a client of mine located in his city. Even that did no good. He insufficiently apologized, offered no remedy, and finally resorted to saying, "Well, you have to agree it's a great bed, don't you?" I thought it futile to provide a lengthy training seminar on the realities of word-of-mouth marketing. Fact is, it could be the greatest bed ever invented and ever owned by me, delivering the most restful sleep I've ever experienced and liberating me from back pain, and I would still tell everybody in my wake not to buy the damned thing. Which I've done. I killed four sales immediately, within my circle of acquaintances. And now I'm telling you and 100,000 other people my cautionary tale about this company. Because the bed is *expected to be* the greatest bed I ever owned. They promised *that*. So if it is, that meets *minimum* performance requirements. Of far greater importance to me—and I'll wager many affluent consumers—is not having my valuable time abused, not being put through an agonizing and difficult process to resolve problems, not dealing with rude, uncooperative, and incompetent people, and not being lied to. This company has no significant product problems. Even though mine had two major defects, that's not what turned me into a raving critic. The company has severe management problems.

The most powerful force for good or evil in business is word of mouth. *Everybody* says so. But who really does anything to manage it? You should hear one of my Titanium coaching-group Members, Dr. Tom Orent, tell his dentist clients about the "million dollar bathroom" he had in his dental office. Five kinds of little scented soaps and five kinds of scented hand lotions in a little basket. Another basket of sample-sized lipsticks and perfumes, for patients to take as many as they liked and take home. Fresh, neatly folded, high-quality hand towels that had to be laundered every night, not paper towels. And the dentists say: "Five kinds of soap? How much does all that cost? Well, I'm not going to waste money on five kinds of soap. And who has time to wash, dry, and fold towels every day?" And that's why Dr. Tom has million-dollar practices and they don't.

Word of mouth is tricky. First, it has more to do with the five soaps and towels and little cosmetic gifts than with the excellence of the core service, the dentistry. The patients expect excellent dentistry. They tell people about the unexpected. Second, your people and their interaction with your customers have far greater impact than your core products or services.

Third, negative word of mouth is much easier to get, and it spreads faster and in bigger numbers than positive. Spurring a lot of positive word of mouth requires creative thought and deliberate effort. Spurring monstrous amounts of negative word of mouth requires zero creativity, zero planning, and zero effort. Just let customers go away frustrated and angry.

So, you must ruthlessly refuse to tolerate—even for a minute—anything or anyone contributing to negative word of mouth. No equivalent of sticky gum can be permitted.

The other day, I stopped at a chain sandwich shop to pick up a couple salads to go. Waiting, I wandered over to a little display promoting the company's catering service. The large, fancy box they pack sandwiches in when delivered had a layer of dust on its top. Were I the manager when I found it, I would call every employee to it, scream, throw it on the floor and stomp on it, threaten the very lives of anyone leaving dust in this restaurant. I would begin a daily white glove inspection. I would make it abundantly clear that discovery of dust would be closely followed by beheadings. I would not tolerate it, sanction it, make excuses for it. That's an overreaction if you think of it as just a little dust missed that week. It's not near enough of a reaction if you view it as a million-dollar mistake. Further, let a little dust or gum on the floor or goopy scum on a bathroom sink slide and you establish a direction. A policy of tolerance.

> **Again, you must ruthlessly refuse to tolerate—even for a minute— anything or anyone contributing to negative word of mouth.**

Conversely, you should creatively strive to stimulate positive word of mouth, by delivering not only exceptional-quality goods and services, but beyond that, unexpected extras and experiences that people are inspired to tell others about.

Copyright © Dan Kennedy 2007

Vincent Palko
www.AdToons.com

CHAPTER 38

Activity Masquerading as Accomplishment

"It is not enough to be busy. So are the ants. The question is:
What are we busy about?"

—Henry David Thoreau

If you could do nothing else but cut "activity masquerading as accomplishment" by half, you'd skyrocket any company's profits.

Some people intentionally hide their lack of accomplishment behind the mask of activity—even frantic activity. Others just can't tell the difference between the two.

So, let's begin with definitions. Defining *activity* is easy. You see it all around you and you engage in it, pretty much every minute of every day. There can be a lot of people putting in 40 hours a week and even running around while doing it with nothing getting done. Meetings held. Paper moved. Warner Brothers® Tazmanian devils stirring up their own little tornadoes—but when the dust settles, there's nothing to show for it.

Defining *accomplishment* is a bit more difficult because it needs something to be measured against. It requires context.

In something like a football game, it's easy to discern the difference. A team can have a lot of activity inside the 20-yard line and never score. It can even win the game statistically, in rushing yards, passing yards, first downs, and time of possession, but still manage to lose the game on the scoreboard. Accomplishment is getting the ball into the end zone. And putting more points on the board within 60 minutes of play than the opposing team. The question of accomplishment has one answer evident to everybody in the game and everybody watching the game. It's a clear picture.

In business, it's a lot cloudier. Why?

First of all because, usually, victory or defeat can't be measured within 60 minutes. This, however, can be fixed and the intensity and accuracy of the football game's 60 minutes can be approximated and simulated in business. Doing so is a breakthrough in personal productivity, individual productivity, and team productivity. We'll come back to that. For now, just make a mental note: A major management mistake is measuring accomplishment in too big measurements over too long a span of time. Annual or bi-annual performance reviews and quarterly earnings reports stretch the game clock out way too long and make it ridiculously easy for confusion, deliberate or accidental, of activity and accomplishment.

There's a famous story of industrialist Andrew Carnegie's right-hand man, Charlie Schwab. Charlie came up with a simple invention to increase productivity in the steel mill—a piece of chalk. After the day shift ended, and before the night shift got to the mill, Charlie wrote a big number on the floor with chalk, the numerical measurement of the amount of steel produced during the shift. The night shift workers didn't need it explained. They understood what it was—a challenge. And when they finished

one of them erased the old number and wrote their superior number on the floor in its place. The competition continued, night and day after day and night. I doubt something as simple would motivate many of today's factory employees. It requires competitive spirit, pride, and work ethic. But its brilliance in its time consisted of quick, simple, clear measurement. A 60-minute game. An eight-hour shift.

Second, it's cloudy and confused because of the aforementioned absence of nitty-gritty standards set up to accurately, ruthlessly judge accomplishment. If you don't know what a deer looks like, deer hunting is a waste of time and quite possibly dangerous. If you don't know what accomplishment is supposed to look like—today—how will you know whether it's sipping from the puddle in your backyard or not?

Recommended Resource #4

Complete information about the other books in the *No B.S.* series, free sample chapters and video interviews with Dan Kennedy by Kristi Frank from Donald Trump's *The Apprentice* are available at www.NoBSBooks.com. Books are available at bookstores and online booksellers. See page 379 for more information.

Let me make this personal. I tend to get a whole lot more accomplished every day than most people do in a week or a month. There are many ways for me to know this and I'm not going to bore you with all of them—for the sake of efficiency here, in getting to what could be useful to you, I'll ask you to take my word for it. One subjective way I know, though, is that everybody who gets to know me much, in person, or just observing my prolific work performance and output by reading my newsletters, wants to know how the devil I do it. So many wanted to know, I wrote an entire book about it: *No B.S. Time Management for Entrepreneurs.* But here's one of the main secrets, and it's a simple one. I decide what I am going to GET DONE . . . not start, not work on, not try to get done . . . GET DONE each day, then each item gets assigned blocks of time from five or ten minutes to a couple hours for its completion. I assign time slots and script my day in advance to the minute, then I bar all interruptions and distractions and do those things within the time allotted.

If you are willing to so organize, hold yourself ruthlessly accountable, and refuse interference, then you can get just as much accomplished as I do. Then if you want to move others up to higher levels of accomplishment, you can teach them this modus operandi and insist they use it—evidenced by sharing their day's scripts with you, at the starting gate and at the finish line.

If you are unwilling to do these four things—and unwilling to insist your key people do these four things—nothing else will save you. You are forever doomed and destined to the monstrous frustration that comes from unending, frantic activity but little accomplishment.

---

1. Decide what you are going to Get Done.

2. Assign each item a block of time for its completion.

3. Script your entire day minute by minute in advance, incorporating the Get Done items and their assigned blocks of time.

4. Bar all interruptions and distractions until you are Done.

One study of a large Fortune 1000 corporation's top 25 executives found that, by their own accounts, they average fewer than 40 minutes a day of actual accomplishment. Most put in 10 hours a day. Nine hours and 15 minutes a day, by their own account, could not evidence any accomplishment. It is, as they described it, time that gets away (as if a prison break); time sucked up by others; time lost forever with nothing in exchange. I don't doubt their assessments. I suspect most business owners operate with similarly depressing ratios. Yet, there's also reason for hope there. If you are only getting 40 minutes of accomplishment time out of day, you need only get to 1 hour and 20 minutes—about the same amount of time as given to a lunch break—to triple your personal productivity. If you're at 40, it's a safe bet most of the key people working for you are at 20. This means there's a whole lot of room for more accomplishment!

So, still, exactly what *is* Accomplishment?

Something that must be done, done. Something done that either immediately produces profits or can be measured and tracked as directly contributing to sustaining or increasing profits. A problem interfering with maximum productivity or maximum profits solved. A decision made and acted upon. A person fired or hired, a needed vendor found and contracted with, a marketing campaign implemented. A sale made, a client acquired. **A litmus test: Accomplishment is always described presently in past tense.**

Conversely, activity includes: things done that don't produce profits, but more so, things in progress moving along toward an uncertain end with an uncertain arrival time. Activity is a nagging or reoccurring problem thought about, mulled over, discussed, handed off to a committee, or otherwise kept stewing. A decision unmade. Activity is always described presently in present or future tense.

The Lesson of My First Storyboard

The Storyboard is a time- and task-management tool that comes from moviemaking and has migrated into management largely thanks to the teaching and advocacy of the late Michael Vance, a close associate of Walt Disney's for a number of years. Mike used it for what he called "visual thinking." I like the device personally and have used it, off and on, over the years. To describe it in brief, it's a wall or other surface like a bulletin board, divided into three main columns: DO, DOING, and DONE or DO, DOING, DELEGATING, and DONE. Then ideas, items, and so on are written on little cards, displayed, moved around, and ultimately migrate to DONE.

The first time I set one up for myself was in 1979. It ran the entire length and height of a large wall in my office. I spent a lot of time getting it set up, for multiple major projects, each with a four-column layout. I had a bunch of items written out on little color-coded cards arranged on it. The same day I put the whole thing up, a very tough, grizzled veteran of managing companies in crisis, which is what I was doing at the time, dropped by my office at day's end to share a Scotch. (I drank at the time. A lot. And had a bottle of good Scotch at hand.) He surveyed my wall, asked a few questions about how it worked, and said, "You've got one thing really f***ed up here."

"What's that?" I asked grumpily, having spent all day on this work of art.

"Too damn much space for DOING, not near enough space for DONE."

He went on to say: "Most people allow too much space and time and have way too much tolerance for DOING in their

> Jeff Bezos once told an employee daring to raise the issue of work-life balance: "We are here to get stuff DONE— and that is the top priority. That is the DNA of Amazon. If you can't excel and put everything into it, this might not be the place for you."
>
> On another occasion, he told a group, "I don't want this place to be a country club. What we do is hard. This is not where people go to retire."
>
> Source: *The Everything Store: Jeff Bezos and the Age of Amazon*

businesses, in their days, with their people, and all that does is delay the DONE. You only get to pay the bills with DONE. If you got a lotta bills, you need a whole lotta DONE. And if you got a lotta unpaid bills, it just might be cuz you ain't got much DONE."

Ah-ha.

Don't Tell Me about the Labor Pains—Show Me the Baby

Recently I worked in-depth with a fairly large and bureaucratically hamstrung corporate client on a major overhaul of its entire advertising, marketing, and sales efforts—a project targeted for completion in four months that drug on painfully for over 12. This is a rarity for me, and I became increasingly frustrated with the client and the five-person team underneath the CEO who were responsible for implementation. The only real good news was that the CEO became increasingly frustrated with them instead of me. One day he asked me why I thought every little thing was taking so long. I said, "Because you are not holding any of these buffoons responsible for accomplishment. They are telling you what they are DOING, you are telling me what they're DOING, but nothing's ever DONE." Every day he was getting an update on the labor pains. But no baby ever popped out.

I realized early in my business life that the only way to get much DONE was to stop reveling in my labor pains and to refuse listening to others'. I first heard the axiom in a meeting in a client's office in 1976. I was waiting to discuss something with him. Two of his regional sales vice-presidents were there, one started to speak and got about eight words out when the President showed him his hand and yelled, "Stop. Just show me the baby and get the hell out of here. If you haven't got work to do, I do." I got the message about how this leader wanted to be communicated with, and, in fact, how really successful entrepreneurs need to be communicated with.

The Last and Most Important Lesson about This

A lot of activity has to do with attempting perfection or attempting mistake-proof, criticism-proof, ass-fully-covered, fail-safe implementation.

Some of this may be your fault. If you manage in a way that makes people fearful of making mistakes—rather than in a way that is focused on profitable Dones—then you are to blame. If you prize perfection and are thin-skinned about criticism, you are your business's worst enemy. I tell people that success gets cooked up in a messy kitchen. When you and/or your people are breaking new ground, it has to be OK for messes to be made, misfires to fizzle, and cleanups done on the run.

Bill Gates is, by most accounts, the richest man in the world. Has Microsoft *ever* released a completely debugged, perfect product? Apple sold over 200,000 iPhones the first day knowing AT&T could never possibly get everybody's service turned on, but confident the frustrated consumers' grumbling and media reporting about it would not be enough to dampen the carefully orchestrated demand for their new, hot, and imperfect product. These companies separate getting to market and racking up huge sales as Done, fixing the product as another Done.

DONE prematurely, even badly, is almost always more profitable than DOING, DOING, DOING, endlessly DOING and never DONE.

Every cent of my personal wealth and business's success has infinitely more to do with speed than with perfection. I know how easy it is for worthwhile projects to die in the Doing, so I'm eager to get them Done in a first version, not exactly right, certain to warrant later improvement and get them launched, out the door, into the marketplace. The world that I and most of my clients live in would be very troubling to by-the-textbook MBAs. In fact, I have one client, the CEO of a franchise company, who admits his MBA is his worst enemy, because he's been conditioned to do things sequentially while we do things simultaneously. Our world is full of 24-, 36-, and 48-hour launches of new products that bring in a million dollars or more before the product is done. Our world is about managing chaos, not creating order. It's a hard thing for people who come from traditional academic and corporate environments to wrap their heads around. Not everybody can handle it. So beware the great resume; it may represent somebody who'd be great in a conventionally run corporation but unable to function in a high-performance, high-accomplishment entrepreneurial environment.

Being Unflinchingly Accomplishment Oriented

The cliché is: "Leadership is top down." I suppose it's true. Certainly you set the tone for what goes on around you—or at least you should. The people working for you and around you should be strongly influenced by you, not the reverse. I think the best thing you can exhibit is an unflinchingly accomplishment-oriented attitude. If you cut every DOING conversation short and demand to either see a DONE or be left alone so at least you can be productive, people will get the idea.

Be sure you've got that space on your actual or figurative storyboard allocated correctly!

CHAPTER 38 / ACTIVITY MASQUERADING AS ACCOMPLISHMENT

CHAPTER 39

The Speed Imperative

"Faster than a speeding bullet, leaps tall buildings
in a single bound . . ."

—THE GREATEST DESCRIPTIVE LINES EVER WRITTEN

FOR A SUPERHERO

I'm a Jack Welch fan, despite the fact that I think he blathers on too much about "leadership." You can't argue with the facts of his accomplishments while at General Electric. And, underneath the "leadership talk," there's a tough-minded, demanding, aggressive guy all about progress and profit.

One of the things Jack brought to GE was an understanding of the need for speed. He took over a big, bloated, bureaucratic, and therefore horribly slow-moving creature with the determination to trim it, whip it into shape, and make it faster. He talked a lot about "the penalty for hesitation in the marketplace." Today, that penalty is much greater than it was when Jack remade GE. If you are slow today, by the time you get there, the rewards are all gone.

Just about everybody I've ever met in business frequently has good ideas. CEOs of big companies, owners of small companies, solo entrepreneurs, and my own peers in the information-marketing field, like authors, speakers, conference promoters, and publishers. All these good ideas are useless and valueless until they are DONE. Compressing the time between idea and action, and between action and completion, is where all the profit is.

I have a friend, for example, who came up with a truly outstanding idea for a book virtually certain to be a bestseller, land her on *Oprah,* and make her famous and richer than she already is. But she's working on (Doing) the book. Now, months after the idea. I don't think she grasps the Speed Imperative. The idea is very vulnerable during each minute it is incomplete. First of all, there are at least one million other people coming up with ideas for new books, including authors of previous bestsellers with agents and publisher relationships, hour by hour. There are a lot fewer slots for new books each year than there are new books being pitched to publishers. The likelihood of her being the only one with this idea is slim. The question is: Will somebody else get to completion first—a deal, a book done, a book in the market in the same space, in her way?

Second, ideas have a way of losing their power as their owners lose passion and enthusiasm for them over time. They sort of dissipate. If you have an idea you'd like to own a little farm 50 miles or so outside Of town and be a weekend farmer, it's much, much, much, much more likely to EVER happen in your life if you run out there the very first weekend the thought occurs to you and buy one even if you overpay and even if you're not ready, than if you wait and ponder and wait and ponder. Or, if you feel a need to be a bit more prudent and methodical, you at least set a relatively short time frame to get a farm bought and, that first weekend, bolt yourself away with all the information you can assemble, build the complete to-do list in steps, assign completion times to each step, list obstacles to overcome, people to find, build the whole plan, and implement at least some of it first thing Monday morning. Like hiring a real estate agent to find you a farm.

My attitude is that you can always stop a project once started but completing a project not started is pretty much impossible. So, if my friend were really serious, she'd have cleared her calendar for a week immediately upon falling in love with the idea, sent her husband packing, and gotten to work. Not necessarily writing the book, but doing all the research into what's out there in that category, shopping for the right agent, developing the book proposal, and so forth. All business projects and initiatives are the same as this book project. At the beginning they are nothing more than ideas with potential. Napoleon Hill, author of *Think and Grow Rich,* was not completely truthful when he stated "Thoughts are things." Most thoughts are just fleeting thoughts; most projects never exit the womb. Thoughts certainly have the potential to be things *if* quickly and decisively acted on.

It was a pleasure working with Bill Glazer at the helm of what was then Glazer-Kennedy Insider's Circle, now GKIC™, for about ten years because he was usually willing to put things into motion before ready, start multiple projects simultaneously recognizing only some of them would succeed, and push everybody around him for speed. Most of my clients work this way, too, and I'm continually ridding myself of those who don't.

Jack Welch told everybody at GE that "speed is EVERYTHING. It is THE indispensable ingredient in competitiveness."

At GE, he earned the nickname Neutron Jack for blowing up all the middle management levels he saw slowing things down. He streamlined and simplified communication, delegated authority even to dangerous extremes, and got rid of 10% to 20% of the entire workforce by rote each year, continually culling the slow ones from the herd. Maybe his most important and least understood tactic was that he launched many, many new initiatives simultaneously rather than sequentially. This is a key principle I emphasize in my Renegade Millionaire System®. It's contrary to your entire upbringing and conditioning; you've been incessantly warned that "haste makes waste" and taught to do things "one step at a time," not "all steps at the same time." But that's not how accomplishment *really* happens, not how entrepreneurial wealth is *really* created.

Recommended Resource #5

Information about the Renegade Millionaire System® is available at www.GKIC.com/store. The System incorporates strategies in common from several hundred first-generation, from-scratch millionaire, multimillionaire, and seven-figure-income entrepreneurs I've worked with in depth for many years. The experience-based strategies encompass marketing, management, entrepreneurship, and wealth.

It's easier to understand this if in a turnaround situation with a troubled company. If Iacocca had approached Chrysler's troubles pedantically and sequentially, he'd have first made cuts in operations, *then* worked on financial restructuring, *then* turned his attention to improvements in the product line and new products, *then* developed better advertising and better offers for consumers—and by then, there would have been no Chrysler. I was at a little meeting at Lee Iacocca's house in Palm Desert, California, when somebody asked him if he could list the steps he took to turn around Chrysler in order. "Order?" he huffed contemptuously. "There was no order. We did it all at once." And at the speed of light.

Iacocca simultaneously put two new products on the road with virtually no research, restructured financing, sold the government and banks on a bailout, cut fat, changed pricing, boldly offered consumers a new, better warranty with no earthly way of predicting its future cost, and took on the spokesperson role to sell his cars and his company to consumers himself. Jack Welch said he tried to infuse GE with a "small business soul" so it "could be run like a corner grocery store." Iacocca pretty much ran Chrysler like a corner grocery store or at least like an entrepreneur running his own small business. In a much smaller but comparably pressured turnaround situation, I honed my own "simultaneous, not sequential" approach and skills. Then I reasoned, if this works with a horribly troubled company barely escaping extinction day by day, under this kind of extreme pressure, imagine how well it can work in better circumstances! To this day, I look at every business as a turnaround situation.

Ironically, many small-business owners operate what should be agile little speedboats as if they were gigantic freighters, even while the savviest CEOs who inherit big, sluggish freighters try remaking them into flotillas of agile speedboats.

To manage for maximum profit—and survival—today, you must bring The Speed Imperative into your business. The Speed Imperative is a philosophy and an attitude, an overriding idea of how your business is to be operated that has to be crystallized in your own mind, embraced emotionally, and communicated to everybody around you, relentlessly. This, more than anything else, is what Jack Welch brought to GE, and it's what you can bring to your business. The Speed Imperative is then applied in practical ways in many different aspects of your business, from marketing to innovation to testing new strategies to expansion.

With all this said about speed, I'd be remiss skipping the two big caveats.

Caveat 1: Everything, every relationship is easier to get into than to get out of. Never go in anywhere without a predetermined escape route. Never enter any relationship without a prenegotiated exit. Prenups are infinitely easier to negotiate and infinitely less costly than are postnups. You will be tempted to ignore this advice with any number of justifications: *Bob and I have been buddies for 20 years . . . . We have an understanding; there's no need to bother with a lot of paperwork and legal mumbo jumbo . . . . I don't want to offend him . . .* yadda, yadda. Each and every one of these justifications is unjustified. Each time I've made this dumb mistake (hey, only three times in 30 years), it's been very expensive and troublesome. I have had to pay somebody I'd been a buddy with a lot of money just to go away at a time I could least afford it. I have gone through a very costly divorce without a prenup. No need to bore you with the details.

Caveat 2: Don't be afraid to reverse yourself and kill a project or get out of a business situation as soon as you determine, for whatever reason, that it is more trouble than it's worth. A little egg on your face now is preferable to a 1,000-pound anchor chained to your ankle while in shark-infested waters later. Never stay in a bad or deteriorating or unreasonably dangerous situation out of ego. You need to be just as fast in reverse as you are in forward.

CHAPTER 40

**Are You a
"Control Freak"?**

"To avoid criticism, say nothing, do nothing, be nothing."

—Elbert Hubbard

Negative labels are often applied to exceptionally successful people, often for being or doing what is required for exceptional success.

In my book *No B.S. Business Success in The New Economy*, I write about the "workaholic" label. This is most often affixed to somebody who is passionately interested in his work and finds it infinitely more interesting than virtually all other activities, to the distress of family and friends. The label is awarded by people miserable in their jobs or businesses, bored by their work, and often financially unsuccessful as well who resent the happy entrepreneur. It is arguably the same as the population of an insane asylum deciding the doctor, who has a stable home life, a high income, and gets to climb into his Porsche and zip to his lake cottage on weekends, is a nut—because he isn't incarcerated like them. Yet, individuals can be intimidated, shamed, and manipulated by the negative labeling.

"Greedy" or, harsher, "greedy money-grubber," is another label, used in a very similar way for very similar reasons and motives. I debunk it in *No B.S. Wealth Attraction for Entrepreneurs*.

The critical label of "control freak" is similarly applied to a successful, demanding, critical leader by people who resent being compelled to perform as agreed or at the highest level and resent accountability and consequences for their failures, and more broadly, by people whose lives are out of control so they envy and resent anyone who is not like them. Secret admiration is usually expressed as criticism or ridicule. I have heard this control freak labeling my entire life, and more stridently the more control I exercised over subordinates, vendors, clients, time, access to me, and interaction with me. My practice of never randomly taking unscheduled inbound calls and requiring preset phone appointments with preset end times rubs a lot of people the wrong way. Especially those who are so insecure in their businesses they feel compelled to suffer unlimited and entirely uncontrolled interruptions at all hours.

My entire manifesto for control is in my book, *No B.S. Time Management for Entrepreneurs*. I sometimes get comments or letters about it from people saying either that they could never go through life as such a control freak or that they could never train customers or clients to behave as I've described. The first comment suggests there's something wrong with me because of their inability or absence of courage—an amazing idea! The second idea is patently false. All sorts of businesses successfully train and condition all sorts of customers to engage in bizarre behavior. Go to a Panera Bread® restaurant. There, customers not only clean up after themselves and cart their trays, dishes, and napkins to a work station, they also separate the food scraps and paper and dispose of it in one hole, and separate silverware from dishes and place those items in two different places. Their customers are doctors, lawyers, salespeople, suburban moms, old, young, and so on, all "clearing the table and doing the dishes" without thought or complaint despite being paying customers. You most certainly *can* control others' behavior.

You can do it *mechanically*. Disney® hurries people out of the parks at night by altering the tempo of the music and utilizing lighting, dimming it in some places, brightening it in others. You can do it *culturally*. Again, people are so much better behaved at Disney® parks than anywhere else. Per person, they throw far less trash on the ground than they do at a ball game, stadium, or shopping center. You can do it by *stated rules of engagement*, such as I have with my clients, my coaching group members, and at my events. You can do it by *carrot-and-stick*, reward and punishment, positive and critical recognition. Control is exercised over people constantly. That's not open to question. The only question has to do with how much control you exercise!

Legendary Control Freaks

Steve Jobs was labeled a "control freak" by associates, employees, and biographers. He did, in fact, exercise macro and micro control over Apple's design, hardware, software, amount of memory in a product, colors, online services, ad copy and illustrations, TV commercials, as well as food choices in the company cafeteria, parking spots, and hiring and firing of low-level staff. Psycho-babblers have theorized his control freakedness ties to his abandonment by his birth parents. The fact is, it was very good for business.

Walt Disney was labeled a control freak. He walked the park early in the morning, noting the smallest deviations from set standards or things that just "seemed off." He was known to call and have executives and workers dropping what they were doing and rushing from all points to a spot, to hear Walt rail against a chip in paint, some off-kilter lighting, someone not doing their job. He personally poked into every aspect of every film made while he was alive. He told Annette Funicello not to wear a bikini, even though all the other girls in the movies with her did. He personally went and negotiated the contract for the rights to *Mary Poppins*. Big or small, Walt weighed in. Walt's control-freakishness remains as a part of the entire Disney® organization, where supervisory attention to micro detail is unrivaled.

These men created work environments that were anything but "laid back." Arguably, they could have made their own lives less stressful by being less controlling, less invasive, and less demanding. The question is: *Could they have made their products better or their companies more successful by letting "little" things slide, being less rigid, being less interfering in everything?* Elsewhere I quote General Norman Schwarzkopf, who educated me about the axiom: "Shined shoes save lives." He said the top commander needs to care that the lowest-ranking soldier has perfectly shined shoes and adheres to every other micro standard, for, if that discipline erodes, bigger failures follow as certain as night follows day.

They Hated Seeing Me Coming

For many years, I did a lot of professional speaking engagements, at which I sold resources from the stage. In situations where measurement was possible, I always outsold all others. Many audiovisual crew employees, event planners, and hotel staffs labeled me a terrorist, a diva, a control freak, and hated seeing me on the speaker roster. I micromanaged everything, insisted on things being "just so," publicly ridiculed the a/v guys if a microphone faltered, and, as one said, "made everybody's life a living hell." Other speakers suffered being started late, introduced ineptly, technology screw-ups, incorrect stage setups, sloppiness at the back of room sales stations—and their results suffered too. They were far more laid back and far better liked by the crews. I preferred and prefer results. Pick your poison.

Even when working with the same backstage and a/v crews again and again and again, each and every time I insisted on meeting with each and painstakingly reviewing how things were supposed to be and go. On occasion, I have checked a meeting room late at night on arrival, for a speech the next morning, and rousted crews to reset the entire room. Really good and dedicated people appreciated this and responded well to it. Most had to be bullied. I'd rather not bully, but I'd rather be a bully than a failure. Leaving one of these places without every single dollar that might be obtained constituted failure. I devoutly believe this is a key reason I got rich and others didn't from the very same work—including others with more talent. They left things up to others. I was a control freak.

You Can't Afford to Be Laid Back

There have been periods of time in America when money ran uphill. There may be again. This, now, isn't one of them. We have an economy with negligible growth; most businesses have rising costs and shrinking margins; competition is keen and often desperate, therefore dangerous; and each and every prospective customer, client, or patient matters. Shrugging your shoulders at any preventable loss is an unaffordable luxury.

One of the things I push business owners very, very hard on is having their employees' handling of inbound calls expertly, frequently, mystery-shopped and recorded, to personally review transcripts, and to invest in ongoing calling-on-the-carpet of employees who violate scripts and standards, coaching the coachable, summarily firing the recalcitrant. You need to be a control freak about every word, the tone of voice, the impression the caller gets. Whatever standard you decide is appropriate for every function in your business must be met and must be micromanaged and enforced by somebody who is a control freak.

The more of this you do and the more you build it into an organization, the more you will be criticized, openly and behind your back. This is the least important thing you could ever try to control, and surrendering to mediocrity or worse in an effort to try and be liked *by poor performers* is a failure wrapped in futility. A lot of people still won't like you. And you'll have a less successful business. Being criticized and negatively labeled comes with the taking and ownership of territory.

An important question is: Why shouldn't you be in control? Of your time, of the way people access and work with you, of the way your phones are answered, of the cleanliness of your floors, of anything and everything that you decide matters. Why should you tolerate others' sabotage? I suppose there are places, jobs, limited ambitions where you can be laid back. Maybe as a college professor, or even as a department head at a college. Maybe as a fishing charter boat captain in the Florida Keys. And if you want to be laid back, I advise relocating and choosing an activity where you can do so. Being an entrepreneur building or leading a business just isn't such a place.

Nice 'n Easy Doesn't Do It

It's a pleasant Sinatra song, "Nice 'n easy does it." It's not a good business or career strategy, and, by the way, Sinatra was never nice 'n easy about his career. You need to be on top of things and in things and examining things from every angle.

CHAPTER 41

How They Should Communicate with You

"Executives who get there and stay suggest solutions
when they present problems."

—MALCOLM FORBES

T he number-one complaint I have about people and always had about my employees, and that I hear from my clients about their employees, is they can't communicate.

The complaint has validity. Generally, people have no idea how to communicate effectively and efficiently. Enormous time gets wasted. Here's an example: I called one of my two CPAs, got his voice mail and left this exact message: "I need to know when you will have my Kennedy Sports Corporation tax work done so I can tell the other CPA when to expect it. Call and tell me."

Here's the message he left me in return: "I'm working on the taxes. Call me if you have any questions."

Do I have any questions? Well, yes, I do. The same one I called with the first damned time that he didn't answer.

Aaaargh. And this sort of thing goes on all the time. In my case, I cut down on it a lot three ways. First, I try very hard to train people in how they should communicate with me. Second, I try very hard to eliminate people from my life who prove incapable of or unwilling to learn how to communicate with me as I want to be communicated with. Three, I rarely engage in telephone communication like the above fruitless exercise with the accountant at all; I force people to communicate with me in writing by fax, never email, which forces them to stop and think and be coherent. I communicate with everybody the same way.

For your purposes, let's talk about the first remedy, the training.

How to Communicate with You about Problems

I once had 47 employees in a troubled company environment where there was some sort of crisis every hour on the hour. I gradually trained the people I kept not to bring me a new problem without simultaneously bringing me the basic information I needed to make an intelligent decision plus at least three possible solutions. That template looked like the one in Figure 41.1.

When you force people into a process like this, you accomplish quite a bit. First of all, it stops people from bursting into your office screaming or sending you a hysterical and incomprehensible email. Second, it forces the person with the problem to actually think about it before they can dump it in your lap or anybody else's. If they're worth having around at all, they'll wind up deciding on a solution and handling the whole matter on their own some percentage of the time. Third, you can actually have an intelligent conversation about the problem and potential solutions if you must, rather than always having at least three or four consecutive conversations.

FIGURE **41.1:** Problem-Solution Communication Template

Name of Problem or Crisis: _____

Five Key Facts You Need to Know about It:

1. _____

2. _____

3. _____

4. _____

5. _____

Two Possible Solutions to Consider:

Solution 1 _____

Pros	Cons
_____	_____
_____	_____
_____	_____

Solution 2 _____

Pros	Cons
_____	_____
_____	_____
_____	_____

We also developed a code, sort of like Homeland Security's colorful terror alert thing. If you arrived with a problem, the first thing I asked you for was its numerical ranking, from 1 to 5. Five meant that life on this planet might end if it wasn't dealt with immediately. One meant that it's bugging you, but a day or two probably wouldn't matter much. After a while, people got that they had to accurately answer that question. This reduced the number of emergencies, led to more thinking on their part, and kept me from committing suicide. I should mention that, at the time, I was experimenting with the "open door management" idea highly recommended in most of the management books I'd hurriedly consumed when I woke up with all these employees. And if there's a dumber management idea, I'd like to see it. You might want a glass door so you can see 'em and they know you can, but you'll still want to shove a really heavy couch in front of it to keep them out.

The point is not so much whether you like this specific technique or any other I might use or recommend. The point is that you need a set way that you permit employees and vendors to communicate with you, that works best for you. You may have one method or different methods for different situations or even for different people. Whatever works best for you. Think of it as a little instruction manual for communicating with you: *The Care and Feeding of Information to the Boss.* The point is that you teach it to everybody who has to communicate with you and get them to use it.

But what if they won't follow your instructions?

Step 1: Off to remedial reading class they go. You refuse to accept their communications if presented in a noncompliant way. You gently say, "Sorry, but that's not how I take in information. Good-bye." Maybe you hand them another copy of your little instruction manual. Under no circumstances—unless you can actually see the place on fire behind them as they are yelling "Fire!"—do you permit them to ignore your instructions. Not once. No exceptions. Rebuff them. Send them away. Hang up on them.

Step 2: If Step 1 fails, forget gentle. Sit them down and read them the riot act.

Step 3: Fired. Next. I promise, you will wind up with people who can follow directions eventually, if you insist on it.

CHAPTER 42

How to Hold Meetings

"The Law of Meetings: There's an inverse relationship between the number of people in a meeting and what will be accomplished."

—Dr. Gene Landrum, Founder of Chuck E. Cheese Pizza,
author of Profiles of Power and Entrepreneurial Genius

I n the May 2007 issue of GQ magazine, writer Cecil Donahue said this: "Nothing crushes the soul—or your productivity—like a day full of meetings . . . pure torture. Not only a wearying time suck, but also a double whammy: Every minute wasted in mind-numbing boredom was also a minute lost attacking the various stacks on my desk." He went on to describe the people most often found populating the endless meetings everybody seems to be in whenever you call a company. Included, some from his list, some from mine, are the following individuals:

- *The Bloviator.* He has an MBA, and wants to be sure you know it. *Tick-tock, there goeth the clock.*

- *The Merry Quipster.* A little fun's fine. But he thinks the meeting's being held in a comedy club. *Tick-tock, tick-tock, around your neck a rock.*
- *The Yes-Men and Brown-Nosers.* Since they are bobblehead clones of the boss, they are an entire waste of time, air, and doughnuts. *Tick-tock, tick-tock, tick-tock, the urge to gag as great as if, in your mouth, a sock.*
- *The Killer.* He's never met an idea he doesn't hate and can't come up with 402 reasons it won't work. *Tick-tock, shoot the clock.*
- *The Mover.* He prevents any decisions or resolution of anything in favor of more research, committees formed, items tabled for future meetings, and more meetings scheduled for items tabled. *Tick-tocks, roadblocks.*
- *Mr. Meetings.* The worst of all. The boss or project manager who loves the sound of his own voice, loves hearing what a genius he is, secretly loves pitting people against each other, loves avoiding any real work, loves covering his ass with groupthink he can later blame for anything that goes wrong (while taking full credit for anything that goes right), and most of all, loves those little deli sandwiches. *Tick-tock, tick-tock, tick-tock, tick-tock, sell your stock.*

It's up to you to prevent this B.S. from taking over your company.

The Best Meeting May Be No Meeting

The first thing to do is to avoid having all these meetings in the first place. There are other options for collecting input and disseminating information. For example, posing a question to people and making each one respond separately in writing forces them to think; avoids emotions linked to interpersonal conflicts and jockeying for position from coloring the input; eliminates all the time consumed by bloviating, joke telling, arguing; and gives you something you can quietly consider, say while being driven home by your chauffeur or sitting on the can. Improves everybody's productivity.

If you can't cut out a meeting, consider cutting down on the people in it. Not everybody with two cents to offer or a need to know needs to be there. Some can contribute in advance in writing; some can be informed after the fact.

If You Feed 'Em, They Might Move In

The second thing to do: stop feeding them. Another consultant and I used to love joining one company's employees at their lengthy new product brainstorming meetings because the food was just outstanding. On arrival, five different kinds of bagels, flavored cream cheeses, doughnuts, fruit, imported cheeses. Only a couple hours later, lunch! Little deli sandwiches with the crust cut off, gourmet potato salad, fresh veggies and dips. In the afternoon, bakery (not grocery store) cookies, brownies, and miniature cream puffs. If this guy had added masseuses giving shoulder massages, we'd still be there. Of course, we were also getting paid our hefty daily fees. But for the employees it was a soul-draining, mind-numbing, woefully unproductive experience just as the *GQ* writer described his. Productive people hate these things. Unproductive people love 'em. You can reduce their appeal by taking away the food.

You can further reduce the appeal of minimeetings by making them stand-up meetings. At the very least, resist the urge to create a Taj Mahal conference room with plush, comfortable chairs. Decorate with clocks.

Insist on Outcomes

The third thing you can do is actually manage the meeting. Have a preset agenda with defined objectives, time pre-allocated by topic, and the decision to occur by meeting's end predefined. Participants need to know the meeting has a purpose.

Copyright © Dan Kennedy 2007

Vincent Palko
www.AdToons.com

CHAPTER 43

Friendly as Long as You Feed Them

"Sooner or later you sleep in your own space."

—BILLY JOEL, "MY LIFE"

As the owner of a business, ultimately you are alone. You may have a hundred employees around you, you may get nice gift baskets from your vendors, you may be the local hero at the Chamber meeting, you may even be famous to your peers in your industry or profession. Never let any of that fool you. Let something negative and cataclysmic happen, and you'll find nearly all of these folks gone missing.

At least once every summer, there's a story in the news about some numb-nut in a national park who sits on a ledge tossing jelly doughnuts to a couple bears. The bears happily eat the treats and behave like big, friendly dogs. Until the idiot runs out of doughnuts. Then the bears eat the idiot. This is a useful thinning of the herd, but it's also a true and accurate representation of how most employees behave, too. Friendly as long as you feed them.

In one of the early Presidential debates in 2007, Rudy Giuliani was struggling to explain his pro-life/pro-abortion position when electric shocks came through the microphone, mimicking lightning. He quipped such a thing was frightening to somebody who'd gone to parochial schools. The other candidates joked by all moving steps away from him. Well, that's exactly what goes on in real business life when things go awry. Ask Martha Stewart or Arnold Taubman how quickly people distanced themselves when they were arrested, prosecuted, publicly pilloried, and sent off to jail. Ask Donald Trump to compare the numbers of people eager to be around him at the height of his *Apprentice*-fueled popularity vs. the years he spent teetering on the brink of bankruptcy.

Given that this is true—and it is—then you must ultimately always do what you judge to be in *your* best interest. You have to give yourself full permission to do that, no qualms, no strings attached.

A few years ago, I had a confrontation in a meeting with the account executive representing a client's current ad agency. I made a simple suggestion: He could put up $50,000.00 out of his pocket to run the ad he'd prepared against the one I'd prepared, which I'd run with $50,000.00 out of my pocket. Whoever won would get $50,000.00 from the other and be reimbursed by the client for the $50,000.00 spent running the superior ad. The loser would eat his ad cost and pay the winner. He sputtered like an old, bad lawn mower running on politically correct ethanol. He was insulted by the unprofessional nature of my proposal. And, of course, he wanted no part of the wager.

This is the way it is. Every single day you, the business owner, put yourself at risk. The others who disapprove of your actions put nothing at risk.

Everybody has lots of opinions, but hardly anybody is willing to put themselves on the line to accept consequential responsibility for them. Lots of people are willing to privately and publicly pass judgment on you, your decisions, your business practices, but few will offer to open up their own checkbooks to wager on being right. It's also very important to keep in mind that most people expressing opinions, generously offering you their wise counsel free of charge, and gifting their criticisms have their own agendas—some practical, some emotional.

Every employee thinks he's smarter than the boss. Your employees think they are overworked and underpaid, making a much greater contribution to your business than you are, smarter than you are, and therefore well justified in ignoring or circumventing your directives, standards, and procedures. And should you be delusional about your business being some sort of all-for-one, one-for-all exception, try this experiment: Call everybody in, tell them you just lost a major account or had some other economic reversal, announce that you're taking a 20% pay cut for an indeterminate length of time, and ask for volunteers to do the same. If you like, take it further and give everybody a day to privately let you know whether 1) he is willing to take that 20% pay cut to save everybody's jobs and keep the ship afloat or 2) he prefers 100% of his pay and having others laid off. Unity will be in short supply.

Consider a U.S. automaker like General Motors, Ford, or Chrysler. I can't recall a month passing in recent years without the recall of thousands of cars with various manufacturing defects being announced. I had a new car with seven different recalls in 18 months. When these occur, do you suppose all the employees who actually worked on these cars and put all the brake lines in backwards or neglected to seal the moonroofs all come forward, march over to the CEO's office, and say, "Hey, my bad. Our screw-up. Please dock our pay appropriately, so all the stockholders who've invested here with the perfectly reasonable expectation that we're going to be awake while assembling these cars don't suffer." Does the head of the union call a press conference to announce the employees' eagerness to share responsibility for the recall costs, damage to the company's brand, and inconvenience or danger and harm to the customers?

Should you find anyone willing to book the bet, you may wager your life savings on this never happening in complete safety, with as much certainty as betting against Paris Hilton ever receiving an Oscar (or any other recognition of talent) or of Al Gore ever again using the word *lockbox*.

Profits of businesses are shared, by paying salaries, bonuses, and benefits to employees at every level; by paying taxes to local, state, and federal governments; by purchasing goods and services from vendors; by paying for advertising in media, and on and on. After all that profit sharing, you, the owner, get to keep whatever's left over. That might be about 2% of all the money if, say, you own supermarkets or certain kinds of industrial manufacturing companies. It might be as much as 20% if you own a professional practice or service business. Regardless, it's a long, long way from 100% of the money. But 100% of the responsibility is yours and yours alone. Don't ever lose sight of this fact.

This knowledge has to empower you: To think about yourself; to view your business as a means of achieving your personal goals; and to always do what you judge to be in *your* best interest. You have to give yourself full permission to do that, no qualms, no strings attached. This flies in the face of plentiful advice about putting customers first and others' equally zealous advice about putting employees first. Nonsense. He who puts his chips on the table and neck in the noose every day gets priority.

One of the many objects I have in my office as reminders to myself is a miniature wooden hanging platform with a noose suspended from its top. It's prominently displayed on a bookshelf, to catch my eye and jog my memory, telling me it's my neck in the noose.

CHAPTER 44

Why I Can't Do
These Things

"The price of progress is trouble."
—Charles F. Kettering

The reasons business owners tell me they can't do the obviously patently logical and sensible things described in this book include:

1. My employees won't do it.
2. My employees won't accept this kind of environment.
3. Bertha (ONE employee) won't let me.
4. It's bad for morale.
5. It makes me look like a tyrant.
6. What will people think?
7. My business is different.
8. I don't have time for this kind of management.

Regarding excuses 1, 2, and 3: One of the saddest, most pitiful things I ever hear from business owners is, "But my employees won't let me." I hear it a lot. It seems the inmates are running the asylums, and the wardens have surrendered, north, east, south, and west. Of course, it is possible to present your new Program in such a negative, belligerent way that you spark mutiny—and deserve it. This does have to be *sold*. But it is also likely you are living in tyranny in your own business, and you really should stop. Employees are replaceable. Lost profits are not.

Regarding excuse 4: Morale is a funny thing. It's subjective and variable. While a definite Program and supervisory enforcement are hated and resented by some employees, it is welcomed by others. There are plenty of people who prefer working in an environment with strong leadership, good management, a well-defined Program, clearly defined opportunities and rewards and penalties, and elimination of bad employees around them. They actually want to do the work, do the work well, and have accurately measured accomplishment. Everything I've talked about here is absolutely awful for the morale of noncompliant, unprofitable employees. But you may be surprised at its effects on the morale of productive, profitable employees!

Regarding excuses 5 and 6: The only opinions that really matter are those of the customers, clients, or patients who make deposits to your bank account. I have two books to recommend on this issue of sensitivity to criticism, to be read in this order: *The New Psycho-Cybernetics,* which I co-authored with the late Dr. Maxwell Maltz, then *Thick Face, Black Heart* by Chin-Ning Chu. You need to read the first to be prepared for the second.

Regarding excuse 7: No, it isn't.

Regarding excuse 8: If you decide to put a small herd of cattle in your backyard, you'd damn well better make time to feed them, water them, care for them, and constantly repair your fences. If you are going to have employees, they come with a collection of responsibilities. If you are going to have profitable employees, these responsibilities cannot be ignored.

Copyright © Dan Kennedy 2007

Vincent Palko
www.AdToons.com

CHAPTER 45

What Is "Profit," Anyway?

"A company's No. 1 responsibility is not to the customer but to the
shareholder. It doesn't mean that the customer isn't important. But the
people who invest in a company own it—not the employees, not
the suppliers, not the customers, and not the community."

—ALBERT DUNLAP, TURNAROUND WIZARD AND AUTHOR OF *MEAN BUSINESS: HOW I
SAVE BAD COMPANIES AND MAKE GOOD COMPANIES GREAT*

Accountants can make fabulously unprofitable companies seem profitable. Enron leaps to mind, but almost every quarter some big company is "restating its earnings." A lot of small-business owners are similarly confused. I've certainly had clients who couldn't differentiate between gross and net. Since this is a book about managing for profit, I thought it might be worth a stab at definition.

There are different kinds of profit.

One is the amount of money that you, the owner, remove from the business in cash as yours. This might include your salary, bonuses, contributions to your retirement accounts, and your health benefits. It might also include the salaries paid your wife, mistress, unemployable brother-in-law you'd have to support anyway, and that "fact finding junket" you went on to Las Vegas. You need to be reasonably honest with yourself about all this, or you may be unhappy without just cause. One client complained to me that he was only keeping $300,000.00 a year from his $3 million business. Quizzed, he wasn't counting $100,000.00 put into his retirement accounts, a large low-interest loan he was using to invest in very profitable real estate, rental payments he got from his company for his vacation home and boat when he hosted meetings there, and, of course, the salary paid to his unemployable brother-in-law.

On the other hand, it's important not to fool yourself either. The fact that your business rented your vacation home or bought you first-class tickets to Vegas, where you did drop in on a trade show, well, that's nice. But it's still money that's gone altogether or disappeared into an asset like your vacation home and boat that may have questionable future worth as investments. In short, there's "total net profit" and then there's "net cash profit, retained." It's this second number, "net cash profit, retained," that matters most, because this is the only number that can translate into financial security for you and your family.

I firmly believe it a mistake to let all or most of your wealth accumulate and be tied up in your business, for the dreamt-about day when some big, dumb company or deep-pocketed investor arrives to buy you out at a nice multiple of all that accumulated value. A business is a thing to take money out of. A business owner must measure his success, in large part, by the amount of the gross that runs through his hands he is able to get out of the business and into untouchable and reasonably secure investments, such as cash in Federal Deposit Insurance Corporation (FDIC)-insured banks, top-rated bonds, and real estate in stable markets. Most business owners err in thinking they'll take care of such things "later." They should be done from day one, done every day, week, or month, every payday. This all-important number should be managed and made to grow on a schedule.

The other type of profit is equity.

Equity can be confusing, too. A lot of what gets put on balance sheets and counted as accumulating equity actually has diminishing and little or no cash value to the business owner if and when he needs to borrow against it or goes to sell the business. I bought a company once that had over $3 million of a particular so-called asset on its balance sheet, certified as worth exactly that by a famous name Big-Eight accounting firm. However, these assets had value only to the business as it was operated, and lost value with age rapidly—a loss never calculated by the accountants. As a practical matter, the asset was worth somewhere between $0.00 and about $50,000.00 for the raw material. This is really quite common. Owners con themselves, accountants confuse them, and owners and accountants lie to stupid bankers about these things.

An asset is worth only what it could be sold for, today.

If you have, for example, a building full of perfectly functional equipment you're happy to use but that has been antiquated by two newer generations of technology, it is not worth the million dollars you paid for it less your accountant's formulaic depreciation. It's only worth what you could get for it today at auction, with an ad in the paper, or on eBay. If you have, for example, a half-million dollars in inventory you carry, but it's only useful in the products you make, and they're only useful providing your chief account keeps buying them, you do not have a half million dollars. You have hope worth a penny, plus whatever the raw material would sell for as is, today, on the auction block. This is why I've always said that inventory is evil.

However, there is an asset that gets short shrift on balance sheets, that is worth much more than any bean-counter formula allows, that you should be aggressively investing in acquiring and nurturing: customers and good, active relationships with them.

Buildings burn down. Locations go from great to awful because of road construction. Products and services are vulnerable to competition, commoditization. Technology can be antiquated. Every single thing most business owners think of as solid assets are actually paper-thin.

The only asset that can be kept safe from every threat and made to appreciate in value year after year is the relationship you have with your customers. Not just a list of customers. *Relationship* with customers.

Most business owners do a terrible, terrible, terrible job managing this asset. They take it for granted. They refuse to invest in it. They abuse it by only communicating with it when asking it for money.

Customer relationship depends on a number of factors. An important one is frequency of communication. A customer

Recommended Resource #6

You can obtain a FREE subscription to my *No B.S. Marketing Letter* along with a special package of other gifts at www.DanKennedy.com/managementbook or by following the instructions on page 379 of this book. This will help you implement a profitable customer relationship program.

(or prospect) list loses about 10% of its value every month it is neglected. In 11 months, it's worth less than random names pulled from the white pages. Communication needs to be as frequent as it is welcomed, by being interesting, informative, entertaining, and personal, as well as commercial. In my businesses, my best customers hear from us through a variety of means and media 232 times a year—not including overt promotions and offers. The minimum I set for my clients is 52, once a week. Most businesses' number is zero to a few. A few might as well be zero. You cannot sustain relationship with an occasional, random drive-by and a kiss thrown from the window of your car.

Another factor is consistency. Some aspect of your relationship ought to be ritualized and dependable. Like maintaining relationship with the relative who lives a long distance away with the phone call every Saturday morning. The media devices we use most often for this are consistently published customer or member newsletters; customer birthday, anniversary, and seasonal greetings; and periodic events. These are appropriate for every business and every sales professional, and the most profitable business with the highest customer values in over 256 different categories I have direct interaction with use them.

Another factor is quality of communication, creativity, and personality. In my book *The Ultimate Marketing Plan*, I make my case for the Ultimate Marketing Sin: being boring.

Customer Relationships as Equity

For every business, there is a Present Bank and a Future Bank. Both require attentive management.

The Present Bank has to do with today's sales and profits. At the restaurant, Present Bank statistics to manage might include the number of tables turned per shift, or the number of extra desserts or fine wines sold. Those will immediately affect the sales and profits deposited that day. The Future Bank has to do with customer relationships initiated or nurtured. Statistics to manage that might include the number of Birthday Club Cards completed by customers or the number of customers who join the VIP Club. These have Future Bank Value. The thing to wrap your head around, that few business owners ever do, is that managing the Future Bank is as important or more important than the Present Bank, because the Present Bank is merely income, the Future Bank is equity. You can't, for example, sell me the income you've already spent. But you can sell me the *facts* that you have 2,300 people in your Birthday Club who will all, obviously, be having a birthday sometime in the next 12 months and again within 24 months and again within 36 months, and historically you get 70% of these Club Members to come in for their free dinner and bring three people with them producing average checks of $100.00 . . . so there's 2,300 x 70% = 1,610 x 3-year average customer life span = 4,830 x $100.00 = $483,000.00 in the Future Bank. That's equity.

Believe it or not, the same principle applies whether you're a manufacturer of spud nuts or an equine podiatrist or a zebra stripe remover. There's a way to manage the Future Bank in nearly every business. You need to figure it out in yours.

The next chapter deals with other numbers you need to manage by.

Let me conclude here by saying that I think you ought to get rich. As rich as your business can possibly allow under the very best of created circumstances. Nothing less should be acceptable. It is my experience that just about any business, even small businesses, have the potential to make their owners quite rich— and a lot richer than those owners think. But it doesn't happen by accident. It requires very smart marketing and very tough-minded management. That's the work that's necessary for a business owner, service provider, or self-employed professional to move from just making a good living to creating real wealth.

I think we'd have a better society if all the rich people really knew and experienced how poor people live and all the poor people knew and understood how hard the rich people work.

CHAPTER 46

Management by the Numbers
(The Right Numbers)

"Paying attention to numbers is a dull, tiresome routine, a drudgery. The more you want to know about your business, the more numbers there will be. They cannot be skimmed. They must be read, understood, thought about and compared with other sets of numbers which you have read that day, that week, or earlier that year."

—HAROLD GENEEN, FORMER PRESIDENT OF ITT, AND AUTHOR OF *MANAGING*

"How can you govern a country which produces
246 different kinds of cheese?"

—CHARLES DEGAULLE

I 'll begin by saying that I personally hate everything that has to do with mathematics except counting money. If you do, too, I understand. I would also much rather be involved in creative activity than number crunching. If you are like that, too, I understand. However, we have to be mature enough not to let our want-tos totally control us.

The fact is, in 30 years, with well over 1,000 clients, those who've made the most money and gotten wealthiest are the ones who know their numbers inside out, upside down, backward and forward, minute by minute, day by day.

When I meet with most business owners, I can stump them with the first three numbers questions I ask.

Most business owners also spend a lot of time looking at useless numbers. Most accountants give you history books and banker's numbers that are of little value in making good day-to-day decisions or even in accurately understanding what's going on in your business. The income statements and balance sheets prepared for the bankers and tax authorities reflect neither real income nor real worth.

Here are some of the most important numbers you need to monitor and manage in your business:

CPL = Cost Per Lead
CPS = Cost Per Sale
ATV = Average Transaction Value
CVs = Customer Values
LCV = Lifetime or Long-Term Customer Value
CTP = Contribution to Profit
PB = Present Bank
FB = Future Bank
EC/PC = Expense Creep/Problem Creep
QC = Quality Control
SE = Sales Effectiveness

And for yourself:

WA = Wealth Accumulation
EIEND = Enough Is Enough Number Deficit

As you might instantly guess, an entire book could be written just about this. In these few pages, I'll do my best to explain each category of statistics and why they're important.

Let's start with ATV, CVs, and LCV.

ATV, Average Transaction Value, has several uses. Average FIRST Transaction Value gives us a big-thumb number you may be willing to spend part, all, or 110%, 150%, or more of to acquire a customer—and determining the maximum allowable cost of acquisition needs doing before ever spending a dime on advertising and marketing. Beyond that, ATV as a continuous measurement gives you a blink-of-an-eye look at how well or how poorly your selection of customers, sales process, and salespeople are doing overall, against same time prior year, and during special promotions.

Increasing ATV is one of the few ways a mature business or a business at or near 100% capacity can actually increase income. And small ATV increases can equate to large net profit increases; if all fixed expenses are covered by, say, a $100.00 ATV and you can bump ATV by just $10.00 or 10%, the only deduction is cost of goods at, say, 50%, leaving $5.00. If the regular $100.00 loses not only cost of goods but another 30% to overhead and fixed expenses, you only net $20.00 from the regular or old $100.00 ATV. The little $10.00 bump to ATV at the top gives you $5.00, a 25% increase in net. The constant "what can we do to increase ATV?" question is important. So is measuring and monitoring ATV.

CV, Customer Value, takes into consideration multiple transactions and buying behavior over a period of time, You need a way to monitor your average Customer Value within a prescribed time period, so you can segment your list into A-, B-, and C-level customers, to invest in them and communicate with them differently. This can also help you choose media, methods, and sources of customers better, by watching where A customers come from and where C customers come from; if there's a difference, upping the use of the things attracting A's and dropping the things attracting C's. Sometimes even field salespeople differ in the value of the customers they bring in; the one bringing in A's and B's should be kept, while the one bringing in mostly C's and a few B's has to go.

Then, CTP, Contribution to Profit, delves even deeper. It takes into consideration what they buy and even how they behave. In most businesses, different products and services are more profitable than others, so naturally different customers are more profitable than others. And different customers spending the same amounts on the same products and services require different amounts of care. A big long-distance carrier made news and public controversy in mid-2007 by "firing" thousands of its "worst" (least profitable) customers, based on their excessive need for human customer service. Its average customer used a couple hours of customer service a month while these undesirable customers used 10, 20, or even 30 hours. So they sent them letters of termination and sent them elsewhere. The public and media outcry was: How dare they deprive these people of phone service? The smart shareholders' thought was: Finally. If you aren't measuring CTP, you are undoubtedly servicing customers who are actually costing you money to keep.

LCV, Lifetime Customer Value, needs to bundle CV and CTP, consider the length of time you keep customers active, and provide a number measuring the total value of a customer. This ultimately controls your decisions about what you will invest in obtaining your customers. It's also the number you deposit in your Future Bank the day you secure a new customer—or, possibly, re-activate a lost one. Knowing this number also helps keep you real about the costs of losing customers, and helps you determine what you are willing to invest in keeping them.

Specific to managing your marketing and sales, there are three important numbers. When consulting with a client, I need to know and be able to manipulate CPL and CPS, Cost per Lead and Cost per Sale.

CPL is the money spent to get a prospect to raise his hand, step forward, and start down the path we've constructed for him. So, if you pay $1,000.00 a month for your Yellow Pages ad and it gets ten people a month to call or go to your website, you have a CPL of $100.00 from that media. CPL differs by media but can also be greatly affected by what I work on most—the advertising and marketing message itself. CPL can be deceptive, as the source with the highest CPL may provide the lowest CPS.

So this is a predictive but not definitive stat to watch and manage. **CPS is the truly critical number, because it reflects all the costs of putting the prospect on the path, moving him along the path, and ultimately converting him to a customer, client, or patient.** CPS will also vary by source, method, and the effectiveness of the path itself. From the previously described numbers, you have a MA-CPS, a Maximum Allowable CPS, and you work to get as many ways of bringing in customers as possible to perform at or below that number. I should tell you, hardly any business owner knows these numbers, although quite a few think they do. When somebody starts digging in, investigating, analyzing, and monitoring these numbers, they are usually amazed at how little they knew about what was really going on in their business.

I often get questions asked of me that can't be answered intelligently without these numbers. For example: "My Yellow Pages ad works pretty good. The rep is urging me to increase from a quarter page to a half page. Should I?" My questions then have to do with what "pretty good" really is:

1. What is the CPL from the ad?
2. What is the CPS from the ad?
3. What is the LCV of the customers obtained from the ad?
4. How do they compare to the CPL, CPS, and LCV from all the other means you use to get customers?

And that's just the beginning, but if you can't at least answer those, I can't tell you whether to increase that ad's size, shrink it, eliminate it altogether, or, heck, buy two full pages!

And if you're buying ad media and investing in marketing without tracking these numbers, you aren't *managing* your business at all. You are *guessing* your business.

The other number related to this is SE, for Sales Effectiveness. It's not really *a* number, but a collection of numbers. For example, the number of people who call in and are converted to kept appointments is an SE number, and its movement up or down will dramatically affect CPS. Also, the number of visitors to a website induced to provide their full contact information and invite follow-up vs. those providing only an email address vs. those providing no information at all, this is an SE issue. Of course, the biggest SE number is what happens when the prospect comes to your store, office, or showroom or invites you or your sales representative into his home or office and a sales presentation occurs. Here, the closing percentage and the size of the transaction combine to create SE. Tolerating subpar performance with either number backs up through the entire system, making your CPS and CPL too high from some or all sources. Improving performance in either or both closing percentage and transaction size allows for higher CPL, providing competitive advantage in marketing, and provides better profits as well.

SE applies, incidentally, not just to situations where a salesman designated as a salesman is making a formal sales presentation to a prospect. It's broader. In a retail store in the mall, the number of people who walk in vs. the number who leave empty-handed after just browsing vs. the number who buy is an important SE statistic. So via recording every "ding" of a person walking across the threshold or from surveillance cameras, you have to know how many people walked in today. Then you look at how many different customer transactions there were. If 100 people walked in and you have 20 different purchases, you have, to be sloppy, a 20% SE number. With that in hand, you can begin working on merchandise, display, signage, offers, and staff—Sales Design® and Sales Choreography®—to improve the 20%. Without knowing it and monitoring it, you can't do anything about it. You would also measure ATV in that same store as another SE number.

Next, there are two numbers related to managing operations rather than managing marketing: EC/PC and QC. EC/PC stands for Expense Creep and Problem Creep. If freight was 8% of your gross in the first quarter of 2012 but is 11% for the same quarter in 2013, it bears investigation. EC happens many ways. Vendors can inch prices up without being questioned, comparison shopped, or negotiated with. Theft can start occurring or increase. (I have a client whose freight bill went up nicely when his shipping clerk was shipping quite a bit of goods she was selling on eBay through his UPS and FedEx accounts. To add insult to injury, she was stealing the merchandise from him, too.) EC alarm bells should trigger investigation.

PC is even more interesting. It's a way to try and quantify your mostly hidden "people costs" with employees, vendors, and customers alike. For example, let's say a vendor is late on promised deliveries 1 out of 20 times. But over time, it's 1 out of 16, 1 out of 12. Unchecked it'll be 1 for 1. The sooner stopped or the sooner the vendor gets replaced, the better. I have a big rule about all this you may have seen in my other books or heard me discuss: If I wake up three mornings in a row thinking about you and we aren't at least occasionally having sex, you gotta go. But managing relationships by PC can usually rid you of such problems before they reach the three-mornings-in-a-row stage.

QC, Quality Control, is again about translating vague ideas about how you're doing into quantifiable data about how well you're doing. There are a lot of tools to measure QC. Customer questionnaires and surveys, "How are we doing?" calls to a certain number of randomly selected customers each week, close monitoring of customers gone inactive and direct contact with them, mystery shopping, surveillance systems. QC is about compliance with your Program as well as customer perceptions and feedback. It's easier in manufacturing than in sales or service businesses. In manufacturing, you can, for example, random pull and check x number of items from each job or each shift, rate them on a set criteria, and numerically grade the quality for the job, shift, day. You can monitor returns of merchandise for refunds due to defects. In nonmanufacturing environments, you have to work harder to assemble meaningful statistics.

A quick, amusing QC story. I had a very bad day in an upscale chain hotel, in Boston. I rather angrily filled out its full-page satisfaction survey with a thick, bold black marker, and continued my comments on its back. I vented. In the morning, I forgot to take it downstairs and left it lying on the top of the desk in the room, with piles of other papers. When I returned that afternoon, it—and only it—had been removed by the maid. Gee, do you think she turned it in for me?

Finally, there are four money numbers I suggest managing carefully. PB and FB, Present Bank and Future Bank, have to do with income and equity. Most business owners focus entirely on the first and ignore the second. Simply, you not only need a set of numbers you watch every day relevant to your business, reflective and predictive of income, you also need a set means of evaluating whether you've increased the value of the business today or not. I've discussed this earlier in the book.

Finally, WA and EIEND. WA, Wealth Accumulation, is the first number that actually gets to your primary responsibility as a business owner and primary purpose for business ownership (unless you very consciously and deliberately decide otherwise, as in, *This little antique shop is really my hobby, and I don't care about the financial results*). If you are in business for business reasons, then **your personal WA is really what it's all about**. This means you have to be measuring your success by the amount of money you are able to take out of the business and put somewhere smart and safe, ideally in appreciating or income-generating assets. You should have preset goals for WA and be very, very grumpy if not meeting them and ruthless about making whatever changes are required to meet them. There's also a discipline for this, usually called "pay yourself first."

> # Recommended Resource #7
>
> For a basic primer on "pay yourself first," I urge you to get and read a copy of a classic book *The Richest Man In Babylon* by George Clason. To move into more advanced territory and likely dramatically alter your thinking about money and wealth, read my book *No B.S. Wealth Attraction for Entrepreneurs.* Info, a sample chapter, and a video interview are available at www.NoBSBooks.com. For more information, see page 379 of this book.

EIEND is a very interesting measurement hardly anybody uses but me. Years back, I determined what my Enough-Is-Enough Number was. The EIEN is that sum of money you have invested in income-producing "untouchables," that will allow you to never need to earn another dollar as long as you live. Your EIEN has to take into consideration whether you want to leave a certain size estate to your heirs or are happy on the "die broke plan," eventually eating all the principal, ideally with your very last check bouncing as they close the lid . . . exactly how much you want to spend every month . . . reserves for health care . . . and other factors. It is admittedly an imprecise number, due to semi-unpredictable matters like inflation, divorce, suddenly deciding at age 80 you want to take up hot air balloon racing. But a well-considered number is a lot better than no number at all. And you may reset the number if you get close quicker than expected, although constantly pushing the number higher defeats its purpose.

Anyway, once establishing this number, I kept it on every page of my checkbook and deducted from it the amounts of money moved out of my business into my personal WA accounts and investments. Every day, or at least every time I used the company checkbook, I saw the EIEND, the Deficit, the gap between where I was and where I aspired to be, and the shrinkage of that gap (or lack thereof). This motivated me in many ways, but most importantly to move money out of my business to my personal WA.

To offer full disclosure, I went nearly the first two of three decades of my prime business years without EIEND monitoring, or effective use of many of these other numbers. As a result, I was a high-income, underinvested guy. I think I made some very poor decisions as a result. Literally the minute I started evaluating myself in this way, I rapidly got better at investing, and I dramatically accelerated my personal wealth accumulation. I went way past my original EIEN number several years ago, and again went several years without such measurement, only to recently reinstate it, and again, immediately recognize positive changes in my decision making, my personal motivation, and my wealth accumulation.

As I said, I hate math. But I've learned to be very, very interested in this kind of "money math." And as I said, business owners who aren't, aren't really *managing* their business. They are *guessing* their business.

CHAPTER 47

How To Profit from the Age of Tolerated Mass Incompetence and the Coming Monster Recession

"Following a nuclear attack on the United States, the United States Postal Service plans to distribute Emergency Change of Address Cards."

—U.S. Federal Emergency Management (FEMA) Executive Order #11490

When I was in my teens, I came across a book I've since lost and can no longer remember the exact title or author of, but its title was something like *How To Profit From The Coming Crash.* I read it and was fascinated. It was the first time it was made clear to me that there was such a thing as "crisis investing," that one man's crash was another man's boom, and that you could, in fact, profit from circumstances everybody around you viewed as "awful." One of the chapters in the book profiled people who got rich during the Great Depression that began in 1929, some by buying real estate and hotels and businesses, some by starting particular types of businesses. In history classes I was shown a Great Depression that encompassed all of America and everyone in it; pictures of shoeless people in camps eating beans from cans; desolation, destruction, and despair. But in this book I was presented with a different picture of that same time—a picture of ambitious, optimistic investors and entrepreneurs eagerly embracing a whole new array of opportunities to get rich. This came in handy later when Jimmy Carter got elected and single-handedly created the second Great Depression. (Many readers will be too young to recall this and have no frame of reference. Summary: double-digit interest rates, double-digit inflation, double-digit unemployment, and mile-long gas lines to boot.) By then I knew that there is no such thing as a "good" economy or "bad" economy for the person agile of mind and action, who creates his own economy.

N₀ B.S. Ruthless Management Truth #9

To paraphrase Napoleon Hill, in every crisis lie the seeds of one or more equal or greater opportunities. The person agile of mind and action can create his own economy

---

Crisis Opportunity

"Crisis opportunity" actually comes around frequently and repeatedly in different sectors of business and economy. Recessions of a sort limited to a single segment of the business world and public economy. For example, as I was putting the finishing touches on the first edition of this book, we were in the early stage of a potential tidal wave of residential real estate foreclosures and forfeitures, flooding banks and lenders with a predicted 1.2 million to 1.6 million properties in an 18-month period. That's over 65,000 a month. Over 2,000 every day. A crisis if you owned, managed, or owned stock in a lending institution that had been aggressive and "loose" with its lending standards. The opportunity of a lifetime if you knew how to buy foreclosures, how to "flip" and sell or rent properties, had some capital and time. If you did, you could buy dollar bills for 40 to 60 cents each.

It was my belief there was a "crisis opportunity" rapidly developing and likely to explode in the very near future, that would destroy many businesses and destroy the profit margins of many others, but present incredible opportunity to a relatively small number of businesses in each category who readied themselves to profit.

Any "crisis opportunity" has two parts, converging at a meeting point visible on the horizon.

One is an utter and complete collapse of even minimally acceptable service and basic competence. You can see it coming. Wherever possible, businesses are replacing and will continue to replace incompetent, unreliable, expensive humans with automation. That was once restricted to the factory, but it is now part of the ironically titled customer service environment. The Industrial Revolution is long over but the Service Revolution has just begun. Automation is replacing service people just as it did factory workers. Beyond that, consumers are forced into pumping their own gas, banking at ATMs and online rather than face-to-face with a teller. Even pizzas are ordered online by customers doing their own data entry.

In each application, it began or is beginning as a choice for consumers. In every application the goal is to make it the only choice. Wherever possible, other customer service jobs are being outsourced overseas to cheaper labor. Every place from the retail store to the casino floor has fewer and fewer service people, more and more do-it-yourself options, longer waits, poorer service. This will kill some businesses. But, for all businesses that participate in this trend, it will fully and completely commoditize them, end all consumer preference, and liberate consumers to go wherever the cheapest price is offered. There will be nothing to influence buying but price. That, of course, shrinks margins to the bone and further thins the herd.

The second is an overall, broad, across-economic-segments recession. You can see them coming, too. Too much of the most recent boom was based on "irrational exuberance" (to quote Alan Greenspan) and ridiculously profligate spending, drunken sailor use of consumer credit, conversion of all home equity into depreciating assets like boats and vacations, and Taj Mahal kitchen remodeling. All made possible by nonsensically suppressed interest rates and the impact of President Bush's tax cuts. This produced a remarkably resilient economy, able to thrive even under the burden of an incredibly expensive war. But if ever there was an overinflated balloon just waiting to burst, this was it. Add much pressure, say, from a liberal President and Congress eager to tax the pants off "the rich," lay on a bank-breaking socialist health-care system, make "free" preschool and college available to all; or from finally rising interest rates and stagnating or dropping real estate values; or from stock market correction backward by 1,000 or 2,000 or more possibly partly spurred by liberals' announced desire to raise capital gains taxes to equal income taxes; or—well, the list went on. Any of many ignition switches would do.

So, when these two freight trains collide head-on, as I fear they will, is it possible not only to survive but actually to thrive in business? Yes, you can prosper to a greater degree than ever before. There are only two key things you need to do. First, be providing an ever escalating, exceptional, even phenomenal level of customer service, delivered by exceptionally competent, highly trained, highly incentivized, and well-policed humans. Go in the opposite direction of the masses of businesses in your field and in general. As they cut back on service, as they increasingly disappoint consumers and sanction incompetence from their employees, you be the one to increase, expand, and improve service, to invest more in providing service and in employees who perform. Second, design your business and aim your marketing at the affluent consumers who are least affected by overall economy ups and downs, who do not use price as a decision factor, who have a demonstrated preference for exceptional service and a willingness to pay for it.

In short, the business pyramid is going to change in shape to something with a starving, struggling, barely surviving crowd of commoditized businesses delivering little or no service and selling at minimum margins at the bottom, no middle, and at the peak, very different businesses selling at premium prices and enjoying higher than ever margins by delivering extraordinary service to affluent customers. Now, there's a big middle—think moving from Walmart to Target to Kohl's to J.C. Penney to Dillard's and Macy's to Nordstrom and Nieman-Marcus. The middle will disappear. Not permanently, of course, but long enough to do serious damage. (See Figure 47.1 on page 352.)

The difference determining whether you fall to the bottom or rise to the top will not be in products or brand names or physical location or any factor other than the existence or nonexistence, and extent of and quality of your customer service. If you follow the crowd on its current path of shrinking service, sanctioning incompetence, and merely trying not to be worse than others in your category, you'll follow the crowd off the cliff. If you turn your back on the crowd and head in the exact opposite direction, you'll soon arrive at the land of milk 'n honey.

The only other option is to devise a business requiring few or zero people involved in any way other than yourself, but

FIGURE **47.1**

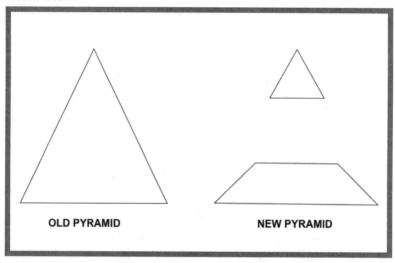

OLD PYRAMID   NEW PYRAMID

that cannot be automated and commoditized. This applies, for example, to very high-priced professionals providing a service. If this is you, then you may have opportunity to shrink your business' size and get rid of all employees, raise your fees even more, and deal with a small, select number of clients. "Concierge" medical and dental practices represent a small, current, controversial trend that moves doctors in this direction. But failing this, if you are going to compete in the big marketplace, all your middle choices will disappear, and you will choose to either 1) "bottom feed," providing minimalist service and rock-bottom prices, a place where extinction always looms as there's always some big, dumb, unprofitable but well capitalized company or some small-business fool willing to sell cheaper, or 2) step way up to the tiny peak of the pyramid, providing truly extraordinary service to a small segment of the market. Better to choose now than wait until you must do so under crisis circumstances.

Incidentally, this movement can be seen in certain industries and companies already. Disney® has a thriving business with personal, VIP guides at its parks in the $200.00-per-hour price range. It's only one of many examples of Disney® creating new "for the affluent options" in goods and services, at its resorts and parks. Luxury hotels are adding ultraluxury suites with personal chefs and butlers. And hotels are adding upscale hotels inside themselves, such as the Four Seasons inside Mandalay Bay in Las Vegas. The boom in "marketing to the affluent" that I began focusing my newsletter subscribers and clients on beginning in 2005 is actually a precursor to the entire disappearance of the middle of the pyramid, a movement of forward-thinking companies and entrepreneurs to the top of the new pyramid.

Last, I'd be remiss if not mentioning the related antiproductivity, antiwork crisis developing. A piece on the *Today Show* that I saw was titled "Friday Is The New Saturday." It revealed the quiet surrender of hundreds of big U.S. corporations to a four-and-a-half day workweek, inviting people to come in only one hour early Friday mornings then leave at noon because "nobody does any work Friday afternoons." Employees spend Friday afternoons planning their weekends, thinking about their weekends, calling and texting and emailing people about their weekends, so these employers have acquiesced and written off those Friday afternoons. Fools—now nobody will do any work Friday mornings. And when all of Friday is surrendered, Thursday afternoon will be the new Friday afternoon. Where does it end? Probably where Outback Steakhouse's® TV ads are the day I completed this book: They have proclaimed Wednesday as the new Friday. An entire generation of workers is making it abundantly clear they do not value work, do not equate work to honor, have no work ethic, and have very little interest in work. Their jobs are evil inconveniences. Our society is becoming French, all about leisure and lifestyle. For quite some time, the hottest "business" (I use the term loosely) book was

Tim Ferriss' *The 4-Hour Workweek*. Personally, I like Tim, and Tim writes about me as having great influence on him, which I appreciate. But frankly, this title resonated with so many people that it made the book a huge bestseller, and that so many people never questioned the plausibility of its premise, does not bode well for anybody trying to get 40 hours of honest productivity out of people. The warning signs are all around you. While it is difficult to get productivity from people now, that's only going to get a whole lot worse before it gets better, if it ever does.

The only way to turn *that* to your advantage is to design a business that needs fewer employees and can pay them overly generously, so that you can attract and keep the absolute cream of the crop and can deliver the truly extraordinary service that will keep you at the peak of the new pyramid. And you will need every trick in this book to make that work!

CHAPTER 48

In the Next 12 Months

> "In my first 12 months we marketed 107 new product initiatives across 22 countries. Every existing product was repackaged and most were reconceived, reformulated, or relaunched."
>
> —ALBERT DUNLAP, TURNAROUND WIZARD AND AUTHOR OF *MEAN BUSINESS: HOW I SAVE BAD COMPANIES AND MAKE GOOD COMPANIES GREAT*

If you have read this far, congratulations. Most people who buy business books never actually read them! But the next step is action. The real question is: What will you DO—what will you get DONE—as a result of your thinking spurred by having read this book?

My friend, speaking colleague, and author the late Jim Rohn said, "Poor people have big TVs. Rich people have big libraries." That's true as far as it goes. But the entrepreneurs I know and hang out with who develop amazing businesses and create exceptional wealth can, as I can, walk you through their big libraries and tell you what actions they took as a result of each of the hundreds and hundreds of books on the shelves.

And I would pose an even tougher question to you: What will get DONE in the next 12 months?

Foolish people try to escape pressure. Successful people deliberately put themselves under pressure to perform. Extremely successful people put themselves under extreme pressure to perform—and thrive on it.

I frequently work with entrepreneurs on triggering what we call The Phenomenon—a time when you accomplish more in 12 months than in the previous 12 years. That's possible. It happens a lot. It happens to just about every ambitious, hard-working entrepreneur at some time in his life. But it can be *made to happen* immediately. One of the most powerful triggers is the *deciding*. Determining everything you will get DONE in the next 12 months, the next 12 weeks, the next 12 days, the next 12 hours, even the next 12 minutes, then racing the calendar and the clock, declaring war on the resistance, opposition, and sluggishness of those around you, and placing yourself and others under extreme pressure to perform. (Those who crack under the pressure need to be discarded and replaced.) So I urge you not to put this book away on a shelf or lend it to a friend until you first bolt yourself in a room with nothing but it, a legal pad, a pen, and caffeine, and go through it again page by page, and think, and decide what you will get DONE in your business in the next 12 months, 12 weeks, 12 days. Your lists may include things you've been tolerating that you will no longer tolerate, people who should have been replaced who now will be, new initiatives in marketing, sales, training, and supervision, reshuffling of priorities and people, and more.

Don't just read the book. Make the lists. DO. Get DONE. Fast. Ruthlessly when need be.

CHAPTER 49

Your Support Circles

"Help. I need somebody! . . ."

—JOHN LENNON AND PAUL MCCARTNEY, *HELP!*

Owning, leading, and running a business can be a lonely business, and the isolation of entrepreneurship can have many negative consequences. While I personally appear to work alone to the casual observer, I have actually created "support circles" around me, and I believe you need to do the same.

We'll start closest to you and work out. See Figure 49.1 on page 362.

Circle 1 is your inner, inner, inner circle. Lee Iacocca talked and wrote about his "five horses," the people closest to him who he trusted, was on the same page with, who understood him, who were qualified and able to offer worthwhile advice and ready and able to facilitate and implement his decisions. This inner, inner circle must be small to be valuable. It may (or may not) include your spouse, your business partner, a "wise old man" mentor, and the people may (or may not) be employees, paid advisors, or friends. You need to exercise enormous care about choosing the members of this team as well as great vigilance toward their developing any agendas in conflict with your own.

Circle 2 is comprised of experts, specialists, and providers of information. For many of my clients, this includes me. For me, there is one person above all others I rely on for information and advice about online marketing, another for the securing of celebrities for my clients' advertising campaigns, another for printing and publishing. And so forth. For me and probably you, this has to include at least one CPA, one or more other financial advisors, and one lawyer.

Either Circle 1 or Circle 2 needs to include The Man Who Makes You Defend Your Position. This is someone with considerable successful and relevant experience, no interest in mollifying or pleasing you, no agenda, little tact, and a great ability for asking tough and provocative questions. Someone willing to tell you he thinks you're making a huge mistake, with enough credibility you'll consider his position even though it displeases you. This is not the same as the buffoon who always has 100 reasons something can't be done but never has any ideas about how to accomplish anything. That's a minimum-wage loser. Here, I'm talking about high-value talent; someone of real authority with whom you can argue your ideas, to improve them.

Circle 3 is made up of conduits and liaisons. For some of my clients, I'm on this list, too. These are people who know people you do not, who can refer you to reliable vendors you do not know, who can broker introductions for you with others. When I need to know something in the area of real estate, there are a few experts in my Circle 2 that I can call on, and there are others in Circle 3 that I can call on who can connect me to the right people. This Circle should be as large as you can make it, your Rolodex® of useful and potentially useful contacts.

Circle 4 consists of high-performance, high-reliability vendors and suppliers. You'll have your own nuanced definitions of *high performance* and *high reliability,* but, for me, these are providers of essential goods and services who perform with little or no supervision, who can think, who make promises they can keep and keep the promises they make as a matter of honor not just due to a contract, and who practice the kind of management I've described in this book so they actually have the internal capability to do the job right the first time, on time. As an aside, you rarely get such vendors and the cheapest prices. I advise my clients to adjust the prices, margins, and economics of their businesses so they can afford paying premium prices and fees to top-notch vendors. If you surround yourself with cheapest price suppliers in this circle, you better stock up on Tums® and Tylenol®.

It is vital not to get lazy or complacent about maintaining the best possible Circles 2 and 4. Here, as with your employees, they all go lame. You must be demanding, critical, measuring of performance and value, alert for slippage in attentiveness to you and performance, willing to fire, to churn 'n burn without procrastination, and always searching for the next, better replacement.

Circle 5 is a "looser" group of mentors, consultants, coaches, peers, and colleagues, paid and unpaid; essentially, the people you select to associate with. Association is one of the most powerful factors influencing or sabotaging personal and professional success. Being deliberate about whom you do NOT associate with is as important as choosing whom you do associate with. "Lie down with dogs, wake up with fleas" is a ruthlessly truthful Japanese proverb. And it only takes one cohabitation to get infested with fleas. By "fleas," I mean negative and unproductive thoughts, limiting or erroneous beliefs, guilt, doubt, complacency, procrastination, weakened resolve, poverty thoughts, etc. You need to associate exclusively with people who reinforce your personal motivation, encourage and celebrate your achievement, and are qualified through successful and relevant business or life experience to offer opinions and ideas worthy of your consideration. To be simplistic, and to paraphrase Donald Trump, there are winners and there are losers. You win by hanging around winners. You lose by hanging around losers. No one you associate with leaves you untouched.

Recommended Resource #8

You can obtain a FREE GUEST PASS to a GKIC™ local Chapter meeting, if there is a Chapter in your area, by accessing the Directory of Advisors/Chapters at www.GKIC.com. FREE two months' membership with my newsletter and other benefits; see page 379.

With this in mind, I encourage entrepreneurs to participate in formal associations with other success-oriented entrepreneurs, and GKIC™ provides such opportunities at both a local and international level. We have local Chapters for our Members in more than 80 cities and areas throughout the U.S. and Canada, and local Kennedy Study Groups in many of those same areas, facilitated by our Certified No B.S. Advisors. We also have an international coaching and mastermind group facilitated only by phone, print media, and an online community; a higher international group, our Peak Performers Group, that meets for three two-day meetings a year led by Lee Milteer; and higher-level, small groups led by myself. These are, in a sense, "support groups" for like-minded entrepreneurs utilizing my advertising, marketing, sales, management, and wealth strategies. Other groups I recommend include the C.E.O. Clubs founded by Joe Mancusco, and groups in different niche industries and professions led by the experts I consult with and mentor. If you are unfamiliar with the "mastermind principle" at the foundation of all these groups or should you opt to organize one of your own, I urge reading both *Laws of Success* and *Think and Grow Rich* by Napoleon Hill. You'll discover that these groups go back at least as far as the Industrial Revolution when, for example, Henry Ford, Thomas Edison, and Harvey Firestone deliberately formed their own "mastermind group." And you'll find the ingredients of a successful, productive group or a failed group clearly described.

Circle 6 is comprised of living and dead authors from whom you seek, collect, and organize ideas, information, and sage advice. All business leaders are great readers. If you are not, you are at an extreme disadvantage. Books worth reading including highly successful entrepreneurs' autobiographies and biographies about them (for example, Conrad Hilton's autobiography is free for the taking in the nightstand drawer of every Hilton hotel), legitimate experts' how-to books, and business opinion and strategy books like this one. I don't think you're "with it" if not reading at least one such book a week, and in my peak years, I read one a day. You should also develop a "top shelf" of books you reread once a year or more often, of key authors you choose to get and keep and refer to frequently.

FIGURE 49.1: Support Circles

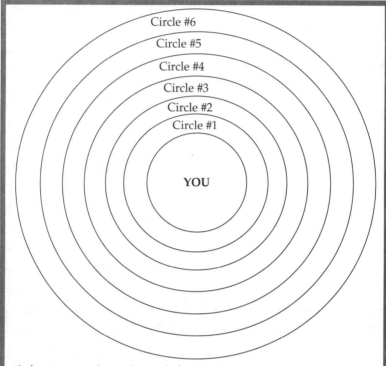

Circle #1: Inner, inner, inner circle

Circle #2: Experts, specialists, and providers of information

Circle #3: Liaisons and conduits

Circle #4: High-performance, high-reliability vendors and suppliers

Circle #5: "Looser" group of mentors, consultants, coaches, peers, and colleagues

Circle #6: Your Dialogue with the Dead

In essence, an advisory board of authors accessed through their writings. You may even come to know a few so well you can ask yourself, "What would _____ do in this position?"—even carry on conversations with them in what Dr. Maltz called "the theater of your mind" (see the book *The New Psycho-Cybernetics*). In addition, there is a wealth of comparable material available in audio CDs, books on CD, seminars on CD, teleseminars, webinars, and current input from your chosen author-experts via their newsletters.

Carefully managing and using all six of these circles multiplies your personal power and enables you to get much more accomplished much faster than the typical business owner who establishes "rut-ines" and sticks with them almost entirely absent of input or outreach.

Recommended Reading on Management

The Everything Store: Jeff Bezos and the Age of Amazon by Brad Stone

Car Guys vs. Bean Counters: The Battle for the Soul of American Business by Bob Lutz

Icons and Idiots: Straight Talk on Leadership by Bob Lutz

Broken Windows, Broken Business by Michael Levine

Sam Walton: Made in America by Sam Walton with John Huey

No B.S. Time Management for Entrepreneurs, 2nd Edition by Dan Kennedy

About the Author

DAN KENNEDY is a serial entrepreneur who has started, bought, built, and sold businesses of varied types and sizes. He is a highly sought-after and outrageously well-paid direct-marketing consultant and direct-response copywriter, coach to groups of entrepreneurs, nearly retired professional speaker, author, equal opportunity annoyer, provocateur, and professional harness racing driver. He lives with his second and third wife (same woman) and a small dog in Ohio and Virginia. His office that he never visits is in Phoenix.

He welcomes your comments and can be reached directly only by fax at 602/269-3113 or by mail at Kennedy Inner Circle, Inc., 15433 N. Tatum Blvd., #104, Phoenix, Arizona 85032. (Do NOT email him via any of the websites presenting his information and publications. He does not use email.)

He is occasionally available for interesting speaking engagements and very rarely accepting new consulting clients. Inquiries should be directed to the above office.

All information about his newsletters, how-to products, other resources, and GKIC™ annual Marketing and Moneymaking

SuperConferences℠ and annual Info-Summit℠ at which Dan appears can be accessed online at www.GKIC.com, and by click-link, the online catalog/web store. A Directory of local GKIC™ Chapters offering networking meetings, seminars, and Kennedy Study Groups in various cities can also be accessed at www.GKIC.com—if you enjoyed this book, you'll enjoy getting together with other business owners in your area applying Kennedy strategies! His horse racing activities can be seen at www.NorthfieldPark.com.

In the *No B.S.* Series, Published by Entrepreneur Press:

No B.S. Guide to Direct Marketing for Non-Direct Marketing Businesses

No B.S. Guide to Marketing to Leading-Edge Boomers and Seniors (with Chip Kessler)

No B.S. Guide to Trust-Based Marketing (with Matt Zagula)

No B.S. Price Strategy (with Jason Marrs)

No B.S. Guide to Marketing to the Affluent

No B.S. Business Success in the New Economy

No B.S. Sales Success in the New Economy

No B.S. Wealth Attraction in the New Economy

No B.S. Time Management for Entrepreneurs

Other Books by Dan Kennedy

The Ultimate Sales Letter (4th Edition—20th Anniversary Edition), Adams Media

The Ultimate Marketing Plan (4th Edition—20th Anniversary Edition), Adams Media

The NEW Psycho-Cybernetics with Maxwell Maltz, M.D., Prentice Hall

My Unfinished Business/Autobiographical Essays, Advantage
Making Them Believe: The 21 Principles and Lost Secrets of Dr. Brinkley-Style Marketing with Chip Kessler, GKIC/ Morgan-James
Make 'Em Laugh & Take Their Money, GKIC/Morgan-James

Other Books

Uncensored Sales Strategies by Sydney Barrows (with Dan Kennedy), Entrepreneur Press

Index

A

absenteeism, 91–92

academic achievement vs. experience, 138

academic approach to management, 1–8, 296

accepting less than you can get, 252–254

accepting unacceptable employee behavior, 21–23

accomplishment vs. activity, 286–297, 300–303, 355–356

accountability, 275–276

accountants. *See* bean-counters

accurate thinking, 16–19

activity vs. accomplishment, 286–297, 300–303, 355–356

advertising budgets, 139–141

advisors, in support circles, 358

affluent people, marketing to, 352

agendas for meetings, 320

Amazon, 29, 83, 244, 293

answering telephones, 207–208, 217, 309–310

approval-seeking managers, 25–30, 310

assets, 330–335

association, 359–360

audio surveillance, 162. *See also* surveillance

authors, 361–363

automation, 83–84, 349–350

average transaction value (ATV), 338–339

B

Ballmer, Steve, 244

bean-counters
  as CEOs, 137
  cutting costs indiscriminately, 144–145
  draining the life out of a business, 141–144
  impact on top performers, 149–153
  as managers, 145–146